W9-CXO-723

Music Theory Translation Series
Claude V. Palisca, *Editor*

OTHER PUBLISHED VOLUMES IN THE MUSIC THEORY TRANSLATION SERIES:

The Practical Harmonist at the Harpsichord, 1708, by Francesco Gasparini, translated by Frank S. Stillings, edited by David L. Burrows.

The Art of Counterpoint, Part Three of *Le Istitutioni harmoniche,* 1558, by Gioseffo Zarlino, translated by Guy A. Marco and Claude V. Palisca.

Hucbald, Guido, and John on Music, Three Medieval Treatises, translated by Warren Babb, edited with Introductions by Claude V. Palisca.

The Art of Strict Musical Composition, 1771–1779, by Johann Philipp Kirnberger, translated by David Beach and Jurgen Thym.

Introductory Essay on Composition, 1782–1793, by Heinrich Christoph Koch, translated by Nancy Kovaleff Baker.

Aristides Quintilianus On Music, in Three Books, translated with Introduction, Commentary, and Annotations, by Thomas J. Mathiesen.

On the Modes, Part Four of *Le Istitutioni harmoniche,* 1558, by Gioseffo Zarlino, translated by Vered Cohen, edited with an Introduction by Claude V. Palisca.

The Florentine Camerata: Documentary Studies and Translations by Claude V. Palisca.

Fundamentals of Music

ANICIUS MANLIUS SEVERINUS BOETHIUS

Translated, with Introduction and Notes by
Calvin M. Bower

Edited by
Claude V. Palisca

Yale University Press
New Haven & London

The preparation of this volume was made possible by a grant from the Translations Program of the National Endowment for the Humanities, an independent federal agency.

Published with the assistance of the F. B. Adams, Jr., Publication Fund.

Copyright © 1989 by Yale University. All rights reserved. This book may not be reproduced, in whole or in part, including illustrations, in any form (beyond that copying permitted by Sections 107 and 108 of the U.S. Copyright Law and except by reviewers for the public press), without written permission from the publishers.

Designed by James J. Johnson and set in Times Roman types by Brevis Press, Bethany, Connecticut. Printed in the United States of America.

Library of Congress Cataloging-in-Publication Data

Boethius, d. 524.
   [De institutione musica. English]
   Fundamentals of music / Anicius Manlius Severinus Boethius; translated, with introduction and notes by Calvin M. Bower; edited by Claude V. Palisca.
   p.   cm.—(Music theory translation series)
   Translation of: De institutione musica.
   Includes index.
   ISBN 0–300–03943–3 (alk. paper)
   1. Music—Theory—500–1400.   I. Bower, Calvin M., 1938–   .
II. Palisca, Claude V.   III. Title.   IV. Series.
MT5.5.B613   1989
781—dc19   88–19939
                                                                      CIP
                                                                      MN

The paper in this book meets the guidelines for permanence and durability of the Committee on Production Guidelines for Book Longevity of the Council on Library Resources.

10   9   8   7   6   5   4   3   2   1

TO
George Boylston
AND
Mildred Ruth Brown
et musici et doctores

Contents

BOOK 2

BOOK 3

Preface by Series Editor

The treatise of Boethius translated here has had a remarkable career over the fifteen centuries since he wrote it. Only recently have we come to appreciate how diversely different historical epochs exploited it. Beginning around the ninth century, *De institutione musica* became established as the foundation of Western music theory, and throughout the Middle Ages Boethius remained the authority most revered for music-theoretic matters. But soon the preoccupation with polyphony and the problems of measured music, for which Boethius was of little help, led to its neglect in the training of musicians. With the rise of universities, however, his became the basic text in music studied as one of the liberal arts of the quadrivium.

The fifteenth century was a time of transition for the *fortuna* of this work. On the one hand, Johannes Gallicus recognized it as a translation of Greek writings, hence a font of knowledge about Greek music but foreign to the Western ecclesiastical tradition. On the other hand, Franchino Gaffurio continued to uphold Boethius as the source of the only true doctrine, though he became aware of contradictory views in other ancient sources discovered by the humanists. (This will be evident in the translation and annotations of his *Theorica musice* of 1492, which are being prepared for this series by Walter Kreyszig.) Meanwhile, *De institutione musica* was one of the first musical works printed—in Boethius's *Opera* (Venice, 1491–92). A more critical text was edited in 1546 by Heinrich Glarean, who used Boethius to bolster his theory of the twelve modes in the *Dodekachordon* of 1547.

From the mid-sixteenth century Boethius was often dismissed as lacking relevance to modern musical practice—for example, by Nicola Vicentino, whose *L'Antica musica ridotta alla moderna prattica* (Ancient Music Adapted to Modern Practice) of 1555 has been translated by Maria Rika Maniates and will soon be issued in this series. At the same time, the valorization of Boethius as a transmitter of Greek music theory, to be consulted along with other ancient sources, reached a high point, and two Italian humanists completed vernacular translations that were never published—Giorgio Bartoli in 1579 and Ercole Bottrigari in 1597. The only published translation is much more recent: that of Oskar Paul (Leipzig, 1872), which, like the standard edition by Gottfried Friedlein (Leipzig, 1867), was a product of the German philological movement.

Today we value Boethius for a multiplicity of reasons. We read him to understand Western medieval theory and how it evolved. He is at the center of the theoretical quarrels of the sixteenth century. As Calvin M. Bower has shown, he appears to have handed down in a glossed translation a massive music treatise of the Hellenic period by Nicomachus that otherwise would not have survived, one of the broader windows that we have on the tonal system of the ancient world. Finally, Boethius appeals to the modern theorist, ever searching for consistent schemes and principles of tonal organization, for in the first four books he lays down such a system in great detail.

For good reasons, then, an English translation of Boethius's *De institutione musica* was the first goal of the Music Theory Translation Series when it was inaugurated by David Kraehenbuehl thirty years ago. However, it was only with the completion of Bower's dissertation "Boethius, *The Principles of Music:* An Introduction, Translation, and Commentary" at George Peabody College in 1967 that the project began its path to fulfillment. A draft by another scholar had been abandoned after receiving a careful review by Professor David Hughes of Harvard University, to whom we are indebted for his valuable counsel. My collaboration with Calvin Bower since that time has been a source of mutual instruction in Greek music theory. We have benefited also from the increasing sophistication concerning the Greek theoretical tradition in the English-speaking world, particularly as represented by the work of Thomas J. Mathiesen, whose translation of Aristides Quintilianus's *On Music* is in this series, and of Jon Solomon, whose translation of Claudius Ptolemy's *Harmonics* will soon be ready for publication in it. Professor Bower has earned our thanks for persevering through these years in investigating the sources and manuscript tradition of Boethius's music theory. The insights and information gained in this research enrich every page of his introduction and annotations.

That Boethius's famous treatise has not been published in English before is understandable to us who have worked with the text. Not that Boethius's Latin is so very difficult; major obstacles have been, rather, his terminology, his antiquated mathematics, his often ponderous explanations, and the diagrams. But most of all the challenge has been to express his thoughts in today's English. The translation we have arrived at here has benefited from the experience of my students in the history of medieval theory at Yale University, who read earlier drafts and wrote often revealing commentaries on selected chapters.

The financial support and encouragement of the National Endowment for the Humanities' Translations Program, directed by Susan Mango and more recently by Martha B. Chomiak, were indispensable for the realization of this volume.

CLAUDE V. PALISCA

Translator's Preface

This translation of Boethius's *De institutione musica* grew out of a doctoral dissertation at George Peabody College under the direction of Robert L. Weaver. After completing the dissertation, however, I continued work with Boethius's text, especially as preserved in the very rich manuscript tradition. Then, about a dozen years ago, I began work with Claude V. Palisca on formal revision of the translation for publication. Continued work with the manuscript tradition made Boethius's Latin more immediate, and further explorations of the Greek background of the treatise clarified many difficult passages. Solutions to problems regarding the diagrams and many textual peculiarities gradually fell into place, and this new version of the translation emerged. Palisca's contribution to this reading has been constant and considerable, and I am indebted to him for his encouragement, patience, and persistence.

A number of colleagues and friends have also contributed to this work in various ways. Dr. Brian Pavlac, who prepared the final version of the diagrams and whose background as a medieval historian and ability as a draftsman made it possible to create diagrams which are clear yet capture the character of the ninth-century codices from which they derive; Jon Martel, who, at an earlier stage, helped me articulate many of the graphic and historical problems regarding the diagrams; Charles Atkinson and Elizabeth Hoger, two of my graduate assistants, who made important contributions to my reading of the text at different stages; Olivia Wu and Fr. Chrysogonus Waddell, O.C.S.O., whose insights and suggestions have shaped the character of this work; and Jean van Altena, whose editorial skills during the final preparation of this manuscript made it into a work perhaps worthy of publication. To all of these I extend my thanks.

London
In festo Sancti Eduardi Confessoris
1987

Introduction

Shortly after the turn of the sixth century a young Roman patrician began to record in Latin the sources and background of his exceptional Greek education. Although it is uncertain that he ever studied in Athens or Alexandria, those fifth-century centers of liberal learning and philosophy fundamentally shaped his thinking, even to the extent of determining his literary and pedagogical objectives. He would lay a scientific foundation by writing on four mathematical disciplines—the *quadrivium* as hè collectively called them. Thereafter he would translate and comment on the Organon of Aristotle and, building on the mathematical disciplines and Aristotelian logic, would finally approach the philosophical writings of Plato and Aristotle and the world of metaphysics.[1]

In this context, Anicius Manlius Severinus Boethius (480–524) wrote the treatise entitled *De institutione musica,* one of his earliest works, probably around the middle of the first decade of the sixth century. It was intended to be read along with the *De institutione arithmetica* and may have been one of four works setting out the foundations of Platonic scientific education: arithmetic, music, geometry, and astronomy. None of the mathematical works—or even the logical works—was considered original by Boethius or his contemporaries. Boethius's early works record in Latin what he was reading in Greek. Reading, translating, writing, and commenting formed an integrated process through which Boethius appropriated for his culture works that not only were unknown but that in most cases surpassed the superficial dabblings in science and logic from the golden and silver ages of Roman civilization. Scholars such as Marius Vic-

1. For a thorough study of Boethius's life, see Henry Chadwick, *Boethius: The Consolations of Music, Logic, Theology, and Philosophy* (Oxford, 1981), pp. 1–68. Also informative is John Matthews, "Anicius Manlius Severinus Boethius," in *Boethius: His Life, Thought and Influence,* ed. Margaret Gibson (Oxford, 1981), pp. 15–43.

torinus and Apuleius of Madaura had produced scientific translations for
Latin readers of the fourth and fifth centuries, but Boethius carried the
genre to new levels of rigor and thoroughness. Written for a cultural elite
already initiated into philosophical literature, Boethius's mathematical and
logical works represent one of the most notable projects in intellectual
history of preserving and transmitting a corpus of knowledge from one
culture to another.[2]

No evidence has been found that Boethius's mathematical works were
read between his short lifetime and the ninth century. But when liberal
learning saw a rebirth in the Carolingian era, Boethius's treatises on arithmetic and music reappeared as authoritative works on these disciplines,
rivaled only by Martianus Capella's *De nuptiis Philologiae et Mercurii*.[3]
When a tradition of independent musical treatises began in the ninth century, Boethius's treatise became the unique source for the thorough mathematical underpinning of Western musical theory. It is ironic that this work
intended as an approach to logic and philosophy would essentially shape
the most illiberal of the liberal arts.[4]

MATHEMATICS, MUSIC, AND MYTH

What is the nature of this treatise which played such an important role
in the development of Western musical thought? In the *Fundamentals of
Music* Boethius intended to treat only peripherally the actual theory and
practice of music; his focus was knowing. His basic goal is articulated clearly
at the end of the first chapter, following an eloquent account of the all-
encompassing influence of music on human life: "From all these accounts
it appears without doubt that music is so naturally united with us that we
cannot be free from it even if we so desired. For this reason the power of
the intellect ought to be summoned, so that this art, innate through nature,
might also be mastered, comprehended through knowledge." The means
of coming to know music is uncompromisingly Pythagorean: number. Bo-

2. Concerning the complex question of Boethius's literary precursors and his audience,
see Helen Kirkby, "The Scholar and his Public," in *Boethius: His Life, Thought and Influence*,
pp. 44–69.

3. See *Martianus Capella*, ed. Adolf Dick, with addenda by Jean Préaux (Stuttgart,
1969); also *Martianus Capella and the Seven Liberal Arts*, vol. 1, William Harris Stahl, *The
Quadrivium of Martianus Capella, Latin Translations in the Mathematical Sciences, 50 B.C.–
A.D. 1250*, and Richard Johnson with E. L. Burge, *A Study of the Allegory and the Verbal
Disciplines* (New York and London, 1971); vol. 2, *The Marriage of Philology and Mercury*,
trans. W. H. Stahl and R. Johnson with E. L. Burge (New York, 1977).

4. For the tradition of Boethius's treatise in the early Middle Ages, see Calvin M.
Bower, "The Role of Boethius' *De institutione musica* in the Speculative Tradition of Western
Musical Thought," in *Boethius and the Liberal Arts: A Collection of Essays*, ed. Michael Masi,
Utah Studies in Literature and Linguistics 18 (Bern, Frankfurt, and Las Vegas, 1981),
pp. 157–74; and Alison White, "Boethius in the Medieval Quadrivium," in *Boethius: His
Life, Thought and Influence*, pp. 162–205.

ethius states and restates the Pythagorean creed, insisting on the quantitative nature of sound.[5] Motion causes things to hit each other, and this percussion or pulsation causes sounds; faster and more frequent pulsations cause high sound, slower and less frequent pulsations low sound. The differences between high and low sound are therefore quantitative. One quantity is related to another as a number compared to a number—that is, as a ratio. By comprehending ratios, one comes to know truths about sounds, their unchanging essences. These truths are classified as "related quantity," one of four classes of truth which the student must understand before ascending the lofty heights of philosophy.[6]

Given the rational nature of Boethius's fundamental premise, one might expect a systematic development of ratios in and of themselves, complete with axioms and proofs, followed by a demonstration of how these ratios can lead to a collection of pitches on the monochord. Such a treatise would be in the best tradition of Greek mathematics, as exemplified by Euclid. But undiluted science does not form the whole substance of Boethius's treatise. Equal in importance to its mathematical core is a mythic element, which affects the character of both musical expositions and mathematical demonstrations. The root of the mythic content lies in the Pythagorean origins of the treatise, and this cultic dimension is exemplified first and most clearly in the parables about Pythagoras himself.[7]

Pythagoras is presented in the opening chapter as a person so wise in musical matters that he is able to restore social order by manipulating the character of music. But in this initial encounter, Pythagoras's bearing is extraordinary; he is introduced as a "night owl" (*nocturnus*) who wanders about contemplating the stars (1.1). He is next encountered discovering the mathematical basis of musical consonance in a smithy. But again he wanders about, led now by divine will, and approaches the smithy in something of a trance (1.10). Only when Pythagoras returns home does he become the scientist carrying out experiments. This account of the discovery of musical ratios must be read as mythical allegory, not scientific discourse. The parable has no basis in scientific reality, and the reasons for associating the

5. Boethius summarizes this position in 1.3, 2.20, and 4.1.

6. Boethius, following the Pythagoreans, divides quantitative speculation into two areas: multitude and magnitude. Multitude represents numerical quantity, magnitude spatial quantity. Arithmetic is first among the mathematical disciplines, and it is concerned with multitude, or quantity, per se; music, the second discipline, is also concerned with multitude, but quantity related to other quantity. Geometry studies magnitude which is fixed, whereas astronomy studies magnitude in motion. See *De institutione arithmetica* (hereafter *Arith.*) 1.1 and *Fundamentals of Music* 2.3. Concerning the place of music in Boethius's scheme of learning, see Leo Schrade, "Music in the Philosophy of Boethius," *Musical Quarterly* 33 (1947): 188–200.

7. Concerning the strong element of myth and cult in ancient Pythagoreanism, see Walter Burkert, *Lore and Science in Ancient Pythagoreanism,* trans. E. L. Minar, Jr. (Cambridge, Mass., 1972).

revelation of ratios with the smithy are lost among the mysteries of Pythagorean lore.[8] At Pythagoras's third appearance, his name is changed to Lycaon of Sammos. "Lycaon" refers to the nocturnal wandering wolf, and, by extension, to a shaman imbued with divine powers, capable of revealing sacred lore. In this meeting Lycaon is credited with adding the eighth string (1.20); but in Pythagorean circles, Pythagoras himself was known for having intercalated this eighth note.[9] Finally, in the epilogue of book 1 (1.33), Pythagoras is described as an authoritative teacher, whose words no one dares to challenge.

The mythic character of this text colors the exposition of even the basic musical elements. An explanation of the set of pitches constituting the ancient Greek musical system is found in every ancient musical treatise. In *Fundamentals of Music* (1.20), this exposition has religious overtones. Music began in a state of grace, as it were, with four strings sounding intervals of the octave divided by a fourth and a fifth, intervals embodying the tetractys 12:9:8:6 discovered by Pythagoras at the smithy. In this age of gods and demigods nothing discordant was found in music. This historical allegory reaches back to the most ancient of Greek prehistory, naming inventors of strings who had been associated with the invention of the modes, themselves named after the three peoples of ancient Greek culture: the Lydian, Phrygian, and Dorian. The tonal genesis brings the development of the musical system to its completion in fifteen notes, but a value judgment is clear throughout: namely, that as music moved away from the state of simplicity and purity expressed in the Pythagorean tetractys, its integrity was compromised.

The Pythagoreans treated number in a manner fundamentally different from that of a pure mathematician like Euclid. They were apt to ascribe dynamic qualities to various numbers and to lapse into rhapsodies concerning the virtues of particular numbers.[10] They viewed inequality, ratios, and proportions as numerical realities emanating from the monad, or "unity," as it is named by Boethius (2.7). Ratios closest to unity—that is, to equality—are judged the most commensurate, or "consonant" ratios (1.31, 2.20). Pythagorean theorists were so enamored of differences between terms in ratios that they ascribed significance to the differences themselves. Philolaus, for example, considered 27, the cube of the first odd number (1 is unity, not a number) to hold the "origin" of the tone; it is, after all, the difference between 243 and 216, terms which are in the ratio

8. See Claude Palisca, "Scientific Empiricism in Musical Thought," in *Seventeenth-century Science and the Arts,* ed. H. H. Rhys (Princeton, 1961), pp. 127–29.

9. See book 1, n. 107.

10. Concerning the nature of Pythagorean mathematics, see Nicomachus of Gerasa, *Introduction to Arithmetic,* trans. Martin Luther D'Ooge, with studies in Greek arithmetic by Frank Egleston Robbins and Louis Charles Karpinski, esp. Robbins's "The Philosophy of Nicomachus," pp. 88–110, and "Nicomachus's Philosophy of Number," pp. 111–23.

of the tone immediately adjacent to the terms holding the ratio of the Pythagorean semitone, 256 and 243. Thus 13—the difference between 256 and 243—is identified with the semitone. This numerical allegory is carried even further by identifying 14—the difference between 27 and 13—as the apotome, and unity—the difference between 14 and 13—as the comma (3.5). This obsession with differences ultimately leads to the one serious mathematical flaw in *Fundamentals of Music*—that is, the manipulation of the difference between the terms in the ratio for the comma to demonstrate its relative size (3.14–16).[11]

Even musical details essentially independent of mythic and mathematical elements are made to blend in with the Pythagorean background. Musical systems and genera taken into the treatise from outside the Pythagorean sphere are combined in a way that yields a set of notes numbering 28, a perfect number according to the Pythagorean credo.[12] No mathematical or mythic basis is given for the chromatic or enharmonic genera in the treatise; but when these divisions are introduced on the monochord (4.7), they are developed using the principle of arithmetic proportion so basic to Pythagorean number theory.[13] Finally, the theory of modes is developed, again with no mathematical or mythical background; nevertheless, a Pythagorean hand is evident even in the treatment given.[14]

The philosophical background of *Fundamentals of Music* might have predisposed the treatise to a nature so rational that the raw material of music, sound heard by the ears, would be excluded from consideration. Yet, while reason is judged superior to the erring senses, the senses are by no means denied a role in musical judgment. The senses serve as an exhortation to reason in much the same way that the mathematical disciplines themselves serve as exhortations to the study of philosophy (1.9). The testimony of the senses, in general, is accepted in the recognition of consonances, but the intervals of consonances—their ratios—are determined by reason (1.9). Moreover, Boethius sees an analogy between the way in which the senses find pleasure in sounds and the way the mind finds pleasure in quantitative relationships (1.32). In book 3, after the mathematical bases of consonances, the tone, the semitone, the apotome, and the comma have been demonstrated by reason, exercises are presented whereby the senses can come to know the intervals as determined by reason (3.9–10). Thus, although the student is urged to rise above the senses and the material world which affects them, sound and sense are not excluded from the study of music.

11. See book 3, n. 31.

12. See 1.22 and n. 122, and 4.13 and n. 68. Concerning so-called perfect numbers, see *Arith.* 1.19, which translates Nicomachus *Eisagoge arithmetica* 1.16.

13. See book 4, nn. 58, 59.

14. Concerning the Pythagorean nature of Boethius's theory of modes and its specifically Nicomachian content, see Calvin M. Bower, "The Modes of Boethius," *Journal of Musicology* 3 (1984): 252–63. See also 4.13, n. 65, and 4.14, nn. 71, 73.

Boethius's *Fundamentals of Music* must be read as a treatise in which there is a dialectical balance between mythic and mathematical poles. Given the Pythagorean articles of faith—in particular, the importance of the ratios contained in the first four integers and the musical incarnation of those ratios in the proportion 12:9:8:6—a series of mathematical proofs can follow to demonstrate the ratios of individual consonances and the sizes of these consonances in relation to each other. The ratios of the consonances can be manipulated to create ratios for intervals smaller than the tone, and the ratios and relative sizes of the minor and major semitone and the comma can be demonstrated. All the ratios, in turn, can be referred to the monochord, so that the senses can appreciate the musical sounds embodying the mathematical ratios.

The synthesis of mathematics, music, and myth found in Boethius's treatise creates an approach to the second discipline of the quadrivium which is, at once, cultic and scientific, subjective and objective. The basic truths—mathematical and musical—are revealed, rather than deduced, and these are presented in a style and with an intensity uncharacteristic of pure mathematics. The revealed truths invoke in the reader belief or disbelief and acceptance or rejection of the exhortation to follow a specific philosophical course of study. Once the basic commitment is made, however, no contradictions arise between revealed truths and logical proofs, and mathematical and musical proofs follow as objective deductions. The treatise thus represents an exercise in faith and reason, and, on this ground alone, it should be no surprise that *Fundamentals of Music* shaped the discipline of music during the Middle Ages.

THE TRANSLATOR AND HIS SOURCES

Boethius composed treatises during his early years by translating Greek works or by writing independent commentaries on Greek or Latin works.[15] The extant works which surround *Fundamentals of Music* all represent this genre: *De institutione arithmetica*[16] is a translation of Nicomachus's *Eisagoge arithmetica*,[17] and the logical works are principally

15. For a chronology of Boethius's works, see S. Brandt, "Entstehungszeit und zeitliche Folge der Werke Boethius," *Philologus* 62 (1903): 152–54; A. P. McKinlay, "Stylistic Tests and the Chronology of the Works of Boethius," *Harvard Studies in Classical Philology* 18 (1907): 123–56; and L. M. de Rijk, "On the Chronology of Boethius' Works on Logic," *Vivarium* 2 (1964): 1–49, 125–62.

16. The edition of Friedlein, *Anicii Manlii Torquati Severini Boetii De institutione arithmetica libri duo, De institutione musica libri quinque, accedit Geometria quae fertur Boetii,* ed. Gottfried Friedlein (Leipzig, 1867), serves as the critical text for both Boethius's arithmetical and musical treatises. A translation of *Arith.* is available in Michael Masi, *Boethian Number Theory: A Translation of the* De Institutione Arithmetica, Studies in Classical Antiquity, vol. 6 (Amsterdam, 1983).

17. *Nicomachi Geraseni Pythagorei Introductionis Arithmeticae Libri II,* ed. Richard Hoche (Leipzig, 1866). For a translation, see n. 10 above.

translations of Porphyry or Aristotle or commentaries on works by Porphyry, Aristotle, or Cicero.[18] All these works—like their sources—seem didactic in character, aimed at preparing Boethius and his readers for the study of metaphysics. Since Boethius's other early works are translations or commentaries, the *Fundamentals of Music* would be expected to fall in the same category.

Boethius candidly expressed his attitude toward translation in the prefatory dedication of *Fundamentals of Arithmetic:*

> I hold to a rather strict rule of translation, but not slavishly to the precepts of another author. When I have wandered a little more freely, I am concentrating on the path another followed, not on his footprints. Those matters concerning numbers that were discussed more expansively by Nicomachus I have brought together with a measure of brevity; those matters which offered a rather limited scope to the understanding—which Nicomachus hurried through with cursory treatment—I have singled out for expanded treatment. Sometimes I have used paradigms and diagrams to make these things clearer.[19]

When reflecting on his logical works, Boethius does not describe his work as literal translation of Greek sources, but rather as "turning [a work by Aristotle] into the Roman style."[20] Careful study of the translations of logical treatises has revealed a further dimension of Boethius's technique of translation: he often incorporated glosses and marginal comments from his manuscript sources into the text, giving no indication that these remarks were peripheral to the original work.[21] Thus, Boethius's translations are more than literal translations of works from one language to another; they represent a scholar's efforts to make a foreign text his own. The textual footprints of the earlier author sometimes become blurred, but his broad path is retraced and recorded by Boethius.[22]

18. For a concise yet complete review of Boethius's logical works, see Jonathan Barnes, "Boethius and the Study of Logic," in *Boethius: His Life, Thought and Influence*, pp. 73–89. Barnes points out that even the logical "treatises" by Boethius are not original but derive from Greek models.

19. *Arith.*, Praefatio (4.27–5.4): "At non alterius obnoxius institutis artissima memet ipse translationis lege constringo, sed paululum liberius evagatus alieno itineri, non vestigiis, insisto. Nam et ea, quae de numeris a Nicomacho diffusius disputata sunt, moderata brevitate collegi et quae transcursa velocius angustiorem intellegentiae praestabant aditum mediocri adiectione reservavi, ut aliquando ad evidentiam rerum nostris etiam formulis ac descriptionibus uteremur. (The translation in the text is my own. Hereafter, if no edition is cited, translations are my own.)

20. Boethius, *Commentarii in Librum Aristotelis Perihermeneias editio secunda, seu maiora commentaria*, ed. C. Meiser (Leipzig, 1880), p. 79: ". . . ego omne Aristotelis opus, quodcumque in manus venerit, in Romanum stilum vertens . . ."

21. See J. Bidez, "Boèce et Porphyre," *Revue belge de philologie et d'histoire* 2 (1923): 189–201; L. Minio-Paluello, "A Latin Commentary (? translated by Boethius) on the Prior Analytics and its Greek sources," *Journal of Hellenic Studies* 77 (1957): 93–102; James Shiel, "Boethius' commentaries on Aristotle," *Medieval and Renaissance Studies* 4 (1958): 216–44; and L. M. de Rijk, *Logica Modernorum* I (Assen, 1962), pp. 28–39.

These principles of translation are evident throughout *Fundamentals of Music*. At times Boethius is compressing extended passages in his source; he acknowledges, for example, that he has abridged Nicomachus's extended discussion of the diapason-plus-diatesseron (2.27). At other times he is turning Greek musical theory into the Roman style: his citations of Cicero and Statius (1.1, 1.27) give the text a distinctly Roman flavor, and his brief nods towards Albinus (1.12, 1.26) relate the text to the Latin tradition of music theory. In several passages, what seem to be "additions" may effectively be explained as glosses that Boethius has appropriated. There is little evidence, for example, that Boethius had direct knowledge of treatises in the Aristoxenian tradition; but his knowledge of the Aristoxenian equation of the tone with the value of 12—not found in the text of his source, Ptolemy—is best explained as an incorporation of a gloss into the Latin text.[23] Boethius's statement that Ptolemy appended the eighth mode in the highest position is difficult to explain if we picture Boethius working from "clean" editions of Nicomachus and Ptolemy; if, on the other hand, this remark is read as a gloss concerning the position of the eighth mode which Boethius has brought into his text, the passage becomes more acceptable.[24]

The specific Greek background of *Fundamentals of Music,* unlike those of *Fundamentals of Arithmetic* and the logical works, is not easily determined. In its extant version the work is incomplete, for the text breaks off in the middle of book 5, while titles exist for eleven further chapters. Only the source of book 5 can be positively identified: it begins a paraphrased translation of Ptolemy's *Harmonica.*[25] No single extant treatise can be identified as the source of the first four books, yet they reflect a coherent point of view and a consistent style of thinking and arguing. These books are obviously derived from a Pythagorean source or sources. The person cited most often in the first four books is Nicomachus, and these books—books 1–3 in particular—exhibit a clear development from and dependence on the *Fundamentals of Arithmetic,* a translation of Nicomachus's *Eisagoge arithmetica.* Nicomachus, in his *Enchiridion,* promised to write an *Eisagoge musica,*[26] a more extended treatise on music which would address such topics as the harmony of the spheres; the additions of notes, their inventors, and the times and circumstances of their inventions; a division of the mono-

---

22. For a discussion of Boethius's appropriation of Greek sources, see Seth Lerer, *Boethius and Dialogue: Literary Method in* The Consolation of Philosophy (Princeton, 1985), pp. 14–32.

23. See below, n. 50, and book 5, n. 54.

24. See book 4, n. 91.

25. For a critical edition of Ptolemy *Harmonica,* see Ingemar Düring, *Die Harmonielehre des Claudio Ptolemaios,* Göteborgs Högskolas Årsskrift 36 (Göteborg, 1930); for a German translation of the work see Düring, trans., *Ptolemaios und Porphyrios über die Musik,* Göteborgs Högskolas Årsskrift 40 (Göteborg, 1934).

26. Nicomachus, *Enchiridion* 1, in Carl von Jan, *Musici Scriptores Graeci* (Leipzig, 1895), p. 238, ll. 6–15 (hereafter JanS.).

chord following Pythagorean principles; fuller discussion of musical proportions; and further discussion of the octave, its merit and its
components—namely, five tones and two semitones, rather than six tones.[27]
These topics all form significant parts of *Fundamentals of Music*. The frequent citations of Nicomachus, the close relationship with the arithmetical
treatise, and the description of a more extended treatise in Enchiridion
have led to the scholarly consensus that the first three books, at least, of
Fundamentals of Music represent a translation of Nicomachus's lost *Eisagoge musica.*[28]

Consensus breaks down when it comes to book 4, however. Extant
sources can be identified for several sections and ideas found in this book:
the introduction is based on a terse Pythagorean treatise, *Sectio canonis;*
the notational theory is comparable to that found in notational treatises;
and the modal theory contains elements reminiscent of passages in Ptolemy.
Some scholars have thus concluded that book 4 represents a collection of
disparate sources assembled by Boethius.[29] But this conclusion is flawed in
two crucial respects. First, it fails to account for the alterations of texts and
ideas found in book 4, alterations which bring the passages in question into
harmony with mathematical and musical positions taken throughout the
first three books. Second, it overlooks the necessity of completing certain
promises and premises set out in the first three books—in particular, the
division of the monochord.

The theory assembled in book 4 is wholly consistent with that found
in the first three books, and Boethius himself described the first four books
as a piece, as a text "setting out basic fundamentals" (5.2). Part of *Sectio
canonis* serves as an introduction to the book, but textual alterations and
additions render the tone of the opening particularly consonant with the
preceding books.[30] The monochord division forms the necessary conclusion
to the plan outlined in the first three books, and the application of arithmetic proportions in the division of the chromatic and enharmonic genera
is distinctly Nicomachian.[31] Some purely musical details of the book point

27. For these specific promises, see respectively Nicomachus *Enchiridion* 3 (JanS.
242.11–18), 11 (JanS. 260.4–12), 11 (JanS. 260.12–17), 12 (JanS. 261.18), and 12 (JanS.
264.1–5).

28. The probability that Nichomachus was the source for the early books of *Fundamen-
tals of Music* was first recognized by W. Miekley, *De Boethii libri de musica primi fontibus*
(Jena, 1898). This thesis was subsequently developed by Ubaldo Pizzani, "Studi sulle fonti
del 'De Institutione Musica' di Boezio," *Sacris eruditi* 16 (1965): 5–164 (hereafter, Pizzani,
"Fonti"). I built on the work of these scholars in "Boethius and Nicomachus: An Essay
Concerning the Sources of *De Institutione Musica*," *Vivarium* 16 (1978): 1–45 (hereafter,
Bower, "Sources").

29. See Pizzani, "Fonti," passim, and L. Gushee, "Questions of Genre in Medieval
Treatises on Music," in *Gattungen der Musik in Einzeldarstellungen, Gedenkschrift Leo
Schrade*, vol. 1 (Bern and Munich, 1973), p. 380.

30. See Bower, "Sources," pp. 12–14.

31. Ibid., pp. 19–26.

only to Nicomachus: the theory of three classes of notes found in chapter 13 is found only here and in *Enchiridion*,[32] and the tracing of species using a regular progression of semitones from lowest pitch to highest is also found only in *Enchiridion* and *Fundamentals of Music*.[33] The testing of intervals at the close of the book—insofar as it omits any test of the diapason-plus-diatessaron—reflects a position consistent with Nicomachus.[34] I have argued, therefore, that the principal assembler of the diverse materials in book 4 is Nicomachus and not Boethius, that Nicomachus shaped these materials to form the logical conclusion to his *Eisagoge musica*, and that Boethius saw his translation of Nicomachus to its end before taking up the work of Ptolemy.[35]

In having recourse to Ptolemy's *Harmonica* as the source for book 5, Boethius takes on an author whose approach and language differ markedly from those of Nicomachus. This difference becomes obvious in the vocabulary and grammatical structures of Boethius's Latin, and the reader is immediately aware that new ground is being broken. Nevertheless, Boethius's principles of translation remain basically the same. Having already discussed much of what Ptolemy covers in his first book, Boethius felt free to condense or omit many passages covering similar ground.[36] Conversely, at other times Boethius appears to be expanding terse statements by Ptolemy with appropriate examples.[37] In two cases Boethius's text includes musical details which cannot be explained in terms of the extant text of Ptolemy, suggesting that Boethius was using a textual tradition of the source no longer extant.[38]

By the beginning of book 5, however, Boethius is firmly established on one intellectual course: he is committed to using music theory—the study of related quantity—as preparation for the study of philosophy. Ptolemy's musical interests, on the other hand, extended beyond the mathematical and the philosophical; Ptolemy was, to a degree, an empirical scientist and was committed to testing various intervals and combinations of intervals with various instruments under controlled conditions. Boethius seems to view considerations of this kind as detours from his principal

32. See book 4, n. 65, and Bower, "Sources," pp. 26–27.
33. See book 4, nn. 71 and 73; also Bower, "The Modes of Boethius," pp. 256–57.
34. See Bower, "Sources," pp. 37–38.
35. Ibid., esp. pp. 38–41.
36. See, e.g., 5.7 and n. 25, and 5.13 and n. 45.
37. See, e.g., 5.2 and n. 6, and 5.10 and n. 30.
38. The Aristoxenian association of the tone with the number 12, as found in 5.16 (see n. 54), and the statement that 22:21 is the ratio for the first interval in the chromatic genus, as found in 5.18 (see n. 59), are not found in Ptolemy's text or in any printed glosses on those texts. Work remains to be done on the textual tradition of Ptolemy's *Harmonica* and commentaries thereon. A fifth-century Pythagorean recension of Ptolemy's *Harmonica*—perhaps even an epitome—may have served as Boethius's source; such a recension would account for the rather arithmetical reading found in Boethius and some additions to the text not present in the extant tradition.

course, however; and in most cases he leaves such passages untranslated. As long as Ptolemy's course coincides with his own, Boethius faithfully retraces the path followed by his Greek source.

Boethius's interest in Ptolemy's work centers on the broad philosophical questions concerning the relation between sense and reason and the subtle mathematical divisions of genera; these discussions Boethius transmits with care. In fact, at the point where the text breaks off, Boethius appears to be making Ptolemy into a Pythagorean; the title of chapter 20 is "How inequality of ratios is made from equality," and the discussion, which is not found in Ptolemy, is very Pythagorean, even Nicomachian, in character.[39] Boethius obviously saw his source as an epistemological, rather than a musical, text. Consequently, many of the steps in Ptolemy's arguments are fundamentally obscured as Boethius appropriates the text for didactic purposes.

STRUCTURE OF THE TREATISE

An overview of the structure of the five extant books should assist the reader in placing the musical details of the treatise in perspective. Book 1 forms a self-contained introduction to the discipline, whereas books 2 and 3 present mathematical demonstrations of propositions introduced in book 1. Book 4 applies the mathematical principles developed in books 2 and 3 to the monochord and presents the theory of modes. Finally, book 5 introduces the reader to the mathematical and musical subtleties of Ptolemy.

BOOK I

Boethius's introductory book covers six broad topics basic to the student of Pythagorean musical theory, framed by two chapters each of prologue and epilogue. The prologue presents a collection of musical lore comparable only to those found in Athenaeus's *Deipnosophistae* and the *De musica* attributed to Plutarch. Myth, fact, and even document are eloquently assembled to persuade the reader that music not only pervades every sphere of human life but governs the universe as well. The text of the prologue may have drawn much of its content from the treatise by Nicomachus, but Boethius's hand is evident, particularly when he appropriates passages from Cicero and Statius. The prologue urges the reader to cease being manipulated by this powerful art and to strive to gain knowledge of its measure. It closes by dividing music into cosmic music, human music, and instrumental music. Instrumental music is designated as the topic to be treated first and is studied in the remainder of the extant text.

---

39. A chapter with this specific content is found in book 2 of *Fundamentals of Music* (2.7), and the topic was treated at length in *Arith.* 1.32, which is a translation of Nicomachus *Eisagoge arithmetica* 1.23.6–17. Ptolemy never treats the arithmetical foundations of the theory of ratios.

The rest of book 1 presents the basic tenets of Pythagorean music theory, for many fundamental premises are to be accepted on faith for now (see 1.9 and 1.33); demonstrations will follow in subsequent books. The organization of book 1 is complex, for many propositions must be set out. The complexity is compounded by the alternation between an elevated style—found in the prologue, the account of Pythagoras and the hammers, the history of notes, and the closing chapter—and the tedious rhetorical style necessary for spelling out basic doctrines. The six sections which form the body of book 1 are as follows:

Chapters 3–8: *Sound as quantity and ratios.*   The first premise of Pythagorean music theory holds that the measure of musical sounds is accomplished through quantitative ratios. These six chapters set out the doctrine that sound is known through number, and that numbers are related through ratios. They introduce the reader to the classes of ratios and provide basic definitions.

Chapters 9–11: *Reason, the senses, and the Pythagoras myth.*   The problem of the role of the senses in music has been apparent since the opening sentence of the treatise. In this section the relative roles of reason and the senses are defined, and the myth of Pythagoras's discovery of musical truths in the smithy follows logically.

Chapters 12–14: *The nature of voice and of hearing.*   In Greek and Latin, the technical terms for "voice" and "pitch" are identical (φθόγγος and *vox*), and clarification of these words was a traditional feature of theoretical treatises. Boethius adds a chapter on the nature of hearing to complete this subdivision. (Chapter 15 organizes the contents of the chapters that follow.)

Chapters 16–19: *Development of intervallic theory.*   The consonances and their corresponding ratios are presented as dogma in these chapters, and the student is introduced to elementary reasoning about intervals and ratios based on Pythagorean principles.

Chapters 20–27: *The basics of music systems.*   Fundamental to the study of music is a knowledge of music systems and their underlying principles. The names of the notes, their inventors and functions, the theory of tetrachords, the division of tetrachords into genera, and the principles of building systems from tetrachords are developed effectively and clearly in these eight chapters. The system of notes is introduced in a tonal genesis in the first chapter of this section, and the system is placed in a cosmic context in the last.

Chapters 28–32: *The nature of consonance.*   A theory of consonance is basic to any theory of music, and this sixth subdivision of book 1 introduces the reader to the relevant Pythagorean techniques. Theories of Plato and Nicomachus are reviewed, and a basis for judging the relative value of consonances is introduced. These chapters give book 1 some symmetry, for here Boethius returns to the topics of quantity, ratios, and knowing. Just as the ear is pleased by sounds, so the reason is pleased by ratios, and those combinations of sounds expressing intellectually satisfying ratios should be judged beautiful consonances.

The epilogue—chapters 33 and 34—asserts the dogmatic nature of the introductory book and recapitulates the central theme of knowing. The true musician is not the one who plays instruments or writes songs but the one who masters and applies the speculative principles of the discipline.

Of all the books in Boethius's treatise, the first is the easiest to read. The alternation of styles, the combination of story with dogma, the variety of topics, and the overall symmetry draw the reader forward. It thus functions as an exhortation to the reader to pursue the abstract theory that follows. The reader is left with three specific expectations: of a return to the topics of human music and cosmic music, of logical demonstrations of the theory presented as dogma, and of a division of a ruler whereby the theoretical ratios can be applied to a string. Books 2 and 3 fulfil the second of these expectations, and book 4 fulfils the third. But the first remains unfulfilled, since the completed version of the treatise is not extant.

BOOKS 2 AND 3

The style and content of Boethius's second and third books are relentlessly technical. Theories which were set out with little comment in the first book now receive lengthy and sometimes painfully thorough demonstrations. These two books make constant reference to *Fundamentals of Arithmetic* and contain the mathematical core of that treatise.

The first three chapters of book 2 place the mathematical disciplines in philosophical context, then secure music within the mathematical disciplines. Thereafter the book proceeds through four clearly demarcated sections.

Chapters 4–11: *Theory of ratios.* Music is defined as the discipline that treats quantity related to other quantity, and such relationship is expressed first in ratios. These chapters, with repeated reference to the *Fundamentals of Arithmetic,* meticulously cover the classes of ratios, the generation of classes of ratios from unity, means for finding continuous ratios within a class, a theory for determining the relative sizes of ratios, and the effects of combining various classes of ratios.

Chapters 12–17: *Theory of means.* The theory of proportion—or the combination of two or more ratios—was considered an essential part of mathematics by the ancients, and approximately a third of the second book of *Fundamentals of Arithmetic* is devoted to this theory, where ten classes of proportion are defined and developed. Theory of proportion is explained in these six chapters as a theory of means—a theory, that is, of different kinds of terms which can be inserted into a ratio, thereby dividing it. Three kinds are central to musical theory: arithmetic, geometric, and harmonic. These means were considered important to the Pythagoreans in the division of the monochord, and the arithmetic mean becomes the principle for the chromatic and enharmonic divisions in book 4.

Chapters 18–20: *Theory of consonance.*   The theory concerning the relative merit of consonances in the fourth subdivision of book 1 receives more thorough examination here. Judgments of Nicomachus are compared with those of other Pythagoreans, Eubulides and Hippasus, and the relative value of consonances is shown to be dependent on the order in which ratios are known.

Chapters 21–31: *Demonstrations of necessary correspondence between ratios and intervals.*   Here each interval—the bis-diapason, diapason-plus-diapente, diapason, diapente, diatessaron, tone, semitone, apotome, and comma—is logically related to a corresponding ratio.

Although book 2 demonstrates the ratios of all intervals, its primary focus is on mathematical axioms and the application of these to the primary consonances. The intervals which are constituent parts of consonances—tone, semitone, apotome, and comma—are covered thoroughly in book 3. A musician writing approximately four centuries after Boethius, in discussing the theory of semitones, said: "If some curious investigator of such profound and perplexing subtlety exists, let him read the third book of the oft-cited *De institutione harmonica* [sic] by Boethius, and there he will very likely not only satisfy his curiosity but will also be able to test his genius."[40]
The book is divided into five sections:

Chapters 1–4: *That the semitone is not half of a tone.*   The theorist Aristoxenus had used language rather loosely and had described the diapason (the octave) as consisting of six tones. Aristoxenus considered the two semitones within the diatonic octave to fill the space of one tone, which did not fit with Pythagorean mathematical rigor. These five chapters belittle Aristoxenian reasoning and might have been entitled *Contra Aristoxenum.*

Chapters 5–8: *The constituent parts of the tone.*   These four chapters are framed by theory attributed to Philolaus, one of the most revered of the early Pythagoreans. The intervals which make up the tone—semitone,

---

40. Regino of Prüm, in Gerbert, *Scriptores Ecclesiastici De Musica Sacra Potissimum* (St. Blasien, 1784), vol. 1, pp. 244–45: "Si quis vero tantae profundatis ac perplexae subtilitatis curiosus investigator existet, legat saepe dicti Boetii tertium librum de harmonica institutione, & ibi fortassis non solum eius curiositati satisfiet, verum etiam suum experiri poterit ingenium."

apotome, and comma—are examined in various combinations, and Philolaus's further subdivisions of tones, semitones and commas receive attention.

Chapters 9–10: *Perception of the parts of a tone with the ear.* A significant contention of Boethius's treatise is that no contradiction exists between the rational theory of intervals and intervals as perceived by the senses. These chapters demonstrate how one can arrive at the parts of tones by singing or playing sequences of musical consonances. The intervals thereby become known to the senses as well as the reason.

Chapter 11: *Archytas's proof that ratios in the superparticular class cannot be divided equally.* A historic axiom attributed to the mathematician Archytas is found in the middle of the third book, presumably because it relates to a theme of book 3—namely, that superparticular ratios cannot be equally divided.

Chapters 12–16: *The relative sizes of parts of a tone.* These chapters compare the intervals of the comma, semitone, apotome, and tone with each other and with other ratios in an attempt to ascertain their relative sizes.

Books 2 and 3 complete the task of developing the basic tenets of Pythagorean theory and demonstrating the quantitative basis for each interval introduced in book 1.

BOOK 4

The second and third books of this treatise proceed so doggedly in examining the intricacies of ratios and intervals that the reader often feels that they are too narrowly focused. Book 4 leaves a different impression. At the heart of the book lies the division of the monochord anticipated since book 1; but this heart is surrounded by theory which, at first impression, seems unrelated.

Book 4 is introduced by a review of Pythagorean mathematical principles, taken from the first part of a short treatise on Greek musical mathematics known as *Sectio canonis*.[41] The prologue and first nine axioms of this treatise were probably chosen to introduce book 4 because they set out the basic principles governing the Pythagorean "section of the canon," or division of the monochord. Yet the text is not lifted verbatim; the wording is sometimes changed to make it more consistent with the first three books, and arithmetical proofs are added to the abstract deductions of the original text. Following the review, book 4 unfolds in four loosely connected subdivisions.

Chapters 3–4: *Notation.* Boethius justifies the use of musical notation on the grounds that it facilitates the division of the monochord. Notation

41. For background and use of *Sectio canonis*, see 4.1–2, nn. 1–14.

indeed appears in the first division of the monochord, and, since no names of notes are given in the text, the notation functions to designate notes. But Greek notation is inappropriate for the second, more complete division of the monochord; the notation presents only one symbol for the second pitch of tetrachords (parhypatai and tritai) in all genera, whereas the second division requires symbols for the enharmonic parhypatai and tritai, which differ from the corresponding notes in the diatonic and chromatic genera. The full reason for considering notation in book 4 does not become obvious until the explication of modal theory following thc monochord division.

Chapters 5–13: *Division of the monochord.* These chapters represent the culmination of theoretical principles developed in the first three books. Here the ratios are seen to govern the structure of the music system itself. There are three parts to this subdivision of the text:

1. Chapter 5: The first division of the monochord. In this division the rule is a simple geometric line, and the ratios determine the points on the line which become specific notes. This division presents only the diatonic genus and employs Greek notation.
2. Chapters 6–12: The second division of the monochord. This division has a distinctly Nicomachian character, for it is a thorough arithmetic division, with a discrete number assigned to each note in each of the three genera. The diatonic genus forms the basis of the remaining two divisions, since the chromatic and enharmonic genera are derived by application of arithmetic means to ratios taken from the diatonic division.
3. Chapter 13: Fixed and movable notes. Boethius here looks back at the division of the system and classifies each note as fixed, movable, or intermediate.

Chapters 14–17: *Modal Theory.* The theory of species of the primary consonances and of transposed dispositions or modes is found in these four chapters. The theory of modes finds its appropriate place following the division of the monochord, for the nature of transposed dispositions could not be discussed without first determining the structure of the disposition as a whole. The notation introduced before the monochord divisions becomes the central means whereby the nature of the modes and the intervals between them are explained.

Chapter 18: *Aural tests of consonances.* The thesis that reason does not contradict sense perception is a recurring motive throughout Boethius's treatise. In this closing chapter of book 4, the first two superparticular and multiple ratios are applied to a string, and the ear is given the opportunity to judge the consonance or dissonance of intervals.

Despite its loose structure, book 4 develops logically from the first three books and is consistent with these books in theoretical attitude and textual detail. Although the book covers several disparate topics, the division of the monochord is necessary to complete the first three books;

modal theory is a topic required of every extended musical treatise; and notational theory must precede the monochord division, since notation is used in that section. Exposition of modal theory must follow the division of the monochord, since the practical system, with its notation, is not complete until the monochord is divided. Finally, a return to the premise that judgments of reason are compatible with those of the senses forms an appropriate close to a Pythagorean exposition of music theory.

BOOK 5

Books 1 through 4 form a unified treatment of "instrumental music," as promised at the close of the prologue to book 1. In book 5, the basic topic remains instrumental music, but Boethius sets out in new directions. Here he discusses matters about which musical scholars have expressed diverse opinions (5.1) and also takes up the question of the nature and function of the discipline of music (5.2).

Throughout the first four books only one voice of dissent was allowed—namely, that of Ptolemy. The latter's reservations concerning Pythagorean theories were noted whenever the interval of the diapason-plus-diatessaron or its ratio (the superpartient ratio 8:3) came into question.[42] When, in book 5, Boethius presents Ptolemy's argument that the ratio 8:3 is the basis for a consonance, it therefore comes as no surprise. Similarly, Ptolemy's more extensive classification of consonances is expected, for Boethius has already noted that Ptolemy's evaluation of consonances was different from that of Nicomachus.[43]

Book 5 opens with a very brief chapter of introduction, following which, Boethius begins retracing the broad course of Ptolemy's first book. The text breaks off abruptly following the presentation of Ptolemy's basic principles for dividing tetrachords. The titles of the last eleven chapters of the book have been preserved, revealing that Boethius intended to follow Ptolemy's first book in both basic content and detail. The theory which the last chapters would have contained can easily be surmised from their titles and Ptolemy's text. The completed book 5 would have filled out the following outline.

Chapters 2–3: *Ptolemy's concept of harmonics.* These chapters weigh the relative roles of reason and the senses in the discernment of musical sounds. The Pythagoreans are pictured as believing only reason, the Aristoxenians as believing only the senses. Ptolemy relies on both but leans toward reason. For him, the senses and reason are tools used by the harmonic faculty which makes musical judgments.

42. Ptolemy's reservations concerning the outright rejection of superpartient ratios are found in 1.5 and 1.6, and his specific dissent concerning the diapason-plus-diatessaron is found in 2.27.

43. Ptolemy's differing views concerning the ranking of consonances are found in 1.32 and 2.18.

Chapters 4–6: *The nature of musical intervals.* Ptolemy sides with the Pythagoreans in asserting that the basis for differences in sounds is quantitative, and that these differences are measured by ratios. Only discrete intervals are appropriate for musical judgment.

Chapters 7–10: *Ptolemy's criticism of the Pythagoreans' judgment concerning ratios.* Ptolemy argues that the diapason-plus-diatessaron is consonant, and that the Pythagoreans' use of ratios is too limited.

Chapters 11–12: *Ptolemy's classification of intervals.* Ptolemy's classification extends categories beyond consonant and dissonant intervals, and his association of interval with ratio is based on this expanded classification.

Chapters 13–14: *Ptolemy's "contra Aristoxenum."* Ptolemy refutes Aristoxenus's estimation of intervals and his contention that the diapason consists of six tones.

Chapters 15–18: *Tetrachord divisions by Aristoxenus and Archytas and Ptolemy's criticisms.* Ptolemy's text is the only record of these divisions of the tetrachord. His criticisms are based on arguments from reason and the senses.

Chapters 19–30: *Ptolemy's tetrachord divisions.* Ptolemy applies his principles to the tetrachord and develops a variety of divisions. Boethius's extant text ends with chapter 19.

Even from the incomplete translation of Ptolemy's first book, it is apparent that Ptolemy does not stand in complete opposition to Nicomachus and the Pythagoreans. The critical issue between Pythagorean and Aristoxenian theory concerns the measure of intervals: the Pythagoreans argue that the measure of intervals should be expressed in ratios, while Aristoxenians approach intervals indirectly—arguing that differences between pitches should be expressed as heard distances (logarithmic measures, as it were). In this conflict Ptolemy definitely sides with the Pythagoreans.[44]

Ptolemy's disagreements with the Pythagoreans are basically three. First, Ptolemy, as a more empirical scientist, cannot accept the unreasonable rejection of the consonance of the diapason-plus-diatessaron on the grounds that its ratio is not multiple or superparticular, given its obviously consonant sound.[45] Second, as a harmonic theorist, he finds the division of pitches into consonant and dissonant too limited; he divides all pitches into unison or non-unison, then subdivides non-unison pitches into equison, consonant, melodic, dissonant, or nonmelodic.[46] Third, as a mathematician with developed aesthetic sensibilities, Ptolemy cannot accept the fact that

44. Ptolemy (*Harmonica* 1.3) argues that the difference between high and low pitch is quantitative, and he expresses intervals in ratios.
45. Ibid., 1.5–6.
46. Ibid., 1.7.

Pythagoreans do not use superparticular ratios past the sesquitertian (except for the sesquioctave) in their division of systems and genera.[47] The first two areas of disagreement involve differences of degree—namely, the degree to which reason should accept the judgment of the sense of hearing and the degree to which pitches are subdivided. The third is more radical; in this area Ptolemy appears to be a more rigorous disciple of Pythagoras than the Pythagoreans, for he insists that the mathematical principles determining all intervals in his computations of genera exhibit the same consistency that the Pythagoreans require only of consonances.

Ptolemy extends the roles of both sense and reason in judgments concerning all classes of musical intervals, not just consonances. Ptolemy accepts the diapason-plus-diatessaron as a consonance because it sounds consonant, then determines its measure by reason;[48] furthermore, Ptolemy rejects certain intervals in divisions of genera because they do not satisfy the ear.[49] Although Ptolemy may misrepresent the Pythagoreans as relying immoderately on reason and as excluding the ears in musical judgment—a description not consistent with the Pythagorean position articulated by Boethius (1.9)—the role of the senses does seem much less passive in Ptolemy's approach, and the balance between sense and reason is consequently more dynamic. Boethius was clearly attracted to this refinement in judgment, for he goes on to suggest that the goal of a harmonic scholar should be to bring these two faculties, sense and reason, into concord.[50] This position, so articulated, has obvious appeal to a scholar compiling a treatise on music centered on the notion of knowing.

Boethius is not known to have taken sides in any intellectual dispute.[51] Nevertheless, while Boethius never rejects outright a doctrine from Nicomachus, he clearly accepts Ptolemy's criticisms and refinements of Nicomachus's position. Boethius could perceive the fundamental agreement between the Pythagoreans and Ptolemy in their quantitative approach to sounds. At the same time he was obviously impressed with Ptolemy's criticisms of Pythagorean positions, and doubtless, he was attracted to the extension of superparticular ratios into the division of genera. Ptolemy's *Harmonica* thus became for Boethius a logical extension of Nicomachus's *Eisagoge musica* as he read and translated music theory.

Boethius's fifth book breaks off with no warning following chapter 19.

47. Ibid., 1.6, 15.
48. Ibid., 1.6, Düring ed., 13.10–23, and 1.7, Düring ed., 16.8–10.
49. See, e.g., Ptolemy *Harmonica* 1.14, Düring ed., 32.3–4.
50. These words may represent Boethius's reading of Ptolemy, rather than Ptolemy's own expression, or they may represent a tradition of text or commentary no longer known. A dynamic relationship between the senses and reason is set down as a principle in Ptolemy *Harmonica* 1.2, and the positions of the Pythagoreans and the Aristoxenians are criticized. But the musical metaphor of this expression is not found in Ptolemy.
51. Concerning Boethius's neutrality, see E. K. Rand, *Founders of the Middle Ages* (Cambridge, Mass., 1928), pp. 145–46.

Titles for eleven more chapters are preserved at the beginning of book 5, and the music theory outlined in these titles follows closely the contents of the first book of Ptolemy's *Harmonica*. Did Boethius merely abandon this project? Or did he complete his treatise, and were the final chapters subsequently lost? No objective answer can be given to these questions. Yet there is reason to believe that Boethius intended to proceed beyond Ptolemy's first book. The *Harmonica* consists of three boks, and the final book presents a very cogent discussion of human and cosmic music. Boethius, at the close of his prologue, promised to return to human and cosmic music, topics not found in the extant text. If Boethius continued his translation of Ptolemy to completion, then he would have returned to these topics at the close of Ptolemy's last book,[52] and thereby have given his musical treatise the symmetry expected from the prologue. The original plan of *Fundamentals of Music* was thus probably for a work consisting of seven books, four based on Nicomachus and three on Ptolemy. These books would have recorded and translated the two ancient writers on music who most thoroughly developed a mathematical basis for the discipline. These authors fit best into Boethius's program for laying a foundation of mathematical science before moving on to Aristotelian logic. I would like to think that Boethius completed his project, and that the last part of the musical treatise—along with the treatises on geometry and astronomy, perhaps—was lost during that dark period between Boethius's death and the ninth century.

THE TEXT

One hundred and thirty-seven manuscripts or fragments of *De institutione musica* are available for study today.[53] These sources date from the ninth to the fifteenth centuries and represent most of the major intellectual and scribal centers of those centuries. The manuscripts often contain marginal glosses revealing careful study of Boethius's text. In these codices one finds evidence of scribes and scholars struggling with the text as they inherited it, of collating a new recension of the text from several earlier

52. "Human music" is treated in Ptolemy *Harmonica* 3.4–9, "cosmic music" in 3.10–14 (or 16).

53. For lists of codices containing the treatise, see Roger Bragard, "Boethiana: Etudes sur le De Institutione Musica de Boèce," in *Hommage à Charles van den Borren,* ed. S. Clercx and A. Vander Linden (Brussels, 1945), pp. 84–139; Michael Masi, "Manuscripts Containing the De Musica of Boethius," *Manuscripta* 15 (1971): 89–95; also Masi, "A Newberry Diagram of the Liberal Arts," *Gesta* 11/2 (1973): 52–56; Michel Huglo, Bulletin Codicologique no. 791, *Scriptorium* 27 (1973): 401–02; Michael Bernhard, *Wortkonkordanz zu Anicius Manlius Severinus Boethius De institutione musica,* Bayerische Akademie der Wissenschaften, Veröffentlichungen der musikhistorischen Kommission, vol. 4 (Munich, 1979), pp. 811–13; and Calvin M. Bower, "Boethius's *De institutione musica:* A Handlist of Manuscripts," *Scriptorium* 42 (1988).

sources, and of altering difficult passages to make them more consistent and intelligible. Considerable work remains to be done on the textual tradition of the treatise.[54]

I have based my translation on Gottfried Friedlein's edition of the text, the first and only critical edition. Michael Bernhard's *Wortkonkordanz zu Anicius Manlius Severinus Boethius De institutione musica*[55] is an indispensable tool for working with Friedlein's edition. For his Latin text, Friedlein basically worked with five manuscripts of south German provenance dating from the ninth to the eleventh centuries.[56] Sorting out Friedlein's editorial procedures from his critical apparatus is difficult; but one can safely observe that mathematical clarity and accuracy were among Friedlein's principal goals. He was willing to sacrifice a reading found in most sources for a "clear" reading found in one later source—even in the face of obvious scribal tampering. Friedlein has thus taken into his text several medieval emendations not found in the one ninth-century source he had at hand.[57]

A peripheral textual problem of Boethius's musical treatise is the Greek decree, written in Spartan dialect, found in the opening chapter. Friedlein worked on the decree, using the German codices he had available, an edition by Gronovius published in Venice in 1732, and notes compiled by André Laubmann from three Paris manuscripts.[58] Since the decree was torn out of the one ninth-century source he had at hand, Friedlein was forced to attempt to restore the text using corrupted versions and second-hand notes on ninth-century sources.[59] Friedlein's edition of the decree is remarkable, considering the circumstances under which he was working.

A major problem for anyone working with Boethius's text is that of the diagrams dispersed throughout the work. These visual representations

54. I am compiling a descriptive catalog of all manuscripts containing the treatise; the catalog will establish clearly definable families of manuscripts within the textual tradition and will link these families to specific locales and periods.

55. See, above n. 53.

56. The manuscripts used by Friedlein are listed on pages 175–77 of his edition (see above, n. 16). Eleven sources in all are listed, but Friedlein does not use the sources from Paris or Cambridge other than for consultation regarding the Greek text. He could use one of the sources from St. Emmeram (*1*, Clm 14,601) only for book 1 and the first two chapters of book 2, and he consulted his latest source (*o*, Clm 367, twelfth century) only when passages were particularly problematic.

57. Friedlein lists Munich, Bayerische Staatsbibliothek, Clm 14,523 (Em. F. 26) as dating from the tenth century; it is now recognized as a source from the ninth century (see below, n. 62).

58. See Friedlein ed., p. 176.

59. The Greek text is no longer extant in Clm 14,523. Friedlein did have secondhand reference to ninth-century sources, however. Laubmann transcribed for Friedlein Paris, Bibliothèque nationale, lat. 7,181 (Friedlein's P_1) and lat. 7,201 (Friedlein's P_3, erroneously listed by him [p. 176] as lat. 7,221), and sent him variant readings from lat. 7,200 (Friedlein's P_2). Judging from notes in Friedlein's apparatus, many of Laubmann's transcriptions and readings were questionable.

of demonstrations may represent one of the few genuinely Boethian contributions to the treatise, for, when describing his editorial procedures in the preface to *Fundamentals of Arithmetic,* Boethius claims to have added diagrams to those arguments which need additional explanation,[60] and he may have done likewise in *Fundamentals of Music.* Scribes reacted to the diagrams in much the same way that they reacted to difficult passages in the text, but here with even more imagination. They added new diagrams, and distinct traditions of diagrams—independent of textual traditions—can be identified in the codices. Although Friedlein's critical apparatus makes some attempt to record variants in these figures, the figures in Friedlein's text are themselves of little value and in most cases reflect neither the style nor the content of the sources. A critical study of diagrams found in all manuscripts would not only be helpful to the study of Boethius's text; it would serve to clarify the codicological history of medieval theory in general.

As a means of checking textual problems and establishing some basis for rendering diagrams, I have selected ten "control manuscripts" for the present translation. These manuscripts—all dating from the ninth century—represent the earliest extant sources of the text. My goal is to present an English version of Boethius's text which reflects as much as possible the earliest extant textual tradition, that of the ninth century. The manuscripts used for this purpose and the sigla I have given them are as follows:

B Besançon, Bibliothèque municipale, 507

This single gathering of a manuscript which originated in France contains only chapters 1–8 of the third book. It has been glossed by a hand from the early tenth century, and glosses, diagrams, and text show it to be closely related to other sources originating in northern France during the second half of the ninth century, particularly *Q* and *V.*[61]

I Munich, Bayerische Staatsbibliothek, Clm 14,523 (Em. F. 26)

This codex was formed by bringing together manuscripts of different origins and dates, and, as a whole, reflects a rich musical history. The gatherings containing Boethius's treatise originated in the ecclesiastical center of Freising during the administration of Bishop Anno (854–875).[62] This is the only ninth-century source used by Friedlein, and its siglum

---

60. See above, n. 19.
61. The dating of this manuscript is that of Professor Bernhard Bischoff, communicated to me by Dr. Michael Bernhard of the Musikhistorische Kommission of the Bayerische Akademie der Wissenschaften. The manuscript is cited in Huglo, Bulletin Codicologique, no. 791.
62. See Bernhard Bischoff, *Die südostdeutschen Schreibschulen und Bibliotheken in der Karolingerzeit,* vol. 1, *Die Bayerischen Diözesen* (Wiesbaden, 1960), p. 127; described in *The Theory of Music,* vol. 3, *Manuscripts from the Carolingian Era up to c. 1500 in the Federal Republic of Germany (RISM, B iii 3),* ed. Michel Huglo and Christian Meyer (Munich, 1986), pp. 113–16.

is *i* in his apparatus. The Doric decree and the diagrams of Greek notation from 4.15 and 4.16 have been torn out of this codex. Minor details in the diagrams and several textual variants distinguish this source from those originating in France.

K   Paris, Bibliothèque nationale, lat. 7,201

This manuscript was written in the first half of the ninth century in a monastic center of northern France, probably at St. Amand.[63] The earliest extant sources of the treatise, its text and diagrams are carefully written, although its gatherings, after the first, have been bound together in reverse order. This manuscript was also used by Friedlein, through André Laubmann, to establish a text for the Lacedaemonian decree; but Friedlein cites it (p. 176) as lat. 7,221 rather than 7,201. Friedlein's siglum is P_3.

M   Paris, Bibliothèque nationale, lat. 7,200

Although some have dated this manuscript as from the tenth century, Bernhard Bischoff has placed it around the middle of the ninth century. It originated in northern France, and formed part of the library at Fleury in the tenth century.[64] Text and glosses in this source reflect the tradition of northern France, but the diagrams differ significantly from those in all other ninth-century sources. The codex also contains an independent quire of diagrams bound at the end of *De institutione musica*. It was used by Friedlein, through Laubmann, to establish the text of the Lacedaemonian decree. Friedlein's siglum is P_2.

P   Paris, Bibliothèque nationale, lat. 7,181

Probably originating in some monastic center of northern France, this manuscript presents a major collection of the works of Boethius: it contains *De consolatione philosophiae* and *De institutione arithmetica*,

---

63. See Louis Royer, "Catalogue des écrits des théoriciens de la musique conservés dans le fonds latin des manuscrits de la Bibliothèque Nationale," *Année musicale* 3 (1913): 212; B. Bischoff, *Die südostdeutschen Schreibschulen und Bibliotheken in der Karolingerzeit*, vol. 2, *Die vorwiegend österreichischen Dözesen* (Wiesbaden, 1980), p. 70.

64. The opinion of Professor Bischoff concerning date has been expressed in print in Hucbaldus Pizzani, "[Bedae Presbyteri] *Musica theorica* sive Scholia in Boethii *de institutione musica libros quinque*," *Romanobarbarica* 5 (1980): 307, and concerning place of origin in Claudio Leonardi, "I codici di Marziano Capella," *Aevum* 34 (1960): 432. The tenth-century dating is attributed to Jean Vezin in Michel Huglo and Claude Durand, "Catalogue de l'exposition des manuscrits notés de Saint Benoît sur Loire," in *Les Sources en musicologie* (Paris, 1981), p. 171. The manuscript is listed in *The Theory of Music from the Carolingian Era up to 1400* [Austria, Belgium, Switzerland, Denmark, France, Luxembourg, Netherlands] (*RISM* B iii 1), ed. J. Smits van Waesberghe, with P. Fischer and C. Mass (Munich, 1961), p. 99.

as well as the musical treatise.[65] This source has played an important role in two editions of the *Consolatio*,[66] where it is given the siglum *P.* The Lacedaemonian decree is moderately well preserved in this source and was used by Friedlein through Laubmann. The codex is P_4 in Friedlein's apparatus for the decree.

Q   Paris, Bibliothèque nationale, lat. 13,908

A codex present in the library at Corbie in the ninth century, this manuscript probably originated in the area around Rheims around the middle of the ninth century.[67] Its text is carefully and accurately written and corrected, and it is rich in glosses also dating from the ninth century. The final gatherings of the manuscript have been lost. Its text breaks off after 4.11. The Lacedaemonian decree is particularly well written in this source, reflecting a significant grasp of the Greek text.

R   Paris, Bibliothèque nationale, lat. 13,955

This manuscript was written in the scriptorium of Corbie, probably during the third quarter of the ninth century.[68] The manuscript is a large and very important collection of texts treating the liberal arts. *R* appears to have been written one generation before *S* and *T,* the other manuscripts originating in the scriptorium of Corbie.

65. Royer, "Catalogue des écrits," p. 211; *Anicii Manlii Severini Boethii Philosophiae Consolationis libri quinque,* Corpus scriptorum ecclesiasticorum latinorum 67, ed. Guilelmus Weinberger, based on work of R. Peiper and G. Schepss (Leipzig, 1934), p. 52; and Ludwig Bieler, "Textkritische Nachlese zu Boethius' De Philosophiae Consolatione," *Wiener Studien. Zeitschrift für klassische Philologie* 52 (1934): 128–41.

66. That of Weinberger (see above, n. 65), and *Anicii Manlii Severini Boethii Philosophiae Consolatio,* Corpus Christianorum 94, ed. Ludwig Bieler (Turnholt, 1957).

67. See Royer, "Catalogue des écrits," p. 234, and Michel Huglo, "L'organum à Landévennec au IXe siècle," *Etudes Celtiques* 23 (1986): 191 (facs. of f. 60 on p. 188). Most of the scholarly discussion of this source has centered on the glosses written in the codex by a scribe known among contemporary scholars as "i²," an Irish scribe active in the circle of John Scottus Eriugena (d. ca. 880). See introduction to Edouard Jeauneau, *Commentaire sur l'Evangile de Jean* (Paris, 1972), pp. 63–80; T. A. M. Bishop, "Autographa of John the Scot," in *Jean Scot Erigène et l'histoire de la philosophie, Actes du Colloque No. 561 du CNRS à Laon, du 7 au 12 juillet 1976* (Paris, 1977), pp. 89–94;; John J. Contreni, *The Cathedral School of Laon from 850 to 930. Its Manuscripts and Masters,* Münchener Beiträge zur Mediävistik und Renaissance-Forschung 29 (Munich, 1978), p. 92; and Marie-Elisabeth Duchez, "Jean Scot Erigène premier lecteur du 'De institutione musica' de Boèce?," in *Eriugena. Studien zu seinen Quellen. Vorträge des III. Internationalen Eriugena-Colloquiums, Freiburg im Breisgau, 27.-30. August 1979* (Heidelberg, 1980), pp. 182–87. For a critical review of the literature on i², see John Marenbon, *From the Circle of Alcuin to the School of Auxerre. Logic, Theology and Philosophy in the Early Middle Ages* (Cambridge, 1981), pp. 89–96.

68. Royer, "Catalogue des écrits," p. 234; *The Theory of Music from the Carolingian Era up to 1400* [vol. 1], p. 119; Leonardi, "I codici di Marziano Capella," pp. 443–44; B. L. Ullman, "Geometry in the Mediaeval Quadrivium," in *Studi di bibliografia e di storia in onore di Tammaro de Marinis* 4 (Rome, 1964), pp. 263–85; Bernhard Bischoff, "Hadoardus and the MSS. of Classical Authors from Corbie," in *Didaskaliae. Studies in Honor of Anselm M. Albareda,* ed. S. Prete (New York, 1962), pp. 52–53.

S Paris, Bibliothèque nationale, lat. 14,080

This source also originated in the scriptorium of Corbie during the third quarter of the ninth century.[69] While it bears a marked resemblance to *T* in appearance, certain aspects of the codex link it with *R*. It also contains textual emendations in book 2 copied from *Q*.

T Paris, Bibliothèque nationale, lat. 13,020

A third source originating in the scriptorium of Corbie during the third quarter of the ninth century, this codex contains a text which seems to be formed in part from *Q* and in part from *R*.[70] The diagrams of this source are executed with particular care.

V Rome, Biblioteca Apostolica Vaticana, Reg. lat. 1,638

This manuscript originated in the second half of the ninth century, perhaps at Fleury-sur-Loire. The major portion of the extant manuscript—gatherings iii–ix and xi—can be dated as late ninth century, whereas the remaining gatherings—i, ii, and x—appear to have been written in the tenth century. Judging from the last folios of the eleventh gathering, the original manuscript suffered serious water damage, and certain of the gatherings were rewritten and replaced.[71] In textual details, glosses, and diagrams, this codex exhibits very close parallels with the sources from Corbie (*Q, R, S,* and *T*). At some point in its history the Lacedaemonian decree was torn away from the codex, but that single folio has been preserved in Leiden, Bibliotheek der Rijksuniversiteit, Voss. Misc. 38.

After reading Friedlein's text against these manuscripts, I am convinced that his text is fundamentally sound. I have chosen readings other than his only when the sense of the passage in question has been changed. I am not suggesting that my emendations be accepted as the critical rendering of Boethius's text but offer them as reflecting the textual tradition in circulation in the ninth century. The version of the Doric decree in this translation is based on the Greek text found in *K, M, P,* and *Q*.[72]

The style of the diagrams in the ninth-century manuscripts is simple and clear, and variations from codex to codex (with the exception of *M*)

69. Royer, "Catalogue des écrits," pp. 234–35; Ullman, "Geometry"; Bischoff, "Hadoardus."

70. Royer, "Catalogue des écrits," p. 234; Ullman, "Geometry"; Bischoff, "Hadoardus."

71. See August Reifferscheid, *Bibliotheca patrum Latinorum italica,* vol. 1 (Vienna, 1870), p. 328; Henry Marriott Bannister, *Monumenti Vaticani di paleografia musicale latina* (Leipzig, 1913), nos. 873, 961, and 1046; *The Theory of Music from the Carolingian Era up to 1400,* vol. 2, *Italy* (RISM, B iii 2), ed. Pieter Fischer (Munich, 1968), p. 118; and Michel Huglo, *Les Tonaires* (Paris, 1971), pp. 316, 381.

72. See 1.1 and Appendix 2.

are remarkably small. Most straight lines are either vertical or horizontal, and the curved lines are usually single arches drawn by hand or with the aid of a curve. I have attempted to reproduce the style of these drawings, while changing Roman numerals to Arabic and translating Latin technical terms into English. The diagrams are numbered according to sequence within books, with the letters A to E indicating the books. Limited notes on the diagrams are found in Appendix 3.

In most manuscripts a list of chapters is given at the beginning of books 2, 4, and 5 (it is from these lists that we know the titles of the concluding chapters of book 5), whereas no such list is given for books 1 or 3.[73] These lists are omitted from the translation which follows, but the complete list of all chapters in each book is found on the Contents pages.

THE TRANSLATION

In translating Boethius's late Latin, I set myself two goals: first, to make the facts and ideas of Boethius intelligible to modern readers of English; and second, to preserve something of the elevated tone of Boethius's Latin. These goals were often irreconcilable, however. If every *quidem, enim, autem,* and *vero* had been translated, the exaggerated tone would have become distracting—if not nonsensical. Logical connectives such as *igitur* are often used by Boethius when no logical connection exists. A clause is often introduced by *sed* when no contrary fact or condition follows. Boethius seems to have used these words as a form of punctuation, as well as a means of elevating the tone, and often they must remain untranslated— even if something of the hortatory character of the original is lost. I have tried, nevertheless, to maintain the excited tone that the teacher Boethius communicates, even in the most tedious, scholastic demonstrations of books 2 and 3. The tone of the original is an integral part of the treatise, exhorting the student to forsake enslavement of the senses and rise to the study of philosophy.

73. Of the control manuscripts, *I, K, M,* and *T* follow this pattern, and *Q* follows the pattern in its four extant books; *P* presents lists of chapters for all books except the fifth, *V* has no list of chapters for book 4, and *R* and *S* contain no lists of chapters. (Since *B* is only a fragment of book 3, no comparison can be offered.)

Fundamentals of Music

ANICIUS MANLIUS SEVERINUS BOETHIUS

BOOK 1

1. *Introduction: Music forms a part of us through nature, and can ennoble or debase character*

Perception through all the senses is so spontaneously and naturally present in certain living creatures that an animal without them cannot be conceived. But knowledge and clear perception of the senses themselves are not so immediately acquired through inquiry with the mind.[1] For it is indisputable that we use our senses to perceive sensible objects. But what is the nature of these very senses according to which we act? And what is the property of the sensible objects? Answers to these questions do not come easily to anyone; nor can they become clear unless appropriate inquiry has guided one in reflection concerning truth.

Sight, for example, is present in all mortal beings. Whether sight occurs by images coming to the eye or by rays sent out to sensible objects is a point of disagreement among the learned,[2] although this dispute escapes the notice of the ordinary person. Further, when someone sees a triangle

1. In this philosophical prologue, Boethius uses the word *animus* ("mind") to refer to the seat of reasoning, a function which stands in contrast to the functions of the passive senses. But *animus* is likewise used as the seat of feelings and emotions, the seat of courage and morale, and as the moral constitution of the person, all of which are affected by the senses, particularly the sense of hearing. Literary style further obscures precision of meaning, for *mens* is used as well as *animus* to give variety. Words such as "mind," "intellect," "reason," and even "soul" will be used to translate these two terms.

2. This dispute concerning sight was between the Epicureans, who held that vision was the result of images coming to the eye, and the Stoics, who held that vision took place by means of rays emitted from the eye. See Epicurus, in Diogenes Laertius *De vitis philosophorum* 10.49–50 and Lucretius *De rerum natura* 4.26–109; see also Zeno, in Diogenes Laertius 7.157; Gellius, in *Stoicorum veterum fragmenta*, ed. von Arnim, 2.871, and Cicero *Ad Atticum epistulae* 2.3.

I

or a square, he recognizes easily that which is observed with the eyes. But what is the nature of a triangle or a square? For this you must ask a mathematician.

Now the same can be said with respect to other sensible objects, especially concerning the witness of the ears: the sense of hearing is capable of apprehending sounds in such a way that it not only exercises judgment and identifies their differences, but very often actually finds pleasure if the modes[3] are pleasing and ordered, whereas it is vexed if they are disordered and incoherent.

From this it follows that, since there happen to be four mathematical disciplines,[4] the other three share with music the task of searching for truth; but music is associated not only with speculation but with morality as well. For nothing is more characteristic of human nature than to be soothed by pleasant modes or disturbed by their opposites. This is not peculiar to people in particular endeavors or of particular ages. Indeed, music extends [180] to every endeavor; moreover, youths, as well as the aged are so naturally attuned to musical modes by a kind of voluntary affection that no age at all is excluded from the charm of sweet song. What Plato rightfully said can likewise be understood: the soul of the universe was joined together according to musical concord.[5] For when we hear what is properly and harmoniously united in sound[6] in conjunction with that which is harmoniously coupled and joined together within us and are attracted to it, then we recognize that we ourselves are put together in its likeness. For likeness attracts, whereas unlikeness disgusts and repels.

From this cause, radical transformations in character also arise. A lascivious disposition takes pleasure in more lascivious modes or is often made soft and corrupted upon hearing them. On the other hand, a rougher spirit finds pleasure in more exciting modes or becomes aroused when it hears them. This is the reason why musical modes were named after certain peoples, such as "Lydian" mode and "Phrygian," for in whatever a partic-

3. "Mode" here is a translation of the Latin *modus*, words with broad spectra of meaning in each language. Properly speaking, the Latin term *modus* implies measurement, and in musical contexts a musical measurement or temperament or tuning. *Modus*, as used by Boethius, does not denote "mode" as the term was used in the later Middle Ages; nor does it have the rather specific connotation of octave-species that it carries today. In this treatise the word has various meanings: it may refer to tuning and temperament (as in the present context) or to the Greek *harmoniae* (as later in this chapter in reference to Plato) or to transposed systems or *tropoi* (as in 4.15–17).

4. The four mathematical disciplines are arithmetic, music, geometry, and astronomy. For an account of the derivation of these disciplines from the kinds of quantities, see 2.3. The four mathematical disciplines are defined as the *quadrivium* in Boethius's *Arith.* 1.1 (Masi trans., p. 73); they represent a fourfold path which leads the mind away from sense perception to abstract knowledge. As such, they are propaedeutic to the study of philosophy.

5. Plato *Timaeus* 35B.

6. Friedlein ed., 180.7: *quod in senis* should read *quod in sonis*. The *e* of *senis* is an obvious typographical error, confirmed by all manuscripts.

ular people finds pleasure, by that same name the mode itself is designated. A people finds pleasure in modes because of likeness to its own character, for it is not possible for gentle things to be joined with or find pleasure in rough things, nor rough things in gentle.[7] Rather, as has been said, similitude brings about love and pleasure.[8] Thus Plato holds that the greatest care should be exercised lest something be altered in music of good character. He states that there is no greater ruin of morals in a republic than the gradual perversion of chaste and temperate music, for the minds of those listening at first acquiesce. Then they gradually submit, preserving no trace of honesty or justice—whether lascivious modes bring something immodest into the dispositions of the people or rougher ones implant something warlike and savage.[9]

Indeed no path to the mind is as open for instruction as the sense of hearing. Thus, when rhythms and modes reach an intellect through the ears, they doubtless affect and reshape that mind according to their particular character. This again can be perceived in various peoples; those who are rougher delight in the rather uncultivated modes of the Getae,[10] whereas those who are more gentle delight in more moderate modes—although in these times this hardly ever occurs.[11] Since the human race has become lascivious and impressionable, it is taken up totally by representational and theatrical modes.[12] Music was indeed chaste and modest when it was performed on simpler instruments.[13] But since it has been squandered in var- [181]

7. The terms *mollis* and *durus* (translated from μαλακός and σκληπός) are technical terms in ancient theory. At the more general level of discussion, *mollis* describes music that is soft, tender, and effeminate in character, whereas *durus* describes music that is firm, austere, and masculine. At a more technical level, *mollis* denotes intervals, particularly semitones and quarter-tones, that are small and compact, whereas *durus* denotes intervals, particularly tones, that are broader and more expansive (see 1.21). For a broad survey of these terms in Western music, see Carl Dahlhaus, "Die Termini Dur und Moll," *Archiv für Musikwissenschaft* 12 (1955): 280–96.

8. Plato *Symposium* 187.

9. Plato *Republic* 424.

10. The Getae were the most northerly branch of the Thracian people. The province of Getae is described in Strabo *Geographica* 7.295, 304. This reference to their "uncultivated modes" is without precedent in ancient sources.

11. Boethius (or his source) may not be commenting directly on the actual music of his time in this passage; he is repeating a literary topos which was popular in musical writings of a more philosophical bent. For other examples, see Athenaeus *Deipnosophistae* 14.631E–632B and Plutarch *De musica* 1136B. This does not imply that the literary topos did not apply to music in the second century (the century of Nicomachus) or the sixth century (that of Boethius).

12. Complaints such as this are generally associated with the rise of "popular" theatrical innovations in music, such as those of Melanippides, Cinesias, Phrynis, and Timotheus, all musical innovators of the fifth century B.C. Concerning the role of audiences in determining musical tastes and values, see Athenaeus *Deipnosophistae* 14.631E–632A.

13. Idealization of an ancient simplicity is another topos of ancient theory; see Plutarch *De musica* 1135D for a statement very similar to this one. For a "history" of music in its ideal (i.e., simple) state, see 1.20.

ious, promiscuous ways, it has lost its measure of dignity and virtue; and, having almost fallen into a state of disgrace, it preserves nothing of its ancient splendor. Hence Plato prescribes that children not be trained in all modes, but only in those which are vigorous and simple.[14] This rule must be most carefully adhered to, for if henceforth anything should somehow be altered ever so slightly—albeit not noticed immediately—after some time it will make a considerable difference and will sink through the ears into one's character. Plato holds music of the highest moral character, modestly composed, to be a great guardian of the republic; thus it should be temperate, simple, and masculine, rather than effeminate, violent, or fickle.[15]

The Lacedaemonians guarded this tradition with greatest care and at considerable expense when the Cretan Thaletas of Gortyne[16] imbued children with the discipline of musical knowledge. This, in fact, was the custom [182] among ancient peoples and persisted for a considerable time. Thus, when Timotheus of Miletus[17] added one string to those that were already established, thereby making the music more capricious, a decree was drafted to expel him from Laconica. I have inserted this decree concerning him in the original Greek; since the inscription is in the Spartan language, the letter C (sigma) is changed to P (rho).

ΕΠΕΙΔΗ ΤΙΜΟΘΕΟΡ Ο ΜΙΛΗΣΙΟΡ
ΠΑΡΑΓΙΝΟΜΕΝΟΡ ΕΤΤΑΝ ΑΜΕΤΕΡΑΝ ΠΟΛΙΝ,
ΤΑΝ ΠΑΛΑΙΑΝ ΜΩΑΝ ΑΤΙΜΑΣΔΕ
ΚΑΙ ΤΑΝ ΔΙΑ ΤΑΝ ΕΠΤΑ ΧΟΡΔΑΝ ΚΙΘΑΡΙΖΙΝ
ΑΠΟΣΤΡΕΦΟΜΕΝΟΡ,
5   ΠΟΛΥΦΩΝΙΑΝ ΕΙΣΑΓΩΝ ΛΥΜΑΙΝΕΤΑΙ ΤΑΡ ΑΚΟΑΡ ΤΩΝ ΝΕΩΝ
ΔΙΑ ΤΕ ΤΑΡ ΠΟΛΥΧΟΡΔΙΑΡ ΚΑΙ ΤΑΡ ΚΕΝΟΤΑΤΟΡ ΤΩ ΜΕΛΕΟΡ,
ΑΓΕΝΝΗ ΚΑΙ ΠΟΙΚΙΛΑΝ ΑΝΤΙ ΑΠΛΟΑΡ ΚΑΙ ΤΕΤΑΓΜΕΝΑΡ
ΑΜΦΙΕΝΝΥΤΑΙ ΤΑΝ ΜΩΑΝ ΕΠΙ ΧΡΩΜΑΤΟΡ ΣΥΝΕΙΣΤΑΜΕΝΟΡ
ΤΑΝ ΤΩ ΜΕΛΙΟΡ ΔΙΑΣΚΕΥΑΝ ΑΝΤΙ ΤΑΡ ΕΝΑΡΜΟΝΙΩ
10   ΠΟΤΤΑΝ ΑΝΤΙΣΤΡΟΦΟΝ ΑΜΟΙΒΑΝ,
[183]   ΠΑΡΑΚΛΗΘΕΙΣ ΔΕ ΚΑΙ ΕΝ ΤΟΝ ΑΓΩΝΑ ΤΑΡ ΕΛΕΥΣΙΝΙΑΡ ΔΑΜΑΤΡΟΡ

14. Plato *Republic* 399C.

15. Plato *Republic* 399, 410–11.

16. In Plutarch *De musica* 1134B-C Thaletas of Gortyne on Crete (fl. seventh century B.C.) is said to have been one of the musicians responsible for the second establishment of music in Sparta. He is also said to have appeared in Lacedaemonia on the advice of a Delphic oracle (Plutarch *De musica* 1146C). Concerning the Spartan character of his music, see Plutarch *Lycurgus* 4. See also *Lyra Graeca,* a collection of fragments of Greek lyrical texts edited and translated by J. M. Edmonds, 2d, enlarged ed. (Cambridge, Mass., and London, 1928), vol. 1, pp. 35–37.

17. Timotheus of Miletus (fifth to fourth centuries B.C.) is the most infamous musician of antiquity because of his innovations; see Pausanius *Descriptio Graeciae* 3.12 and Plutarch *De musica* 1135C-D, 1141C–1142B, 1142C. Athenaeus *Deipnosophistae* 634E presents a somewhat different version of Timotheus's expulsion from Sparta, wherein he vindicates himself through rather ingenious means. See *Lyra Graeca,* vol. 3, pp. 280–333, and Timotheos Milesius *Die Perser,* ed. U. von Wilamowitz-Möllendorff (Leipzig, 1903), pp. 69–80.

ΑΠΡΕΠΗ ΔΙΕΣΚΕΥΑCΑΤΟ ΤΑΝ ΤΩ ΜΥΘΩ ΔΙΑCΚΕΥΑΝ
ΤΑΝ ΤΑΡ CΕΜΕΛΑΡ ΩΔΙΝΑΡ
ΟΥΚ ΕΝΔΙΚΑ ΤΩΡ ΝΕΩΡ ΔΙΔΑΚΚΗ;
15 ΔΕΔΟΧΘΑΙ ΦΑ ΠΕΡΙ ΤΟΥΤΩΝ
ΤΩΡ ΒΑCΙΛΕΑΡ ΚΑΙ ΤΩΡ ΕΦΟΡΩΡ ΜΕΜΨΑΤΤΑΙ ΤΙΜΟΘΕΟΝ:
ΕΠΑΝΑΓΚΑΖΑΙ ΔΕ ΚΑΙ ΤΑΝ ΕΝΔΕΚΑ ΧΟΡΔΑΝ
ΕΚΤΑΜΩΝ ΓΑΡ ΤΑΡ ΠΕΡΙΤΤΑΡ
ΥΠΟΛΙΠΟΜΕΝΩΝ ΤΑΡ ΕΠΤΑ.
20 ΟΠΩΡ ΕΚΑCΤΟΡ ΤΟ ΤΑΡ ΠΟΛΙΟΡ ΒΑΡΟΡ ΟΡΩΝ
ΕΥΛΑΒΗΤΑΙ ΕΤΤΑΝ CΠΑΡΤΑΝ
ΕΠΙΦΕΡΗΝ ΤΙ ΤΩΝ ΜΗ ΚΑΛΩΝ ΕΟΝΤΩΝ
ΜΗ ΠΟΤΕ ΤΑΡΑΡΕΤΑΙ ΚΛΕΟΡ ΑΓΟΝΩΝ.[18]

This decree sets forth the following: The Spartans were indignant with [184] Timotheus of Miletus, because, by introducing a capricious music to the minds of the children, he had thwarted those whom he had accepted to teach and had steered them away from the moderation of virtue, and because he had changed the harmony,[19] which he had found temperate, into the chromatic genus, which is overrefined. Indeed, the Spartans were so attentive to music that they thought it even took possession of minds.

It is common knowledge that song has many times calmed rages, and that it has often worked great wonders on the affections of bodies or minds. Who does not know that Pythagoras, by performing a spondee, restored a [185] drunk adolescent of Taormina incited by the sound of the Phrygian mode[20] to a calmer and more composed state? One night, when a whore was closeted in the house of a rival, this frenzied youth wanted to set fire to the house. Pythagoras, being a night owl, was contemplating the courses of the heavens (as was his custom) when he learned that this youth, incited by the sound of the Phrygian mode, would not desist from his action in response to the many warnings of his friends; he ordered that the mode be changed, thereby tempering the disposition of the frenzied youth to a state of absolute calm.[21] Marcus Tullius relates the story in his book, *De consiliis*

18. The text of this decree, as printed here, is based on manuscripts *K, M, P,* and *Q*. Appendix 2 provides notes on this text, a critical apparatus, and an English translation by T. Burgess.

19. *Armonia* (ἁρμονία), like *modus* (see above, n. 3) is a term with both general and specific denotations: it can refer, like *modus,* to the general arrangement of pitches in a system (particularly an octave), or it can denote the seven octave-species which form the basis of the seven tonoi. In certain contexts (e.g., Aristoxenus *Harmonica* 1.2, 23, and Boethius 1.15 of the present treatise) the word can even refer to the enharmonic genus. In the present context Timotheus is reprimanded for changing the structure of pitches in the octave, thereby changing the genus from enharmonic to chromatic.

20. Friedlein 185.1–2: *subphrygii modi sono incitatum* should read *sub phrygii modi sono incitatum*. The appropriate reading is clear, as is the grammar, in the manuscripts and in earlier editions; several lines later the mode is again identified as "Phrygian" (185.6). To read this as a latinization of "hypophrygian" (Pizzani, "Fonti," pp. 162–63) is to legitimate a misprint in Friedlein.

21. For the story of the frenzied youth, see Quintilian *Institutio oratoria* 1.10.32, Sextus

suis, but somewhat differently, as follows: "But I would compare something trivial with something important, since I am drawn by a likeness between them. When drunken youths, incited by the music of auloi,[22] as happens, were about to break in the door of a chaste woman, it is said that Pythagoras admonished the aulete to perform a spondee. When this was done, the severity of the rhythms and the seriousness of the performer caused the raging fury of the youths to subside."[23]

To cite some similar examples briefly, Terpander[24] and Arion of Methymna[25] saved the citizens of Lesbos and Ionia from very serious illness through the assistance of song. Moreover, by means of modes, Ismenias the Theban[26] is said to have driven away all the distresses of many Boeotians suffering the torments of sciatica. Similarly it is said that Empedocles altered the mode of music-making when an infuriated youth attacked one of his guests with a sword because this guest had condemned the youth's father by bringing an accusation. Thereby Empedocles tempered the wrath of the youth.[27]

This capacity of the musical discipline had become so familiar in the doctrines of ancient philosophy that the Pythagoreans, when they wanted

---

Empiricus *Adversus musicos* 6.8, Aristotle Elias, *Prolegomena philosophiae* 2 (ed. Adolf Busse, *Commentaria in Aristotelem Graeca,* vol. 18 [Berlin, 1890], p. 31), and Ammonius *In Porphyrii isagogen sive v voces* (ed. Adolf Busse, *Commentaria in Aristotelem Graeca,* vol. 4, pt. 3 [Berlin, 1891], p. 130).

22. The term *tibia* was used by Latin authors from the period of Ennius *Annales* 299 (293–169 B.C.) to translate the Greek ἀυλός, the principal wind instrument of antiquity. There seems to be no transliteration of *aulos,* as the name of an instrument, into Latin. Of the six appearances of the word *tibia* in Boethius's text, two are in quotations of other authors: the present instance from Cicero and the subsequent quotation of Statius concerning funeral processions. In this translation the word *tibia* will be translated as "aulos," and the performer will be called "aulete." See below, 1.34 and n. 138.

23. This same quotation from Cicero, with minor variants, is also found in Augustine *Contra Julianum* 5.5.23. Cicero's *De consiliis suis,* or Ανέϰδοτα, is no longer extant; see M. Schanz and C. Hosius, *Geschichte der römischer Literatur bis zum Gesetzgebungswerk des Kaisers Justinian,* vol. 1 (Munich, 1927), p. 531.

24. Terpander (of Antissa on the isle of Lesbos), who flourished between 700 and 650 B.C., is probably the most revered musician of antiquity. See *Lyra Graeca,* vol. 1, pp. 16–33. See also below, 1.20 and n. 104.

25. Arion of Methymna (Lesbos) was approximately contemporary with Terpander. This account of Terpander and Arion using music curatively seems to be unique. Concerning Arion, his music, and the dolphin legend, see Strabo *Geographica* 13.2.3, Herodotus *Historia* 1.23, and Hyginus *Fabula* 194. See also *Lyra Graeca,* vol. 1, pp. 136–39.

26. Ismenias of Thebes (fl. third century B.C.) is identified as an aulete in Plutarch *Pericles* 1.152.5 and idem, *Non posse suaviter vivi* 1095F, as well as in Lucian *Pseudologista* 5, although none of these passages treats him with much dignity or respect. Concerning the use of Phrygian, or Thracian, music to cure sciatica, see Athenaeus *Deipnosophistae* 624B. The coupling of Ismenias and the cure is found in no other source from antiquity.

27. This account of Empedocles' curative use of music is found in no other source. Concerning Empedocles' reputation as a physician, see Diogenes Laertius *De vitis philosophorum* 8.60–62, 77.

to relieve their daily concerns in sleep, employed certain melodies so that a mild and quiet slumber would fall upon them.[28] Likewise upon awakening, [186] they purged the stupor and confusion of sleep with certain other modes, for they knew that the whole structure of our soul and body has been joined by means of musical coalescence. For just as one's physical state affects feeling, so also the pulses of the heart are increased by disturbed states of mind. Democritus is said to have related this to the physician Hippocrates, who came to treat Democritus when he was being held in custody by his fellow citizens because they thought he was mad.[29]

But to what purpose is all this? So that there can be no doubt that the order of our soul and body seems to be related somehow through those same ratios[30] by which subsequent argument will demonstrate sets of pitches,[31] suitable for melody, are joined together and united. Hence it happens that a sweet tune delights even infants, while a harsh and rough one will interrupt the pleasure of listening. Certainly people of every age

28. Concerning the Pythagoreans' use of music for sleep, see Plutarch *Isis et Osiris* 31.384, Quintilian *Institutio oratoria* 9.4.12, and Censorinus *De die natali* 12.4.

29. Democritus of Abdera and Hippocrates of Cos both flourished in the late fifth century B.C. Both were known in antiquity for their powers as physicians. Concerning the relationships among Democritus, Hippocrates, and other parties, see documents concerning Democritus in Hippocratic *Corpus*, ed. E. Littré (Paris, 1839), vol. 9, pp. 321–99; concerning authenticity of the accounts, see L. Edelstein, "Hippokrates," in A. Pauly, G. Wissowa, and W. Kroll, *Real-Encyclopädie der klassischen Altertumswissenschaft* (1893–), Supp. 6 (1935), pp. 1290–1345, esp. pp. 1303–05. A brief account of the meeting between these two is recorded by Diogenes Laertius *De vitis philosophorum* 9.42, as well as other keen insights regarding Democritus. The present account concerning the effect of feelings on the pulse seems to be unique.

30. "Ratio" is a translation of the Latin *proportio*, which Boethius translated from the Greek λόγος. Boethius uses the term frequently as technical vocabulary denoting a mathematical ratio. For definition of the term, see book 2.12 and n. 34. In the present context, Boethius is speaking in analogical terms; but ultimately, the text is Pythagorean, and Pythagoreans would argue that the reality of the relation between body and soul is a ratio of numbers.

31. The verb *modulor* ("to modulate") and its substantive form *modulatio* ("modulation") present problems similar to those associated with the word *modus* (see above, n. 3). In fact, *modulor* is derived from *modus* and means the application of measure (*modus*) to the most basic elements of music—pitch and time. Hence the classical Latin definition of music: *musica est scientia bene modulandi* (e.g., Censorinus *De die natali* 10.10). To translate the verb *modulor* as "to sing" or "to play" and the noun *modulatio* as "melody" is to miss the *quantitative* denotation of the words—viz., the application of ratios to pitch and time. To translate the verb as "measure" and the noun as "measurement" seems too abstract, for these terms lack any artistic, aesthetic connotation. Yet to use the English "modulate" and "modulation" is to bring a technical, musical notion into the translation which does not apply— viz., the notion of "changing keys." I will attempt to capture the quantitative and systematic connotation of *modulatio* with such phrases as "arrangement of pitches" or "set of pitches." The verb *modulor* is more difficult. At times it must be translated as "measure" (e.g., at 1.12); at other times it must be given a less quantitative translation. In the next paragraph, e.g., *ipsos modulantur dolentes* (literally, "they modulate their very lamentations") is rendered "they turn their very lamentations into music." See Christoph von Blumröder, "Modulatio / Modulation," in *Handwörterbuch der musikalischen Terminologie*, ed. H. Eggebrecht (1983).

and sex experience this; although they may differ in their actions, they are nevertheless united as one in the pleasure of music.

Why is it that mourners, even though in tears, turn their very lamentations into music? This is most characteristic of women, as though the cause for weeping might be made sweeter through song. Among the ancients it was even the custom that music of the aulos led the procession of mourners, as these lines of Papinius Statius testify:

> The aulos, whose practice it is to lead forth the
>   youthful dead,
> Utters its mournful note from a curved horn.[32]

Someone who cannot sing well will nevertheless sing something to himself, not because the song that he sings affects him with particular satisfaction, but because those who express a kind of inborn sweetness from the soul—regardless of how it is expressed—find pleasure. Is it not equally evident that the passions of those fighting in battle are roused by the call of trumpets? If it is true that fury and wrath can be brought forth [187] out of a peaceful state of mind, there is no doubt that a more temperate mode can calm the wrath or excessive desire of a troubled mind. How does it come about that when someone voluntarily listens to a song with ears and mind, he is also involuntarily turned toward it in such a way that his body responds with motions somehow similar to the song heard? How does it happen that the mind itself, solely by means of memory, picks out some melody previously heard?

From all these accounts it appears beyond doubt that music is so naturally united with us that we cannot be free from it even if we so desired. For this reason the power of the intellect ought to be summoned, so that this art, innate through nature, may also be mastered, comprehended through knowledge. For just as in seeing it does not suffice for the learned to perceive colors and forms without also searching out their properties, so it does not suffice for musicians[33] to find pleasure in melodies without also coming to know how they are structured internally by means of ratio of pitches.[34]

---

32. Statius *Thebias* 6.120–21.

33. The Latin *musicus* carries more weight than the English "musician." For a definition of "musician," see 1.34.

34. "Pitch" is a translation of the Latin *vox*, Boethius's rendering of the Greek φθόγγος (see 1.12). *Vox* is a term with a wide spectrum of meanings, even in musical contexts, for it can mean the human voice, sound in general, or musical pitch. The most common usage in the treatise is the third by far. For the Pythagorean, pitch is an expression of quantity in music (see 1.3), and knowing the ratios of pitches is the goal of the first four books of this treatise.

2. *There are three kinds of music, and concerning the influence of music*

Thus, at the outset, it seems proper to tell someone examining music what we shall discover about the number of kinds of music recognized by those schooled in it. There are three: the first is cosmic, whereas the second is human; the third is that which rests in certain instruments, such as the kithara or the aulos or other instruments which serve melody.

The first kind, the cosmic, is discernible especially in those things which are observed in heaven itself or in the combination of elements or the diversity of seasons.[35] For how can it happen that so swift a heavenly machine moves on a mute and silent course? Although that sound does not penetrate our ears—which necessarily happens for many reasons[36]—it is nevertheless impossible that such extremely fast motion of such large bodies should produce absolutely no sound, especially since the courses of the [188] stars are joined by such harmonious union that nothing so perfectly united, nothing so perfectly fitted together, can be realized. For some orbits are borne higher, others lower; and they all revolve with such equal energy that a fixed order of their courses is reckoned through their diverse inequalities. For that reason, a fixed sequence of modulation cannot be separated from this celestial revolution.

If a certain harmony did not join the diversities and opposing forces of the four elements, how would it be possible that they could unite in one mass and contrivance?[37] But all this diversity gives birth to variety of both seasons and fruits in such a way that it nevertheless imparts one structure to the year. Whence if you imagine one of these things which supply such diversity taken away, then all things would seem to fall apart and, so to speak, preserve none of their consonance. And just as, on the one hand, adjustment of pitch in lower strings is such that lowness does not descend into silence, while, on the other hand, adjustment of sharpness in higher strings is carefully monitored lest the excessively stretched strings break because of the tenuity of pitch, but the whole corpus of pitches is coherent and harmonious with itself, in the same way we discern in cosmic music

35. Concerning cosmic music in general, see Plato *Timaeus* 35–36; idem, *Laws* 889B-C. Concerning the harmony of the heavens, see Pliny *Naturalis historia* 2.22(20).84, Cicero *De re publica* 6.18.18; Plutarch *De musica* 1147, Nicomachus *Enchiridion* 3, Censorinus *De die natali* 12, Macrobius *In somnium Scipionis* 2.1.2 and 6.1–6, and Ptolemy *Harmonica* 3.10–16, 104–11. Concerning the harmony of the elements, see Plato *Symposium* 188A, idem, *Timaeus* 32C; and Macrobius *In somnium Scipionis* 1.5.25. Concerning harmony of the seasons, see Plato *Symposium* 188A.

36. See, e.g., Cicero *De re publica* 6.18.19 and Macrobius *In somnium Scipionis* 2.4.14.

37. There seems to be a lacuna at this point in the text. Given the opening question of the paragraph, a discussion of harmony and the diversity of the elements should follow; but the text skips abruptly to a discussion of the diversity of the seasons. Thus a development of the harmony of the elements and an introduction to the harmony of the seasons are missing. Some scribe may have jumped from one "diversity" to another.

that nothing can be so excessive that it destroys something else by its own intemperance. Everything is such that it either bears its own fruit or aids others in bearing theirs. For what winter confines, spring releases, summer heats, and autumn ripens, and the seasons in turn either bring forth their own fruit or give aid to others in bringing forth their own. But these things ought to be discussed later more studiously.[38]

Whoever penetrates into his own self perceives human music.[39] For what unites the incorporeal nature of reason with the body if not a certain harmony and, as it were, a careful tuning of low and high pitches as though [189] producing one consonance? What other than this unites the parts of the soul,[40] which, according to Aristotle, is composed of the rational and the irrational?[41] What is it that intermingles the elements of the body or holds together the parts of the body in an established order? I shall also speak about these things later.[42]

The third kind of music is that which is said to rest in various instruments. This music is governed either by tension, as in strings, or by breath, as in the aulos or those instruments activated by water, or by a certain percussion, as in those which are cast in concave brass, and various sounds are produced from these.[43]

It seems, then, that we ought to discuss the music of instruments first in this work.[44] This is enough of a preamble; now the basic principles of music must be discussed.

38. Boethius never returns to this topic, in fact.

39. Concerning human music, see Plato *Phaedo* 86; idem, *Laws* 653B; idem, *Republic* 442–43; Cicero *Tusculanae disputationes* 1.10; Plutarch *De musica* 1140B; and Ptolemy *Harmonica* 3.5–7 (95–100).

40. This is the only place where Boethius uses the term *anima* to refer to the soul. See above, n. 1, for use of *animus*.

41. The text here refers only to Aristotle's division of the soul into a rational and an irrational part (*Nicomachean Ethics* 1.13.1102–03); it should not be understood as arguing that Aristotle thought harmony to be a principle in unifying these two parts. Significantly, Boethius does not cite *De anima* 432A-B, where Aristotle finds the division "rational-irrational" less than satisfactory.

42. In fact, Boethius never returns to this topic.

43. Concerning the division of instrumental music into "strings, winds, and percussion," see Cassiodorus *Institutiones* 2.5.6.

44. By the "music of instruments" Boethius understands the mathematical principles that determine the structure of classical systems. The remainder of book 1 presents all the basic elements of the discipline; books 2 and 3 then demonstrate abstract mathematical principles. The "music of instruments" finds its ultimate end in the division of the monochord in book 4. Book 5 (based on book 1 of Ptolemy's *Harmonica*) may be considered a continuation of the "music of instruments," for it presents and evaluates further mathematical principles for division of the system. The implication is clear, however, that "music of instruments" is not the only topic to be discussed by this text. Cosmic music and human music should be discussed for the plan set forth in this chapter to be complete (see above, nn. 38 and 42). For discussion of the complete scope of Boethius's work, see Introduction.

3. *Concerning pitches and concerning the basic principles of music*

Consonance, which governs all setting out of pitches, cannot be made without sound; sound is not produced without some pulsation and percussion; and pulsation and percussion cannot exist by any means unless motion precedes them. If all things were immobile, one thing could not run into another, so one thing should not be moved by another; but if all things remained still and motion was absent, it would be a necessary consequence that no sound would be made. For this reason, sound is defined as a percussion of air remaining undissolved all the way to the hearing.[45]

Some motions are faster, others slower; some motions are less frequent, others more frequent. If someone regards an uninterrupted motion, he will necessarily observe in it either speed or slowness; moreover, if someone moves his hand, he will move it in either a frequent or less frequent motion. If motion is slow and less frequent, low sounds are necessarily produced by the very slowness and infrequency of striking. But if [190] motions are fast and more frequent, high sounds are necessarily produced. For this reason, if the same string is made tighter, it sounds high, if loosened,[46] low. For when it is tighter, it produces faster pulsation, recurs more quickly, and strikes the air more frequently and densely. The string that is looser brings about lax and slow pulsations, and, being less frequent because of this very weakness of striking, does not vibrate very long.

One should not think that when a string is struck, only one sound is produced, or that only one percussion is present in these numerous sounds; rather, as often as air is moved, the vibrating string will have struck it. But since the rapid motions of sounds are connected, no interruption is sensed by the ears, and a single sound, either low or high, impresses the sense. Yet each sound consists of many sounds, the low of slower and less frequent

---

45. Compare this definition of sound with Nicomachus *Enchiridion* 4 (JanS. 242–43). See also the definition of sound below, 1.8 and n. 63.

46. The verbs *intendo* and *remitto,* along with their substantive forms *intentio* and *remissio,* present problems to the translator of medieval Latin theory. *Intendo* implies increasing the tension of a string, adding to the quantity (frequency) of a pitch, and rendering a pitch higher, all at the same time. *Remitto* implies the opposite: viz., loosening the tension of a string, reducing the quantity of a pitch, and rendering a pitch lower. This complex of meaning was particularly important to Pythagoreans, for they viewed pitch as essentially quantitative, and these words functioned particularly well for them as expressions of both the quantitative and the qualitative changing of pitch. In the course of the present chapter, the identification of addition and subtraction of quantity with raising and lowering of pitch forms an important step in a logical derivation of ratios as the essential element in musical expression. Depending on the context, these verbs will be translated "to tighten" or "to loosen," "to raise" or "to lower," and so on. In all cases the quantitative implications of raising or lowering pitch should be kept in mind.

sounds, the high of faster and more frequent ones.[47] It is as if someone carefully fashions a cone—which people call a "top"—and applies one stripe of red or some other color to it and spins it as fast as possible, then the whole cone seems dyed with the red color, not because the whole thing is thus, but because the velocity of the red stripe overwhelms the clear parts, and they are not allowed to appear. But these things will be treated later.[48]

Since high pitches are incited by more frequent and faster motions, whereas low ones are incited by slower and less frequent motions, it is evident that high pitch is intensified from low through some addition of motions, while low pitch is relaxed from high through lessening of motions. For high pitch consists of more motions than low. Plurality makes the difference in these matters, and plurality necessarily consists in a kind of numerical quantity. Every smaller quantity is considered in relation to a larger quantity as number compared to number. Of those things which are compared according to number, some are equal, and others unequal.[49] [191] Therefore, some sounds are also equal, while others stand at an interval from each other by virtue of an inequality. In those pitches which do not harmonize through any inequality, there is no consonance at all. For consonance is the concord of mutually dissimilar pitches brought together into one.[50]

4. *Concerning the species*[51] *of inequality*

Things which are unequal hold within themselves five criteria[52] relating to degrees of inequality. One is surpassed by another either by a multiple

47. For Pythagoreans, the theory that one sound consists of many is yet another step in the logical derivation of ratios as the proper subject of musical theory. Compare this theory of sound and the present argument with those found in Nicomachus *Enchiridion* 4 (esp. JanS. 243.17–244.11).

48. See 1.31 and 4.1.

49. In passages such as this Boethius assumes that the reader is familiar with *Arith*. Concerning these two types of related quantity (equal and unequal), see *Arith*. 1.21.

50. Compare this chapter, a Pythagorean preamble to the study of music, with 2.20 and 4.1. See also Nicomachus's theory of consonance below in 1.31.

51. Although the term *species* appears in the titles of this and the following chapter, in the text of both chapters the term *genus* is used to classify differences in inequalities. The term *genus* is here translated "class."

52. The term *momentum* challenges the translator in many places: Boethius was probably translating the Greek word ῥοπή, which denotes a weight used on a scale, but also connotes the critical moment of judgment, the turn of the scale. In the present context "criterion" conveys the notions of both standard and judgment. The three other instances of this word (1.9 [Friedlein ed., 196.8], 1.10 [Friedlein ed., 196.19 and 197.03]) present somewhat different problems. (Henceforth numbers in brackets will be references to Friedlein ed.) Concerning the term itself and its usage in antiquity, the Middle Ages, and Renaissance, see Paolo Galluzzi, *Momento, Studi galileiani* (Rome, 1979).

or by a singular part or by several parts or by a multiple and a part or by a multiple and parts.

The first class of inequality is called "multiple." The multiple is such that the larger number contains the whole smaller number within itself twice, three times, or four times, and so forth; nothing is either lacking or superfluous. It is called either "duple," "triple," or "quadruple"; and the multiple class proceeds into infinity according to this series.

The second class of inequality is that which is called "superparticular"; it is such that the larger number contains within itself the whole smaller number plus some single part of it: either a half, as three to two (and this is called the "sesquialter" ratio), or a third, as four to three (and this is called the "sesquitertian"). According to this manner in subsequent numbers, some single part in addition to the smaller numbers is contained by the larger numbers.

The third class of inequality is such that the larger number contains within itself the whole lesser number plus several of its parts besides. If it contains two parts more, it will be called the "superbipartient" ratio, as five is to three; whereas if it contains three parts more, it will be called "supertripartient," as seven is to four. The pattern can be the same in other numbers.

The fourth class of inequality, which is combined from the multiple and the superparticular, is such that the larger number has within itself the [192] lesser number either twice, or three times, or some other number of times, plus one other part of it. If the larger contains the smaller twice plus a half part, the ratio will be called "duple-sesquialter,"[53] as five is to two; whereas if the lesser number is contained twice plus a third part of it, it will be called "duple-sesquitertian," as seven is to three. But if the lesser number is contained three times plus its half part, it will be called "triple-sesquialter," as seven is to two. In this same way, the names of multiplicity and superparticularity are varied in other numbers.

The fifth class of inequality, which is called "multiple-superpartient," is such that the larger number has the whole lesser number within itself more than once, plus more than one single part of it. If the larger number contains the smaller number twice plus two parts of it besides, it will be called "duple-superbipartient," as three is to eight; or again a ratio of this class may be called "triple-superbipartient."[54]

---

53. Friedlein, following *I*, gives *duplex supersesqualter* [192.4], *duplex supersesquitertius* [192.6], and *triplex supersesqualter* [192.8] as names of proportions in this class; the reading of *I* is supported by *K, M, P,* and *V. Q,* however, does not contain *super* in the names of the ratios, and *super* is erased or underlined for omission in *R, S,* and *T.* A major branch of the manuscript tradition does not contain *super* (see Friedlein's apparatus, 192.4, 6, 8). When the multiple-superparticular class of inequality is discussed in *Arith.* (1.29), the prefix *super* does not appear in conjunction with names of ratios [61.19–21]. I thus lean toward the reading of *Q,* as supported by *Arith.*

We explain these things cursorily and briefly now, since we elucidated them carefully in the books we wrote concerning the fundamentals of arithmetic.[55]

5. *What species of inequality pertain to consonance*

Of these classes of inequality, the last two may be set aside, since they are a mixture of others; theorizing ought to be carried out within the first three. The multiple seems to hold the greater authority for consonances, whereas the superparticular seems to occupy the next place. The super-partient is excluded from consonance of harmony[56]—as acknowledged by various theorists, with the exception of Ptolemy.[57]

[193]

6. *Why multiplicity and superparticularity are assigned to consonances*

Now those things which are simpler by nature are demonstrated to be harmonious when brought into relationship. Since lowness and highness consist of quantity, those things which can retain the property of discrete quantity will be discovered best to preserve the nature of consonance. One kind of quantity is discrete, while another is continuous. Quantity that is discrete is finite at its smallest point, but proceeds through larger quantity to infinity. For in this kind of quantity, unity[58] is the smallest element, and it is finite, whereas the measurement of plurality extends to infinity, in the manner that number, which begins from finite unity, increases with no limit. Quantity that is continuous, on the other hand, is finite as a whole, but is

54. Friedlein's *ut sunt tres et .XI* [192.17] is a gloss which became a part of the textual tradition in the late ninth and tenth centuries. It is not found at all in *K*, *P*, or *T*, whereas it (or *ut sunt .III. ad .XI.*) is found as a gloss in *I*, *M*, *Q*, *R*, and *V*. The only control manuscript which takes the phrase into the text is *S*. But no concrete numbers (viz., 3 and 11) are given in the original text for this proposition.

55. See *Arith.* 1.21–31, and below, 2.4.

56. "Consonance of harmony," my translation of *armoniae concinentia*, could be construed as redundant. But one must recall that *armonia* in its general meaning implies a well-ordered arrangement of pitches in a system (see above, n. 19). The text should thus be interpreted to mean that the superpartient class of proportion is separated from consonance in a well-ordered, rational system of musical pitch.

57. Ptolemy *Harmonica* 1.7.15; see below, 5.9.

58. Number is defined in *Arith.* 1.3 as a "collection of unities, or a flowing forth of quantity from unities" (*Numerus est unitatum collectio, vel quantitatis acervus ex unitatibus profusus* [13.11–12]). Unity is described as "mother of all number" (*Arith.* 1.14 [30.28], 1.17 [37.18], 2.8 [98.7], and, as implied in the present passage, unity is indivisible (*Arith.* 1.9 [17.12], 1.10 [23.8]. Boethius's *unitas* is a translation of the Greek μονάς. In ancient arithmetic, unity (the monad) had a certain ontological force, as well as a function in calculations. Often the number 1 is not used in arithmetical texts, and the word μονάς, or *unitas*, occurs in its place. In order to preserve the philosophical character of Pythagorean arithmetic, "unity" will be used in the translation where *unitas* designates the number 1 in calculations.

infinitely divisible. For a line—which represents continuous quantity—can be divided at any time into an infinite number of segments (since its length is a foot or some other finite measure). Therefore, number always increases to infinity, whereas continuous quantity decreases to infinity.[59]

Multiplicity, then, since there is no end to its increasing, preserves most of all the nature of number. The superparticular class, on the other hand, since it divides the smaller part into infinity, possesses the property of continuous quantity; it divides the smaller part because it always contains it plus a part of it—whether a half, third, fourth, or fifth. Indeed the very part named by the larger number always decreases (since a third is named by three, a fourth by four, and since four surpasses three, the fourth rather than the third is found to be smaller).[60]   [194]

The superpartient class, in a certain sense, departs from singleness of nature; for it contains two, three, or four parts over and above, and—departing from simplicity—abounds in a certain plurality of parts.

Every multiple ratio, in addition, contains the whole of itself, for a duple takes the total lesser quantity twice, the triple contains the total lesser three times, and so on in the same manner. Superparticularity, on the other hand, preserves nothing undivided, but yields an excess of a half, a third, a fourth, or a fifth; nevertheless the superparticular class achieves division into singular and simple parts. The superpartient ratio, however, neither retains undivided parts nor admits singular parts, and thus, according to Pythagoras, this class of ratios is not brought to bear on musical consonances. Ptolemy, nevertheless, placed even this class of ratios among consonances, as I will show later.[61]

7. *Which ratios should be fitted to which musical consonances*

Meanwhile this should be known: all musical consonances consist of a duple, triple, quadruple, sesquialter, or sesquitertian ratio. Moreover, that which is sesquitertian in number will be called "diatessaron" in sounds; that which is sesquialter in number is called "diapente" in pitches; that which is duple in ratios, "diapason" among consonances; the triple, "dia-

59. Concerning continuous and discrete quantity, see *Arith.* 1.1 [8.15–9.26] and below, 2.3.

60. This passage comparing ratios of the multiple class with discrete quantity and ratios of the superparticular class with continuous quantity seems unique to Boethius's text.

61. See below, 5.7, and Ptolemy *Harmonica* 1.7.15. In fact, Ptolemy does not place superpartient ratios among consonances, but only the multiple-superbipartient ratio 8:3; this is the ratio of the diapason-plus-diatessaron, an interval which Ptolemy believes to be consonant. This chapter is laden with Pythagorean values that will reappear in book 2: singularity, multiplicity, and discrete quantity are all prior to duplicity, superparticularity, and continuous quantity in order of being known and are thus of higher value. See esp. 2.20.

pason-plus-diapente"; the quadruple, "bis-diapason."[62] For the present, let the above be stated generally and without particulars; later, the complete theory of ratios will be brought to light.

8. Definitions of sound, interval, and consonance

Sound is a melodic instance of pitch; it is "melodic" in that it functions within a composition in a given tuning. (At present we do not wish to define sound in general, but only that which is called "phthongos" in Greek from the similarity to speaking, that is, φθέγγεσθαι.)[63]

Interval is the distance between high and low sound.[64]

Consonance is a mixture of high and low sound falling pleasantly and uniformly on the ears.[65]

Dissonance, on the other hand, is a harsh and unpleasant percussion of two sounds coming to the ear intermingled with each other.[66] For as long as they are unwilling to blend together and each somehow strives to be heard unimpaired, and since one interferes with the other, each is transmitted to the sense unpleasantly.

9. Not all judgment ought to be given to the senses, but reason ought more to be trusted. Concerning the deception of the senses in this matter

We propose, concerning these matters, that we should not grant all judgment to the senses—although the whole origin of this discipline is taken from the sense of hearing, for if nothing were heard, no argument what-

62. These terms served as the names of musical intervals in antiquity and the Middle Ages, and they have been retained in this translation: diatessaron for fourth, diapente for fifth, diapason for octave, diapason-plus-diatessaron for eleventh; diapason-plus-diapente for twelfth, and bis-diapason for fifteenth.

63. The term *sonus* in this definition clearly refers to sound as a musical entity and not in the most general sense (see definition of sound in 1.3, also n. 45). The term *vox* and its Greek counterpart φθόγγος are more ambiguous than "pitch," for they refer to the spoken or sung voice as well as to abstract tone; the particular usage of *sonus* and *vox* becomes clear in the complete text of the definition. "In a given tuning" (*in unam intensionem*) establishes the musical context for the melodic sound; that is, it must be at a particular level of pitch and function in a genus and system. Friedlein properly preserves the unique spelling of *intensio* (rather than *intentio*) at this point in the text, although the meaning of the change remains unexplained; the unique spelling is recorded in the control manuscripts, whereas all other occurrences of the word are written as *intentio* (*intencio* in *V*). Compare the use of *vox* in this chapter with that in 1.12. Compare, too, this definition of sound with Nicomachus *Enchiridion* 13 (JanS. 261.4–7) and Aristoxenus's definition of *phthongos* in *Harmonica* 15. Concerning *intentio*, see above, n. 46.

64. See Nicomachus *Enchiridion* 12 (JanS. 261.8).

65. See Nicomachus *Enchiridion* 12 (JanS. 262.1–2); also below, 1.28, 1.30, and 5.1.

66. See Nicomachus *Enchiridion* 12 (JanS. 262.5–6).

soever concerning pitches would exist. Yet the sense of hearing holds the origin in a particular way, and, as it were, serves as an exhortation; the ultimate perfection and the faculty of recognition consists of reason, which, holding itself to fixed rules,[67] does not falter by any error.

But what need is there to speak at length concerning the error of the senses, when this same faculty of perceiving is neither equal in all persons nor equal in the same person at all times? Anyone who aspires to search for truth would to no purpose trust wavering judgment. For this reason the Pythagoreans follow a certain middle path. They do not yield the whole of judgment to the ears, yet certain things are not investigated by them except through the ears.[68] The Pythagoreans estimate consonances themselves with the ear, but they do not entrust the distances by which consonances differ among themselves to the ears, whose judgments are indecisive. They delegate the determination of distances to rules and reason—as though the sense were something submissive and a servant, while reason is a judge and carries authority. [196]

Although basic elements of almost every discipline—and of life itself— are introduced through the impression of the senses, nevertheless there is no certain judgment, no comprehension of truth, in these if the arbitration of reason is lacking. For sensation itself is impaired by excess in greatness and smallness alike. It is possible not to perceive very small things because of the minuteness of the sensible objects themselves, and sense perception is frequently confused by very large objects. In pitches, for example, the hearing grasps with difficulty those that are very soft; but if pitches are very loud, the hearing is deafened by the intensity of the sound itself.

10. *In what manner Pythagoras investigated the ratios of consonances*

This, then, was primarily the reason why Pythagoras, having abandoned the judgment of hearing, had turned to the weights of rules.[69] He put no credence in human ears, which are subject to change, in part through

67. The term *regula* ("rule"), inconspicuously inserted in the opening sentence of this chapter, carries increasing weight as the treatise progresses. The ultimate *regula* (κανών in Greek) for the musical discipline is that of the monochord, the instrument which makes audible the principles which rule reason in musical thinking.

68. The moderation of the Pythagoreans—especially the earliest ones—may be somewhat overstated here; see below, 5.3, and Plutarch *De musica* 1144F. The moderation expressed in this chapter is clarified in 3.10.

69. A subtle play with meanings occurs in this chapter and the next: *momentum* (ῥοπή) implies a standard weight, a weight used in measurement (see above, n. 52). Pythagoras is about to discover his rule, his measure of consonances, in the weight (*pondus*) of the hammers used in the smithy. In the next chapter he will "weigh" (*perpendo*) his theory of consonance. I suggest that subsequent uses of "weigh" in book 1 (1.28 [220.3] and 1.34 [224.19 and 225.8]) reiterate the concept of *momentum* and *perpendo* from these chapters.

nature, in part by external circumstance, and undergo changes caused by age. Nor did he devote himself to instruments, in conjunction with which much inconstancy and uncertainty often arise. When you wish to examine strings, for example, more humid air may deaden the pulsation, or drier air may excite it, or the thickness of a string may render a sound lower, or thinness may make it higher, or, by some other means, one alters a state of previous stability. Moreover, the same would be true of other instruments.

[197]   Assessing all these instruments as unreliable and granting them a minimum of trust, yet remaining curious for some time, Pythagoras was seeking a way to acquire through reason, unfalteringly and consistently, a full knowledge of the criteria for consonances. In the meantime, by a kind of divine will, while passing the workshop of blacksmiths, he overheard the beating of hammers somehow emit a single consonance from differing sounds. Thus in the presence of what he had long sought, he approached the activity spellbound. Reflecting for a time, he decided that the strength of the men hammering caused the diversity of sounds, and in order to prove this more clearly, he commanded them to exchange hammers among themselves. But the property of sounds did not rest in the muscles of the men; rather, it followed the exchanged hammers. When he had observed this, he examined the weight of the hammers. There happened to be five hammers, and those which sounded together the consonance of the diapason were found to be double in weight. Pythagoras determined further that the same one, the one that was the double of the second, was the sesquitertian of another, with which it sounded a diatessaron. Then he found that this same one, the duple of the above pair, formed the sesquialter ratio of still another, and that it joined with it in the consonance of the diapente. These two, to which the first double proved to be sesquitertian and sesquialter, were discovered in turn to hold the sesquioctave ratio between themselves.[70] The fifth hammer, which was discordant[71] with all, was discarded.

Although some musical consonances were called "diapason," some "diapente," and some "diatessaron" (which is the smallest consonance)

70. The above narrative seems construed to make it difficult for the reader to follow the weights and sounds of the respective hammers. The emphasis is on the resounding consonances and the proportions discovered between hammers producing consonances. The Pythagorean tetractys is not introduced until the very end of the chapter, and then "for the sake of illustration." Some manuscripts—e.g., Q—contain the numbers 12, 9, 8, and 6 as interlinear glosses over words in the text, as a means of keeping track of the hammers. Many later sources—e.g., Munich, Clm 18,480—present a diagram at this point, illustrating the possible ratios contained in the four numbers 12, 9, 8, 6. The present translation seeks to keep the character of gradual revelation of Boethius's original text.

71. Boethius uses the term *inconsonans,* which I have translated "discordant." He uses this term in only one other place—in the description of music in its ideal state, which consists of only four notes, which again are related as 12:9:8:6 (1.20 [206.5]). The presence of this term in these two passages further demonstrates the close relationship between them.

before Pythagoras, Pythagoras was the first to ascertain through this means by what ratio the concord of sounds was joined together. So that what has been said might be clearer, for sake of illustration, let the weights of the four hammers be contained in the numbers written below.

$$12 : 9 : 8 : 6.$$

Thus the hammers which bring together 12 with 6 pounds sounded the [198] consonance of the diapason in duple ratio. The hammer of 12 pounds with that of 9 (and the hammer of 8 with that of 6) joined in the consonance of the diatessaron according to the epitrita[72] ratio. The one of 9 pounds with that of 6 (as well as those of 12 and 8) commingled the consonance of the diapente. The one of 9 with that of 8 sounded the tone according to the sesquioctave ratio.

II. *By what differing means Pythagoras weighed the ratios of consonances*

Upon returning home, Pythagoras weighed carefully by means of different observations whether the complete theory of consonances[73] might consist of these ratios. First, he attached corresponding weights to strings and discerned by ear their consonances; then, he applied the double and mean and fitted other ratios to lengths of pipes. He came to enjoy a most complete assurance through the various experiments. By way of measurement, he poured ladles of corresponding weights into glasses, and he struck these glasses—set in order according to various weights—with a rod of copper or iron, and he was glad to have found nothing at variance. Thus led, he turned to length and thickness of strings, that he might test further. And in this way he found the rule, about which we shall speak later.[74] It came to be called by that name, not because the rule with which we measure the sizes of strings is wooden, but because this kind of rule is tantamount to such fixed and enduring inquiry that no researcher would be misled by dubious evidence.[75]

72. Epitritos (ἐπίτριτος), the Greek term for one and a third—i.e., 4/3, or sesquitertian ratio.

73. At this point Boethius introduces the word *symphonia,* a transliteration of the Greek συμφονία, fully equivalent to the Latin *consonantia.* The word had been introduced into Latin vocabulary by Vitruvius *De architectura* 1.1.9, and other writers before Boethius had used the term as equivalent to *consonantia.* Boethius seems to use it for the sake of variety, but always in a context where *consonantia* could just as well have been used. *Symphonia* is here translated, like *consonantia,* as "consonance."

74. Boethius is playing on the double meaning of the Latin word *regula,* a word similar to the English "rule." *Regula* can mean a calibrated stick or a procedural guide and standard of judgment. The musical "rule," which will be revealed in 4.5–12, is so named from the latter meaning, despite the fact that the actual tool, the monochord, is made of wood.

75. Concerning Pythagoras's discovery of these musical ratios and his experiments, see

12. *Concerning the classification of voices*[76] *and an explanation thereof*

Enough concerning these things. Now we should consider the different kinds of voices. Every voice is either συνεχής, which is continuous, or διαστεματική, which it is named when it is sustained by means of interval.[77]

A voice is continuous when, as in speaking or reciting a prose oration, we hurry over words: the voice hastens not to get caught up in high and low sounds, but to run through the words very quickly, and the impulse of continuous voice is occupied with pronouncing and giving meanings to the words.

Διαστεματική, on the other hand, is that voice which we sustain in singing, wherein we submit less to words than to a sequence of intervals forming a tune.[78] This particular voice is more deliberate, and by measuring out differences of pitch it produces a certain interval, not of silence, but of sustained and drawn out song.

To these, as Albinus[79] asserts, is added a third, different kind, which can incorporate intermediate voices, such as when we recite heroic poems

---

Nicomachus *Enchiridion* 6 (JanS. 245–48), Gaudentius *Eisagoge* 9 (JanS. 340–41), Iamblicus *Vita de Pythagora* 1.24, Aristotle Elias *Prolegomena philosophiae* 2 (ed. Adolf Busse, p. 29), and Macrobius *Commentarii in somnium Scipionis* 2.1.9–14. As widespread as this story is in antiquity, most of the observations reported are physically impossible; the ratios supposedly tested by Pythagoras are valid if applied to lengths of pipes or strings, but not to weights of hammers or weights attached to strings. See Mersenne, *Questions harmoniques* (Paris, 1634), p. 166; Claude Palisca, "Scientific Empiricism in Musical Thought," pp. 127–29; and Walter Burkert, *Lore and Science in Ancient Pythagoreanism,* pp. 374–77.

76. In this chapter and the following, the term *vox* is used unequivocally to denote the human voice (see above, n. 34). The distinction between a continuum of pitch built with discrete pitches and a continuum with no discrete steps is something of a standard topic in ancient theory; the same distinction is made in 5.5, there derived from Ptolemy and using a more abstract (pure pitch) notion of *vox.*

77. See Nicomachus *Enchiridion* 2 (JanS. 238) concerning these classifications and descriptions. Boethius chooses the word *suspensa* (*suspendo*) to contrast with *continua* (*continuo*); *suspendo* implies both interrupting and suspending, supporting, or hovering, as in the case of a melody which is both sustained and interrupted by intervals. *Suspensa* has been translated as "sustained."

78. "Sequence of intervals forming a tune" is a translation of *modulis* [199.11] (dative plural of *modulus*), a term which Boethius uses only once. It is obviously related to the *modus/modulatio* complex of meanings (see above, nn. 3 and 31). As a singular noun, *modulus* would imply an interval, but in the plural as in the present context, the term suggests an indefinite number of intervals forming a musical entity. See *OLD* 1124.

79. The musical writings of Albinus, also cited in Cassiodorus *Institutiones* 2.5.10, are not extant. Boethius, in *In librum Aristotelis de interpretatione editio secunda, seu maiora commentaria,* ed. Meiser, pp. 3–4, also cites writings on geometry and logic by Albinus. Concerning this third type of voice, see Martianus Capella *De nuptiis* 9.937.

not in continuous flow as in prose or in a sustained and slower moving manner as in song.

13. *That human nature limits the boundlessness of voices*

The voice which is continuous and that with which we run through song are inherently boundless. For by consideration generally agreed upon, no limit is placed either on flowing through words or on rising to high pitches or sinking to low ones. But human nature imposes its own limitation on both of these kinds of voice. The human breath places a limit on the continuous voice, which it cannot exceed for any reason, for every person speaks continuously as long as his natural breath permits. Human nature [200] likewise places a limit on the diastematic voice, which puts bounds on a person's high and low pitch, for a person can ascend just so high and descend just so low as the range of his natural voice allows.[80]

14. *How we hear*

At this time we should discuss how we hear. The same thing happens in sounds that happens when a stone, thrown from above, falls into a puddle or into quiet water. First it causes a wave in a very small circle; then it disperses clusters of waves into larger circles, and so on until the motion, exhausted by the spreading out of waves, dies away. The latter, wider wave is always diffused by a weaker impulse. Now if something should impede the spreading waves, the same motion rebounds immediately, and it makes new circles by the same undulations as at the center whence it originated.

In the same way, then, when air that is struck creates sound, it affects other air nearby and in this way sets in motion a circular wave of air; and so it is diffused and reaches the hearing of all standing around at the same time. The sound is fainter to someone standing at a distance, since the wave of activated air approaches him more weakly.

15. *Concerning the sequence of subjects,*
that is, of speculations

Having set forth these matters, it seems that we should discuss the number of genera within which all song is composed and which the disci-

80. See Nicomachus *Enchiridion* 2 (JanS. 239–40).

pline of harmonic theory[81] contemplates. They are these: diatonic, chromatic, and enharmonic.[82] These must be explained, but first we must discuss tetrachords and in what manner the augmented number of strings came into existence (to which more are added now). This will be done after we have recalled in what ratios musical consonances are combined.[83]

[201]

16. *Concerning the consonances and the tone and the semitone*[84]

The consonance of the diapason is that which is made in the duple

---

81. Boethius here uses a word from the discipline of rhetoric—viz., *inventio*—to describe systematic musical thought. In rhetorical discourse *inventio* is used to denote the defining of subject matter and the devising of arguments; so I have translated *armonicae inventionis disciplina* as "discipline of harmonic theory." See also 5.2 and n. 4.

82. In this chapter Boethius uses the terms *diatonum, chroma* and *armonia* to designate the genera; these are substantive forms transliterated from the Greek διάτονον, χρῶμα, and ἁρμονία. See Cleonides *Isagoge* 3 (JanS. 181.12), Bellerman's Anonymous II, 14 (originally in F. Bellermann, *Anonymi scriptio de musica* [Berlin, 1841], newly edited in Dietmar Najock, *Drei anonyme griechische Traktate über die Musik* [Göttingen, 1972], 76.10–11), and Anonymous III, 52 (Najock 104.8). This is the only place where Boethius uses *armonia* for enharmonic. *Diatonum* and *chroma* are used again together in 1.21, and *chroma* also appears in 5.16 and 18. Boethius generally uses the adjective forms of these terms: *genus diatonicum, chromaticum,* and *enarmonium.*

83. The purpose of this chapter is to prepare the reader for the chapters which follow: 16–19 consider the structure of musical consonances; 20 discusses basic tetrachords and the addition of strings; and 21 arrives at the genera of song.

84. This chapter begins by stating seven basic tenets concerning ratios of consonances and the tone, accompanied by diagrams for each. These declarations are found in all the control manuscripts and in most later sources, and their character is emphasized through the use of majuscule script in most sources (*I, K, M, Q, T,* and many later sources). Friedlein judged these prefatory elements to be unessential accretions, and he printed them (according to *I*) and a version of the diagrams only in his apparatus. But the text which follows the declarations and diagrams builds on them, and both textual history and context argue that they are an integral part of Boethius's text. I have based my translation on the text as it appears in *K, M, P, Q,* and *T:*

DIAPASON SYMPHONIA EST QUAE FIT IN DUPLO, UT EST HOC.
DIAPENTE VERO EST QUAE CONSTAT HIS NUMERIS.
DIATESSARON VERO EST QUAE IN HAC PROPORTIONE CONSISTIT.
TONUS VERO SESQUIOCTAVA PROPORTIONE CONCLUDITUR, SED IN HOC
    NONDUM EST CONSONANTIA.
DIAPASON VERO ET DIAPENTE TRIPLA COMPARATIONE COLLIGITUR,
    HOC MODO.
BISDIAPASON QUADRUPLA COLLATIONE PERFICITUR.
DIATESSARON AC DIAPENTE UNUM PERFICIUNT DIAPASON, HOC MODO.

ratio, such as this [Fig. A.1]:

DIAPASON

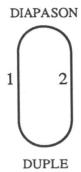

DUPLE

The diapente is that which consists of these numbers [Fig. A.2]:

DIAPENTE

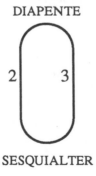

SESQUIALTER

The diatessaron is that which occurs in this ratio [Fig. A.3]:

DIATESSARON

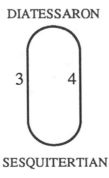

SESQUITERTIAN

The tone is comprised of the sesquioctave ratio, but there is no consonance in this [Fig. A.4]:

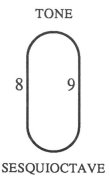

TONE

8   9

SESQUIOCTAVE

The diapason-plus-diapente is brought together through the triple ratio in this manner [Fig. A.5]:

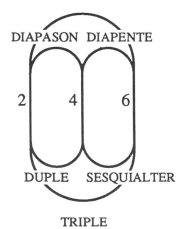

DIAPASON-PLUS-DIAPENTE

DIAPASON DIAPENTE

2   4   6

DUPLE   SESQUIALTER

TRIPLE

The bis-diapason is brought about through the quadruple comparison [Fig. A.6]:

QUADRUPLE

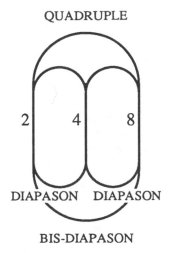

2   4   8

DIAPASON   DIAPASON

BIS-DIAPASON

The diapente plus the diatessaron produce one diapason, in this manner [Fig. A.7]:

DIAPASON

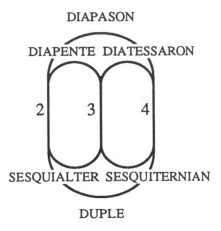

DIAPENTE DIATESSARON

2   3   4

SESQUIALTER SESQUITERNIAN

DUPLE

If a pitch is higher or lower than another pitch by a duple, a consonance of the diapason will be made. If a pitch is higher or lower than another pitch by a sesquialter, sesquitertian, or sesquioctave ratio, then it [202] will yield consonances of the diapente or of the diatessaron or a tone respectively. Likewise, if a diapason, such as 4:2, and a diapente, such as 6:4, are joined together, they will make the triple consonance, which is the diapason-plus-diapente. If two diapasons are combined, such as 2:4 and 4:8, then the quadruple consonance will be made, which is the bis-diapason. If a sesquialter and a sesquitertian—that is, a diapente and a diatessaron, such as 2:3 and 3:4—are joined, the duple consonance, obviously the dia-pason, is formed; 4:3 brings about a sesquitertian ratio, while 3:2 is joined by a sesquialter relation,[85] and the same 4 related to the 2 unities within a duple comparison. But the sesquialter ratio creates a consonance of the diapente, and the sesquitertian that of the diatessaron, whereas the duple ratio produces a consonance of the diapason. Therefore, a diatessaron plus a diapente forms a consonance of the diapason.

Moreover, a tone cannot be divided into equal parts; why, however, will be explained later.[86] For now it is sufficient to know only that a tone is never divided into two equal parts. So that this might be very easily demonstrated, let 8 and 9 represent the sesquioctave ratio. No mediating number falls naturally between these, so let us multiply them by 2: twice 8 makes 16; twice 9, 18. However, a number naturally falls between 16 and 18—namely, 17. Let these numbers be set out in order: 16, 17, 18. Now when 16 and 18 are compared, they yield the sesquioctave ratio and thus [203] a tone. But the middle number, 17, does not divide this ratio equally. For compared to 16, 17 contains in itself the total 16, plus 1/16 part of it—that is, unity. Now if the third number—that is, 18—is compared to this num-ber—that is, to 17—it contains the total 17 and 1/17 part of it. Therefore 17 does not surpass the smaller number and is not surpassed by the larger number by the same parts; the smaller part is 1/17, the larger 1/16. Both of these are called "semitones," not because these intermediate semitones are equal at all, but because something that does not come to a whole is usually called "semi." In the case of these, one semitone is called "major," and the other "minor."[87]

17. *In what smallest integers*[88] *the semitone is ascertained*

At this time I shall explain more clearly what an integral[89] semitone is, or in what smallest integers it is ascertained. For what has been said

85. This is the only time in the treatise that Boethius uses the word *collatio*, a term which functions as a less technical equivalent of ratio, much like *habitudo*. See above, n. 30, and book 2, n. 3.

86. See 3.1–2.

87. Although these ratios are called "semitones" and one is named "major" and the other "minor," they are abstract elements in an argument, rather than concrete entities in a musical system. Boethius further qualifies these ratios as designating "intermediate semitones" (*semitonia media*), thereby associating the ratios with the theory of means developed in books 2 and 3. The same argument—with the same numbers and vocabulary—is developed further in 3.1. See also 3.2 and n. 7.

88. Boethius uses the expression *primi numeri* on three occasions in this treatise: twice in the present chapter and once in 3.14. In *Arith.* 1.13–18, he defines and discusses "prime

about the division of the tone has nothing to do with our wanting to show the measurements of semitones; it applies rather to the fact that we said a tone cannot be divided into twin equal parts.[90]

The diatessaron, which is a consonance of four pitches and of three intervals, consists of two tones and an integral semitone.[91] A diagram[92] of this [Fig. A.8] is set out below:

| 192 | 216 | 243 | 256 |

If the number 192 is compared to 256, a sesquitertian ratio will result, and it will sound a consonance of the diatessaron. But if 216 is compared with 192, the ratio is a sesquioctave, for the difference between them is 24, which is an eighth part of 192. Therefore it is a tone. Moreover, if 243 is compared to 216, the ratio will be another sesquioctave, for the difference between them, 27 represents an eighth part of 216. The comparison of 256 [204] with 243 remains: the difference between these is 13, which, multiplied by

number" (also *primi numeri*); but in the present context he means something other than "prime numbers," for neither 243 nor 256 is prime. Yet 256:243 is the primary expression of that ratio in which the minor semitone is found; thus I have translated *primi numeri* as "smallest integers."

89. Boethius's use of the adjective *integer* presents problems, for he uses it in two ways, each of which has the potential of contradicting the other. At the close of the previous chapter Boethius said that a thing is usually called "semi" when it does not "come to a whole" (*ad integritatem usque non perveniat*). Yet, in this opening sentence Boethius modifies the noun "semitone" with the adjective "integral," thereby applying a qualification to the semitone, the lack of which is precisely what defines it as "semi." Thus, the remainder after two tones have been subtracted from the interval of a diatessaron is an "integral semitone"; that is, it is a constituent, functioning part of the diatessaron, even though it is not an "integral half" of a tone. When Boethius uses the term according to its first meaning, I have translated it as "whole," "complete," or "full"; when he employs it according to its second meaning, as "integral." This confusion in terminology led to textual problems in the present chapter during the Middle Ages (see below, n. 91).

90. See above, 1.16; 18:17:16 do not present the proportion of semitones as constituent parts of a tonal system.

91. Friedlein 203.20: *non integro semitonio* should read *integro semitonio*. The opening sentence of this chapter clearly states that the first possible numbers containing an "integral semitone" will be explained; those numbers are 256:243. The reading *integro semitonio* is found in all the control manuscripts except *I* and *R*, where *non* is added above the line by later hands. The *non* becomes part of the text in one branch of the manuscript tradition during the tenth century, but it was never universally adopted. The introduction of *non* is an example of hypercorrection. The semitone of the present argument, although not a half-tone, is self-contained and complete, a constituent part of the diatessaron.

92. This diagram and the one that follows qualify as "diagrams" and are numbered as figures chiefly because the word *descriptio* occurs in the text. Boethius uses this term consistently to refer to diagrams. In the control manuscripts the numbers occur on the textual line, with no lines or boxes around them. They may have been more elaborate drawings in an earlier tradition, and in later traditions they take on the character of diagrams (see, e.g., Cambridge, Trinity College, R.15.22, ff. 17r and 18r).

8, does not seem to arrive at a mean of 243. It is therefore not a semitone, but less than a semitone. For it might be reckoned to be a whole semitone, rigorously speaking, if the difference of these numbers, which is 13, multiplied by 8, could have equaled a mean of the number 243.[93] Thus the comparison of 243 with 256 yields less than a true semitone.

18. *The distance between a diatessaron and a diapente is a tone*

The consonance of the diapente has five pitches and four intervals, three tones and a minor semitone. Again take the number 192 and compute its sesquialter, which would make a consonance of the diapente with it. This number should therefore be 288. Then let the numbers which were related to 192 above be placed among these numbers: 216, 243, and 256. Let a diagram be formed in this manner [Fig. A.9]:

| 192 | 216 | 243 | 256 | 288 |

Now in the above diagram 192 and 256 were shown to contain two tones and a semitone. Therefore, the comparison of 256[94] and 288 remains, which is a sesquioctave—that is, a tone. Their difference is 32, which is an eighth part of 256. Thus the consonance of the diapente has been demonstrated to consist of three tones and a semitone. Yet a short while ago the consonance of the diatessaron was derived from the number 192 related to 256, whereas now a diapente is extended from this same 192 to 288. Therefore [205] the consonance of the diatessaron is surpassed by the diapente by that ratio which is found between the numbers 256 and 288, and this is a tone. Thus the consonance of the diapente surpasses that of the diatessaron by a tone.

93. The *iure* of this sentence, which I have translated as "rigorously speaking," refers to the kind of Pythagorean mathematical consistency found at the close of the previous chapter, where the ratios 18:17 and 17:16 were called "semitones." If 13 multiplied by 8 had equaled half of 243, then 256:243 would have been a "semitone" in the sense that 18:17 and 17:16 were both semitones—i.e., 256 would be the arithmetic mean between some number x and 243 such that the difference between x and 243 would be an eighth part of 243. Since 13 multiplied by 8 (i.e., 104) is less than the half of 243 (i.e., 121|), 256:243 is less than 18:17— the final demonstration of which is found in 3.13—and, "rigorously speaking," 256:243 is not a semitone. Significantly, Boethius uses the term *medietas,* rather than *dimidium,* in this context, "mean" rather than "half" (concerning means, see 2.12–14). It is clear from this chapter and the previous one that Boethius considers the tone indivisible by 2, and that he is not mistakenly considering any of these ratios a "half-tone" as Pizzani, "Fonti," pp. 55–56, would have us believe. The argument is nevertheless obtuse, which led some frustrated medieval reader to add a *non* where none was necessary.

94. Friedlein 204.21: *comparatio ducentorum ad .CCLXXXVIII.* should read *comparatio ducentorum quinquaginta .vi. ad .CCLXXXVIII.* The latter reading is found in manuscripts and is dictated by the argument.

19. *The diapason consists of five tones and two semitones*

The consonance of the diapason consists of five tones and two semitones, which nevertheless do not make up one tone. For it has been demonstrated that a diapason consists of a diatessaron and a diapente. Furthermore, it has been proved that a diatessaron consists of two tones and a semitone, a diapente of three tones and a semitone. These joined together, therefore, produce five tones (and two semitones)—but since the two semitones were not full halves, their conjunction does not add up to a whole tone. Their sum surpasses a half tone but falls short of a complete tone. According to this reckoning, the diapason consists of five tones and two semitones, which, just as they do not fill a complete tone, so they go beyond a full semitone. But the theory behind these things and how one comes to know these musical consonances will be explained more clearly later.[95]

Meanwhile, belief must be summoned to the present argument to make up for modest knowledge; indeed, a firm credence in all should be summoned, since each thing will be made clear by proper demonstration. Having set these matters in order, we will discuss for a while the strings of the kithara and their names, and also how they were added, since this determines their names. After first coming to an understanding of these matters, knowledge of what will be discussed subsequently will be easy.

20. *Concerning the additions of strings and their names*

In the beginning, Nicomachus reports,[96] music was truly simple, since [206] it was composed of four strings. It continued in this state until the time of

95. The present chapter is pedagogical in purpose, consisting of a review of the doctrines that have been presented up to this point. The reference to later explanations is not specific, but general. Compare this chapter with 1.33, which also asks for credence and reviews the basics of Pythagorean dogma.

96. The account given in this chapter is not found in any extant work of Nicomachus; the development of the musical system presented here is the most thorough of any that have been handed down from antiquity and, as such, is unique. In his *Enchiridion* 11 (JanS. 260.4–12), Nicomachus promised a full account of the growth of the musical system, starting with the tetrachord, an account of each note, and the inventor thereof. I take the present chapter of Boethius to be the history promised by Nicomachus.

The naming of inventors is an important topos in ancient literature. By assigning an agent to a specific invention, an author characterized both the object invented and the person associated with the object, thereby giving an object, profession, or action a sanction that it would otherwise have lacked. In the naming of inventors, the author's interest extended beyond giving a certain historical chronology; it established a cultural context, a function, a value for the object and the inventor. (For a discussion of the naming of inventors in ancient literature, see Adolf Kleingünther, "Πρῶτος Εὑρετής. Untersuchungen zur Geschichte einer Fragestellung," *Philologus,* Suppl. 26, vol. 1 [1934], pp. 1–155.)

The attribution of inventions in ancient musical lore is a subject of great inconsistency and complexity. More than one inventor can usually be found for any given instrument, string,

Orpheus.[97] In this period the disposition of strings was such that the first and fourth strings sounded the consonance of the diapason, while the middle strings each in turn sounded the diapente and the diatessaron with the strings nearest them and those most distant.[98] Indeed, there was nothing discordant in these, in imitation of cosmic music, which consists of the four elements. The inventor of the quadrichord is said to have been Mercury.[99]

At a later time,[100] Toroebus,[101] son of Atys and king of the Lydians,[102]

---

or nomos (see ibid., pp. 22–25, 135–43). The present account is characterized as much by the inventors it leaves out as by those it names; it omits, e.g., Phrynis, Simonides, Thamyris, and Melanippides, all famous inventors associated with "theatrical" music and music of questionable repute. Embedded in the present text is a "tonal genesis" with a consistent point of view: it presents the growth of the musical system as determined by the principle of species of consonances. These species determine the fundamental ethos of ancient music: the modes (see 4.14–15). The indication of these species is revealed through the geographical origins of the inventors named. In almost every case, the attributions can be corroborated by other sources. At each level of development of the tonal system, a Dorian, or native Greek, disposition is expanded into systems which accommodate Phrygian and Lydian elements.

97. Making Orpheus the *terminus ante quem* for music of four strings, or simple music, assigns the "state of grace" of music to the period of the gods and demigods; for Orpheus was the son of Apollo and a muse. Nicomachus *Excerpta* 1 (JanS. 266) reports that Mercury taught Orpheus to play the lyre, but in that account the instrument had seven strings, not four.

98. Concerning the antiquity of the four-stringed lyre, see Terpander *Fragmenta* 5 (*Lyra Graeca*, vol. 1, p. 32), Strabo *Geographica* 13.3–4, Pliny *Naturalis historia* 7.56(57).204, Censorinus *Fragmenta* 12. The disposition of the present instrument is manifestly Pythagorean; the strings are tuned to the same set of pitches discovered by Pythagoras in the weights of the hammers and represented in the ratios 12:9:8:6. The noted absence of any "discordant" (*inconsonans*) element and the tuning of the four pitches resonate strongly with 1.10 (see above, n. 71).

99. In several sources, Mercury is credited with inventing the lyre, but none of the sources calls it a "quadrichord"; see Homer *Hymnus ad Mercurium* 15–63 (seven strings), Nicomachus *Excerpta* 1 (JanS. 266) (seven strings), Diodorus Siculus *Bibliotheca* 1.16.2 (three strings), Apollodorus *Bibliotheca* 3.10.2 (no number given), and Horace *Carmina* 1.10 (no number given).

100. Entering the period of human inventions, here innocently indicated by *post* ("at a later time"), the tuning of the lyre underwent a fundamental change: whereas the four original strings were given no names and were tuned in an octave filled with a fourth and a fifth, the following narrative tells us that the first four strings were the hypate (H), parhypate (pH), lichanos (L), and mese (M). These are the fundamental pitches around which the Greek system was built, the tetrachord with the semitone in the lowest position, a species of fourth with Dorian quality.

$$
\begin{array}{cccc}
1 & 2 & 3 & 4 \\
\text{H} \underline{} \text{pH} & \underline{} & \text{L} & \underline{} \text{M}
\end{array}
$$

1   2   3   4
H __ pH _____ L ____ M
    s   T   T

(I use the diatonic genus in tracing the species since the same genus is used when tracing species in 4.14.)

In describing species of fourth as having a certain "quality," I am following Winnington-Ingram, except that he uses the term *flavor* rather than *quality* (see *Mode in Ancient Greek*

added a fifth string. Hyagnis the Phrygian[103] added a sixth string to these. Then a seventh string was added by Terpander of Lesbia,[104] obviously in likeness to the seven planets. The lowest of these seven was the one called "hypate," the larger and more honorable, as it were; for this reason they name Jove "Hypatos." They also call a consul by the same name because of the loftiness of his rank. This string was attributed to Saturn because of its slow motion and low sound.[105] The second string was the parhypate,

---

Music [Cambridge, 1936], p. 15); but it is important to observe Winnington-Ingram's caution concerning naming tetrachords "Lydian," "Phrygian," or "Dorian" (*Mode,* p. 12).

101. Friedlein 206.8: *post Coroebus Atyis filius* should read *post Toroebus Aetyis filius.* The combination of an adverbial *post* followed by an unfamiliar Greek name gave scribes considerable difficulty. *K,* e.g., reads *posteriobus atyis filius,* and *I* read *postroebus* before it was corrected to *post coroebus. R* also gives *coroebus,* but *M, P, Q, S, and V* all read *post Toroebus Atyis filius.*

102. Toroebus, the Lydian, is named as the inventor of the fifth string; Plutarch *De musica* 1136C, citing Dionysius Iambus and others, names Toroebus as the first to use the Lydian *harmonia.* The fifth string, the trite (T), makes possible the species of diatessaron of Lydian quality, with the semitone in the highest position.

$$
\begin{array}{cccc}
2 & 3 & 4 & 5 \\
\text{pH}\underline{\quad} & \text{L}\underline{\quad} & \text{M}\underline{\quad} & \text{T} \\
\quad T & \quad T & \quad s &
\end{array}
$$

103. According to Athenaeus *Deipnosophistae* 14.624, Aristoxenus named Hyagnis as inventor of the Phrygian *harmonia.* Nicomachus attributes to Hyagnis, the Phrygian, the invention of the sixth string; this string, the paranete (pN), makes possible the species of diatessaron of Phrygian quality, with the semitone in the middle position.

$$
\begin{array}{cccc}
3 & 4 & 5 & 6 \\
\text{L}\underline{\quad} & \text{M}\underline{\quad} & \text{T}\underline{\quad} & \text{pN} \\
\quad T & \quad s & \quad T &
\end{array}
$$

104. Terpander is associated with the heptachord lyre through three traditions: a general association with the heptachord, as found in Aristotle *Problemata* 32, the *Suidas,* and Nicomachus *Excerpta* 1; transformation of the quadrichord into the heptachord through the addition of three strings, as in Terpander *Fragmenta* 5 (*Lyra Graeca,* vol. 1, p. 32), Strabo *Geographica* 13.3–4, and Pliny *Naturalis historia* 7.56(57).204; and the addition of one string (to six), as found in Plutarch *Instituta Laconica* 17 (238C), Plutarch *De musica* 1140F, and the present text. In Plutarch's *De musica* Terpander is credited with having added a "Dorian nete," and it is this that the present text carries forward; for Terpander's addition of a seventh string creates a second tetrachord, a tetrachord—like the first—of Dorian quality.

$$
\begin{array}{cccc}
4 & 5 & 6 & 7 \\
\text{M}\underline{\quad} & \text{T}\underline{\quad} & \text{pN}\underline{\quad} & \text{N} \\
\quad s & \quad T & \quad T &
\end{array}
$$

105. Concerning ὕπατος in reference to Jove (Zeus) and to a consul, see H. G. Liddell and R. Scott, *A Greek-English Dictionary,* 9th ed. (Oxford, 1940), p. 1854. Concerning the association of hypate with Saturn, see 1.27.

being positioned and ordered next to the hypate. The third was the li-chanos, since that finger is called "lichanos" which we call "index." The Greeks call that finger "lichanos" after its tongue-like articulation. And since, when playing, the index finger (which is the lichanos) was found at that string which was third from the hypate, this string itself was likewise called "lichanos." The fourth string is called "mese," since among seven it is always the middle. The fifth is the paramese, since it is disposed next to the middle one. The seventh is called "nete"; neate, as it were—that is, lower.[106] Between this nete and the paramese there is a sixth string, which is called "paranete," being placed next to the nete. Since the paramese is third from the nete, it is also signified by the word "trite." A diagram of

[207] the heptachord [Fig. A.10] is as follows:

HYPATE

PARHYPATE

LICHANOS

MESE

PARAMESE or TRITE

PARANETE

NETE

Lycaon of Samos[107] added an eighth string to these, and, in fact, fitted

106. The position denoted by the Greek νεάτη and the Latin *inferior* is difficult to translate. Νεάτη refers to low or extreme position, whereas *inferior*, also meaning lower in position, can also mean more southerly position (stars) or shorter or may even refer to lowness of pitch. This string is the one most distant from the player; hence it is "extreme" in position, the highest in pitch.

107. Three names are associated with the invention of the eighth string: Simonides of Cos (*Suidas* and Pliny *Naturalis historia* 7.56(57).204), Pythagoras of Samos (Nicomachus *Enchiridion* 5 [JanS. 244–45]), and Lycaon of Samos (the present account). The last is found in no other source, and, it should be remembered, the present text is linked to Nicomachus (see above, n. 96). It is difficult to understand why Nicomachus, the arch-Pythagorean, would credit Pythagoras with the intercalation of the eighth string in one source and Lycaon in a second.

I suggest that the key lies in the meaning of the name "Lycaon." Forcellini, *Lexicon totius latinitatis* (Schneeberg, 1831), "Lucumo," considers the name Λυχάων to be related to the Etruscan *lucumo,* a word associated with both insanity and divine powers. P. Weizsäcker (in W. H. Roscher, *Ausführliches Lexikon der griechischen und römischen Mythologie* [Leipzig, 1894–97], vol. 2, pt. 2, col. 2172, notes same relation. *Lucumo,* both word and name in late Latin sources, connotes king or prince or some form of leader transmitting sacred lore. The name *Lucumo* thus leads back to Pythagoras, for the following hexameter is found in Ausonius *Epistola* 14: *Anticyraeve bibas Samii Lucumonis acumen.* ("Or at Anticyra you

this intermediate string between the paramese—also called "trite"—and the paranete, so that this particular new string would be the third from the nete. And the one which was placed after the mese came to be called simply "paramese." It lost the name "trite" after the third note from the nete, which properly took the name "trite," was placed between it and the paranete. The octachord according to Lycaon's addition is as follows [Fig. A.11]:

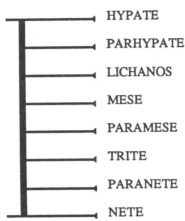

HYPATE

PARHYPATE

LICHANOS

MESE

PARAMESE

TRITE

PARANETE

NETE

In the above two dispositions of a heptachord and an octachord, the heptachord is called "synemmenon," since it is conjunct, whereas the octachord is called "diezeugmenon," since it is disjunct. For in the heptachord one tetrachord is hypate, parhypate, lichanos, and mese; then a second is mese, paramese, paranete, and nete—provided that we count the mese string in the second. Thus the two tetrachords are joined together by the mese. But in the octachord, since there are eight strings, the upper four— [208] that is, hypate, parhypate, lichanos, and mese—complete one tetrachord. An integral tetrachord, disjunct from the first one, begins from the paramese, proceeds through the trite and paranete, and ends on the nete. And there is disjunction, which is called "diazeuxis";[108] and the distance of a tone stands between the mese and the paramese. Therefore, here the mese

should drink in the sharpness of the Samian Lucumo.") Critical opinion concerning this hexameter suggests that "Samius Lucumo" represents Pythagoras of Samos (see discussion of "Lucumo" in Forcellini *Lexicon,* and in *Ausonius,* with an English trans. by Hugh G. Evelyn White [London and New York, 1921], vol. 2, pp. 50–51). "Lucumo" and "Lycaon" were probably cultic names for Pythagoras in late antiquity, and those "in the know" (Boethius?) would have recognized *Lycaon,* particularly *Samius Lycaon,* as a veiled reference to Pythagoras.

108. Concerning diazeuxis, see 1.25. The octachord system with the tone of disjunction in the middle represents the species of octave associated with the Dorian mode, the most Greek of the *harmoniae* (Plato *Laches* 188D) and that which expresses the masculine and majestic ethos (Athenaeus *Deipnosophistae* 624D). In this Pythagorean tonal genesis, it is no accident that the octave of Dorian quality is the first to come into existence.

maintained only its name; it is not the middle by position, for in an octa-chord two middles are always discerned, but a single middle cannot be found.

Prophrastus of Pieria[109] then added one string at the lower end, so that he might make a complete enneachord. Since this string was added above the hypate, it was called the "hyperhypate."[110] At first—as long as the kithara had only nine strings—it was called hyperhypate; now, however, since other strings have been added, it is called "lichanos hypaton." In the present order and technique it is called "lichanos," since it occurs at the index finger; but this will become apparent later. The order of the ennea-chord is, under these circumstances, composed as follows [Fig. A.12]:

109. Prophrastus of Pieria (Periotes) is credited with the invention of the ninth string in Nicomachus *Excerpta* 4 (JanS. 274), as well as in the present account. "Prophrastus" is the most unusual name encountered among musical inventors. It is not found in W. Pape and G. E. Benseler, *Wörterbuch der griechischen Eigennamen* (Braunschweig, 1884), as a Greek proper name, and Meibom, *Antiquae musicae auctores septem* (1652), even changed it to *Theo*phrastus. The word itself would seem to connote some kind of prophet or soothsayer. The geographic location, however, is, more significant than the name, for Pieria is the area around Mount Olympus where the Muses were venerated; and, according to Strabo *Geographica* 10.17, Pieria and Olympus were Thracian territory before they came to be occupied by the Macedonians. (See also Strabo *Geographica* 7.11, and 9.2 for association of Pieria with the Thracian peoples.) The Thracians, the Muses, and the god they worship, Dionysus, are associated with the Phrygian *harmonia;* Prophrastus of Pieria's invention of the ninth string (cf. the nine Muses) brings into existence the species of octave associated with the Phrygian mode.

$$9$$
$$\text{hH} \underline{\quad\quad} \text{H} \underline{\ } \text{pH} \underline{\quad\quad} \text{L} \underline{\quad\quad} \text{M} \underline{\quad\quad} \text{pM} \underline{\ } \text{T} \underline{\quad\quad} \text{pN}$$
$$\quad T \quad\quad s \quad\quad T \quad\quad\quad T \quad\quad\quad T \quad\quad s \quad\quad T$$

110. It is noteworthy that the invention of the ninth string, the name "hyperhypate," and the enneachord disposition are given the status of an independent—not merely a transitional—disposition. Athenaeus *Deipnosophistae* 636F refers to an enneachord as an obsolete musical instrument; and the note named "hyperhypate" is mentioned in Theon of Smyrna *Expositio earum, quae in arithmeticis ad Platonis lectionem utilia sunt* 2.35 (ed. J. Dupuis, Paris, 1892) and in Aristides Quintilianus *De musica* 1.6. Concerning hyperhypate, see also Winnington-Ingram, *Mode*, p. 25.

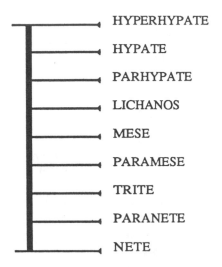

HYPERHYPATE

HYPATE

PARHYPATE

LICHANOS

MESE

PARAMESE

TRITE

PARANETE

NETE

Histiaeus of Colophon[111] joined a tenth string at the lower end, and [209] Timotheus of Milesia[112] an eleventh. Since these were added above the hypate and the parhypate, they were called "hyper-hypaton," as they were the largest of the largest, the lowest of the lowest, or the highest of the

111. Histiaeus of Colophon is also credited with the invention of the tenth string in Nicomachus *Excerpta* 4 (JanS. 274). Histiaeus is a legitimate Greek name, and a certain Histiaeus, a tyrant of Miletus, was associated with the cities of Iona. No references to a Histiaeus have been found in any other musical context. Colophon was one of the twelve Ionian cities captured by the Lydians and was the area particularly associated with Lydian musical culture. The addition of the tenth string brings into existence the species of octave associated with the Lydian mode.

10
pH ____ L ____ H __ pH ____ L ____ M ____ pM __ T
   T   *T*   *s*   *T*   *T*   *T*   *s*

112. No list of musical inventors from antiquity could omit Timotheus (see above, n. 17). Pausanias *Descriptio Greciae* 3.12.10 relates that Timotheus added four strings to the traditional seven, thereby creating eleven; while the *Suidas* attributes the addition of the tenth and eleventh strings to Timotheus. In a fragment attributed to Timotheus, Timotheus places his own name alongside those of Orpheus and Terpander in giving the history of music and associates himself with a lyre of eleven strings (Timotheus *Fragmenta* 19.234–43 [*Lyra Graeca*, vol. 3, p. 324]). The present text and Nicomachus *Excerpta* 4 (JanS. 274) credit Timotheus with the invention of only the eleventh string. Plutarch *De musica* 1144F associates the punishment of the musician in Sparta—Timotheus is not mentioned by name—with the addition of strings and the introduction of the Mixolydian mode. The association of Timotheus with the invention of the eleventh string again links him with the Mixolydian mode; for it is this string that brings into existence the species of octave associated with that mode.

11
H __ pH ____ L ____ H __ pH ____ L ____ M ____ pM
s   *T*   *T*   *s*   *T*   *T*   *T*

highest.[113] Actually the first of these eleven was called "hypate hypaton," the second "parhypate hypaton," since it was disposed next to the hypate hypaton. The third string, which was just called "hyperhypate" in the enneachord, was named the "lichanos hypaton." The fourth kept its old name, "hypate," the fifth "parhypate," the sixth "lichanos" (also having its old name), the seventh "mese," the eighth "paramese," the ninth "trite," the tenth "paranete," and the eleventh "nete."

Thus the hypate hypaton, parhypate hypaton, lichanos hypaton, and hypate form one tetrachord; and the hypate, parhypate, lichanos, and mese form a second. These two are conjunct. The paramese, trite, paranete, and nete form a third tetrachord. But since a middle tetrachord (hypate, parhypate, lichanos, and mese) is now positioned between the higher tetrachord (hypate hypaton, parhypate hypaton, lichanos hypaton, and hypate) and the lower tetrachord (paramese, trite, paranete, and nete), this entire middle tetrachord came to be called "meson," "of the middle strings," as it were. With this addition, the names become "hypate meson," "parhypate meson," "lichanos meson," and "mese." Furthermore, since disjunction occurs between this meson tetrachord and the lower one, that of the nete (namely between the mese and paramese), the lowest tetrachord came to be called "disjunct"—that is, "diezeugmenon." With this addition the names become "paramese diezeugmenon,"[114] "trite diezeugmenon," "paranete diezeugmenon," and "nete diezeugmenon." A diagram of the disjunct
[210]   disposition is as follows [Fig. A.13]:

113. These strings are the largest of the largest with respect to length, the lowest of the lowest with respect to pitch, and the highest of the highest with respect to position.

114. It is exceptional to find the word *diezeugmenon* in conjunction with paramese. The paramese is probably named "paramese diezeugmenon" in this text and the accompanying diagram to stress the disjunction which occurs between the mese and paramese; similarly, the mese in the next diagram is named "mese synemmenon" so as to underline the conjunct nature of that disposition. These combinations of names do not appear in other treatises or elsewhere in the present work.

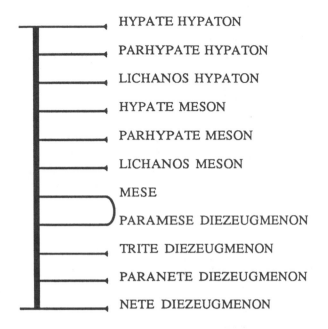

HYPATE HYPATON

PARHYPATE HYPATON

LICHANOS HYPATON

HYPATE MESON

PARHYPATE MESON

LICHANOS MESON

MESE

PARAMESE DIEZEUGMENON

TRITE DIEZEUGMENON

PARANETE DIEZEUGMENON

NETE DIEZEUGMENON

In this instance there is disjunction between the paramese and the mese, and consequently the tetrachord is called "diezeugmenon." If, on the other hand, the paramese is taken away, and the mese, trite, paranete, and nete remain, then the three tetrachords will be conjunct—that is, "synemmena." The last tetrachord will be called "synemmenon," in this manner [Fig. A.14]:

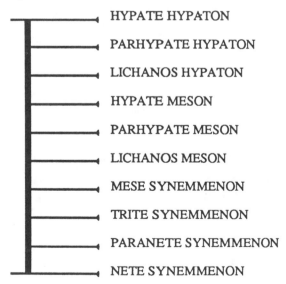

HYPATE HYPATON

PARHYPATE HYPATON

LICHANOS HYPATON

HYPATE MESON

PARHYPATE MESON

LICHANOS MESON

MESE SYNEMMENON

TRITE SYNEMMENON

PARANETE SYNEMMENON

NETE SYNEMMENON

But since in this disposition or in the above endecachord the mese—which
[211] was so named because of its middle location—falls close to the nete, while
it is quite distant from the opposite hypate, and does not hold its characteristic position, one further tetrachord has been added above the nete
diezeugmenon.[115] Because these strings surpassed the earlier established
nete in highness of pitch, the entire tetrachord came to be called "hyperboleon," as follows [Fig. A.15]:

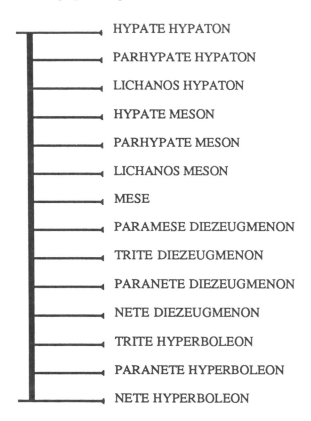

HYPATE HYPATON

PARHYPATE HYPATON

LICHANOS HYPATON

HYPATE MESON

PARHYPATE MESON

LICHANOS MESON

MESE

PARAMESE DIEZEUGMENON

TRITE DIEZEUGMENON

PARANETE DIEZEUGMENON

NETE DIEZEUGMENON

TRITE HYPERBOLEON

PARANETE HYPERBOLEON

NETE HYPERBOLEON

Yet, since the mese was not in the middle place but fell closer to the
hypate, one string, called "proslambanomenos," was added above the hypate hypaton, standing a whole tone from the hypate hypaton; it is, however, called "prosmelodos" by others.[116] Indeed this very string, the

115. With the addition of this further tetrachord, the final three species of the octave
are brought into existence, those of the Hypodorian, Hypophrygian, and Hypolydian modes.
116. Concerning reasons for the addition of the proslambanomenos, see Nichomachus
Enchiridion 11 (JanS. 257–58). I cannot identify the "others" who call the added note "prosmelodos." (See below, 1.22.)

proslambanomenos, is the eighth from the mese, sounding the consonance of the diapason with it. The same sounds the diatessaron, of course at the fourth, with the lichanos hypaton. The lichanos hypaton sounds the con- [212] sonance of the diapente with the mese and is fifth from it. The mese in turn is one tone from the paramese and produces the consonance of the diapente, at the fifth, with the nete diezeugmenon. The nete diezeugmenon produces the consonance of the diatessaron, at the fourth, with the nete hyperboleon; the proslambanomenos renders the consonance of the bis-diapason with the nete hyperboleon [Fig. A.16].

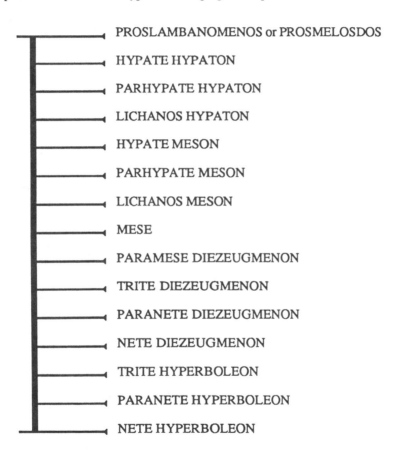

PROSLAMBANOMENOS or PROSMELOSDOS

HYPATE HYPATON

PARHYPATE HYPATON

LICHANOS HYPATON

HYPATE MESON

PARHYPATE MESON

LICHANOS MESON

MESE

PARAMESE DIEZEUGMENON

TRITE DIEZEUGMENON

PARANETE DIEZEUGMENON

NETE DIEZEUGMENON

TRITE HYPERBOLEON

PARANETE HYPERBOLEON

NETE HYPERBOLEON

21. Concerning the genera of song

Now that these things have been explained, the genera of melodies should be discussed. There are three genera: the diatonic, the chromatic,[117]

117. See above, n. 82, concerning use of *diatonum* and *chroma*.

and the enharmonic. The diatonic is somewhat more austere and natural,
[213]   while the chromatic departs from that natural intonation and becomes
softer;[118] the enharmonic is very rightly and closely joined together.

There are five tetrachords: the hypaton, meson, synemmenon, diezeugmenon, and hyperboleon. In all these, according to the diatonic genus
of song, the pitch progresses through semitone, tone, and tone in one
tetrachord, again through semitone, tone, and tone in the second, and thus
in succession. For this reason it is called "dia-tonic," because it progresses,
as it were, through tone and through tone.

The chromatic, on the other hand, is named from "color," inasmuch
as it is the first mutation from the above intonation. It is sung through
semitone, semitone, and three semitones. For the whole consonance of the
diatessaron contains two tones and a semitone (although not a full semitone). This word *chroma,* as has been said, is derived from surfaces[119] which
are transformed into another color when they are turned.

The enharmonic genus is that which is most closely joined together,
for it is sung in all tetrachords through diesis and diesis and ditone (a diesis
is half a semitone).

118. Concerning the terms *durus* and *mollis,* here translated as "austere" and "soft,"
see above, n. 7.

119. The Greek χρῶμα, "color," can likewise mean "complexion," the color of the skin;
in that this genus is the first alteration of the diatonic genus, it is considered a "shade" of that
genus, an alteration which calls attention to the "complexion" or "surfaces" (*superficies*) that
are altered in changing light. Concerning the use of *chroma* for chromatic, see above, n. 82.

A diagram of the three genera progressing through all tetrachords is as follows [Fig. A.17]:

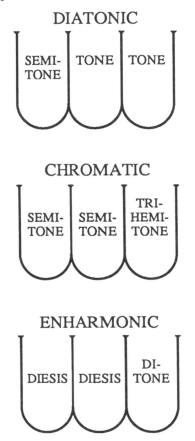

DIATONIC

SEMI-TONE | TONE | TONE

CHROMATIC

SEMI-TONE | SEMI-TONE | TRI-HEMI-TONE

ENHARMONIC

DIESIS | DIESIS | DI-TONE

22. *Concerning the order and names of strings in the three genera*

[214]

Now the order of all the strings—which are altered through the three genera or set out in unchanging order—ought to be set forth.

The first string is the proslambanomenos, which is also called the "prosmelodos." The second is the hypate hypaton, and the third the par-hypate hypaton. The fourth is generally called "lichanos hypaton." But if this string is tuned for the diatonic genus, it is called "diatonic lichanos hypaton"; if it is tuned for the chromatic, it is called "chromatic diatonic"[120]

120. The text in Friedlein and the control manuscripts names this note simply *diatonos chromatice* ("chromatic diatonic"); consistency with the other tetrachords—except for the hyperboleon—would require that this note be named *diatonos hypaton chromatice* ("chro-

or "chromatic lichanos hypaton"; if it is tuned for the enharmonic, it is called "enharmonic hypaton" or "enharmonic diatonic hypaton."

The one after this is called "hypate meson," the one after that "parhypate meson," and the next "lichanos meson"—simply "diatonic meson" in the diatonic genus, "chromatic lichanos meson" or "chromatic diatonic meson" in the chromatic genus, and "enharmonic diatonic meson" or "enharmonic lichanos meson" in the enharmonic genus. The mese follows these.

After this are two tetrachords, sometimes the synemmenon, at other times the diezeugmenon. If the synemmenon is placed after the mese, there follows the trite synemmenon, then the lichanos synemmenon; the same string is called "diatonic synemmenon" in the diatonic genus, either "chromatic diatonic synemmenon" or "chromatic lichanos synemmenon" in the chromatic genus, and "enharmonic diatonic synemmenon" or "enharmonic lichanos synemmenon" in the enharmonic genus. After these is the nete synemmenon.

[215]   If the synemmenon tetrachord is not joined to the mese string, but rather the diezeugmenon, then the paramese is after the mese, then the trite diezeugmenon, then the lichanos diezeugmenon[121]—which is called "diatonic diezeugmenon" in the diatonic genus, sometimes "chromatic diatonic diezeugmenon" and sometimes "chromatic lichanos diezeugmenon" in the chromatic genus, and sometimes "enharmonic diatonic diezeugmenon" and sometimes "enharmonic lichanos diezeugmenon" in the enharmonic genus. The same string is also called "paranete," with the addition of "diatonic" or "chromatic" or "enharmonic."

Above these are the nete diezeugmenon, the trite hyperboleon, and that which is the paranete hyperboleon—called "diatonic hyperboleon" in the diatonic genus, "chromatic hyperboleon" in the chromatic genus, and "enharmonic hyperboleon" in the enharmonic genus. The last of these is the nete hyperboleon.

---

matic diatonic hypaton"). But there are other inconsistencies in designations in this chapter. Only the diatonic lichanos in the hypaton tetrachord is given the more specific designation "lichanos"; in other tetrachords comparable strings are named simply "diatonic"—e.g., "diatonic meson," "diatonic synemmenon," etc. Further, no alternate names are given for altered chromatic and enharmonic pitches in the hyperboleon tetrachord, whereas all other tetrachords have two sets of names for comparable strings—e.g., chromatic diatonic diezeugmenon or chromatic lichanos diezeugmenon. Finally, the naming of notes that change according to genus in the following diagram are not consistent with the names given in the body of the chapter. This, however, is a highly idiosyncratic set of names (see following note). The emphasis on the diatonic terminology in all genera may reflect a conception of the chromatic and enharmonic genera as alterations or shades of the diatonic (see above, n. 119).

121. One might think that "lichanos diezeugmenon" is a misnomer for this note, but for the last statement of this paragraph. This is the only place in ancient theoretical literature where the designation "lichanos" is used outside the hypaton and meson tetrachords. In all other cases the note is named "paranete" with the appropriate modifier.

A diagram may be made in such a way that it contains the layout of the three genera. In it you will become acquainted with both the similarity and difference in names. If those similar in all genera are counted with those that are different, altogether there should be twenty-eight.[122] The diagram below [Fig. A.18, p. 44] demonstrates this.

23. *Which ratios are between pitches in each genus* [216]

In this manner, then, the division is made through each tetrachord according to the special character of the genera, so that we divide all five tetrachords of the diatonic genus into two tones and a semitone. In this genus the tone is called "noncomposite," since it is considered whole, and no other interval is added to it; rather, the tones in each interval are integral.

In the chromatic genus the division is set forth as semitone, semitone, and noncomposite trihemitone. We call this trihemitone "noncomposite," because it is put together in one interval. In the diatonic genus a semitone-plus-tone can be called a trihemitone, but it is not noncomposite, for it is made out of two intervals.

Likewise in the enharmonic genus it consists of a diesis, a diesis, and a noncomposite ditone. We call this ditone "noncomposite" for the same [217] reason, for it is brought together in one interval.

24. *What* synaphe *is*

In the tetrachords so positioned and arranged that a mean of one term holds and joins them together, there is *synaphe,* which can be expressed in

---

122. The number given here is probably determined more by the perfection of 28 than by the disposition of strings. Twenty-eight is a "perfect" number for the Pythagoreans, and it is probably more than coincidence that there are 28 names mentioned in this chapter and 28 notes described in 4.2–3. (Concerning perfect numbers, see *Arith.* 1.20.) In Nichomachus *Enchiridion* 12 (JanS. 264), 33 strings are listed. In the present system of counting and in the system found in 4.3–4 (which is consistent with this), the parhypate/trite are counted only once in each tetrachord; but the enharmonic genus is described as diesis-diesis-ditone, and thus the enharmonic parhypate should not be the same as the diatonic and chromatic parhypate. (The parhypatai and tritai in all genera are notated by the same symbol in notational treatises.)

P ROSLAMBANOMENOS	P ROSLAMBANOMENOS	P ROSLAMBANOMENOS
HYPATE HYPATON	HYPATE HYPATON	HYPATE HYPATON
PARHYPATE HYPATON	PARHYPATE HYPATON	PARHYPATE HYPATON
ENHARMONIC LICHANOS HYPATON	CHROMATIC LICHANOS HYPATON	DIATONIC LICHANOS HYPATON
HYPATE MESON	HYPATE MESON	HYPATE MESON
PARHYPATE MESON	PARHYPATE MESON	PARHYPATE MESON
ENHARMONIC LICHANOS MESON	CHROMATIC LICHANOS MESON	DIATONIC LICHANOS MESON
MESE	MESE	MESE
TRITE SYNEMMENON	TRITE SYNEMMENON	TRITE SYNEMMENON
ENHARMONIC PARANETE SYNEMMENON	CHROMATIC PARANETE SYNEMMENON	DIATONIC PARANETE SYNEMMENON
NETE SYNEMMENON	NETE SYNEMMENON	NETE SYNEMMENON
PARAMESE	PARAMESE	PARAMESE
TRITE DIEZEUGMENON	TRITE DIEZEUGMENON	TRITE DIEZEUGMENON
ENHARMONIC PARANETE DIEZEUGMENON	CHROMATIC PARANETE DIEZEUGMENON	DIATONIC PARANETE DIEZEUGMENON
NETE DIEZEUGMENON	NETE DIEZEUGMENON	NETE DIEZEUGMENON
TRITE HYPERBOLEON	TRITE HYPERBOLEON	TRITE HYPERBOLEON
ENHARMONIC PARANETE HYPERBOLEON	CHROMATIC PARANETE HYPERBOLEON	DIATONIC PARANETE HYPERBOLEON
NETE HYPERBOLEON	NETE HYPERBOLEON	NETE HYPERBOLEON

Latin as *coniunctio* ["conjunction"],[123] as in these tetrachords [Fig. A.19]:

HYPATE HYPATON
PARHYPATE HYPATON
LICHANOS HYPATON
HYPATE MESON
PARHYPATE MESON
LICHANOS MESON
MESE

Here, then, there is one tetrachord: hypate, parhypate, lichanos, and hypate meson; and another: hypate meson, parhypate meson, lichanos meson, and mese. The hypate meson has been counted in both tetrachords, and it is the highest pitch of the preceding tetrachord and the lowest of the latter. This conjunction is one and the same string, so that the hypate meson—linking the hypaton and meson tetrachords—brought together two tetrachords in the above diagram. Thus, *synaphe,* which we call "conjunction," is the middle pitch of two tetrachords, the highest of the preceding and the lowest of the following.

25. *What* diazeuxis *is* [218]

When two tetrachords are separated in the middle by a tone, it is called "diazeuxis," which can be expressed in Latin as *disiunctio* ["disjunction"], as in these two tetrachords [Fig. A.20].

HYPATE MESON
PARHYPATE MESON
LICHANOS MESON
MESON
PARAMESE
TRITE DIEZEUGMENON
PARANETE DIEZEUGMENON
NETE DIEZEUGMENON

123. In this chapter and the next two, Boethius is translating technical vocabulary from Greek into Latin. I give, in each case, Boethius's Latin equivalents to the Greek, followed by English translations in quotations in brackets.

Two tetrachords are clearly set out, inasmuch as there are eight strings. But *diazeuxis*—that is, disjunction—occurs between the mese and paramese, which are separated by a whole tone.

These things will be explained more clearly in subsequent discussions, since at that time we should take up the task of explaining every single thing very carefully.[124] Meanwhile, the more attentive observer discerns five tetrachords, and no more: hypaton, meson, synemmenon, diezeugmenon, and hyperboleon.

26. *By what names Albinus designated the strings*

Albinus translated the names of these strings into the Latin language; thus he called the notes of the hypaton tetrachord *principales* ["principal"], those of the meson tetrachord *mediae* ["middle"], those of the synemmenon tetrachord *coniuncti* ["conjunct"], those of the diezeugmenon tetrachord [219] *disiuncti* ["disjunct"], and those of the hyperboleon tetrachord *excellentes* ["high"].[125] But we should not linger in an extraneous work.[126]

27. *To what heavenly bodies the strings are compared*

At this point it would seem proper to add concerning the above tetrachords that the disposition from the hypate meson to the nete synemmenon is, as it were, a kind of exemplar of the celestial order and specification. The hypate meson is assigned to Saturn, whereas the parhypate is like the orbit of Jupiter. The lichanos meson is entrusted to Mars. The sun governs the mese. Venus holds the trite synemmenon. Mercury rules the paranete synemmenon. The nete is analogous to the orbit of the moon.[127]

Marcus Tullius draws up a different order, for in the sixth book of *De re publica* he asserts: "Nature is so disposed that low sound emanates from its one extreme part, whereas high sound emanates from its other. Therefore that high celestial orbit, that of the stars, the revolution of which is faster, moves with a high and shrill sound, whereas the weak orbit of the

124. This does not seem to point to any specific future passage in which disjunction and conjunction are treated but probably refers to the division of the monochord in 4.6–11.

125. Concerning Albinus, see above, n. 79. These Latin names for the notes were probably included because they are not quite the same as those given in Martianus Capella *De nuptiis* 9.931—a work which probably reflected the standard Latin usage—and 4.3 below. Martianus (and Boethius 4.3) translate *diezeugmenon* as *divisarum* rather than *disiunctarum*.

126. This sentence seems to imply that Boethius is working from one principal source, probably Nicomachus's lost *Eisagoge musica*, and that he has departed from the principal source to pick up Alypius's Latin terminology and is now returning to his principal text.

127. This comparison of strings to the disposition of the heavenly spheres agrees with that found in Nicomachus *Excerpta* 3 (JanS. 271–72) and idem, *Enchiridion* 3 (JanS. 241–42), although in the latter, Mercury and Venus are reversed. See R. Bragard, "L'harmonie des spheres selon Boèce," *Speculum* 4 (1921): 206–13.

moon moves with a very low sound. The earth, in ninth place, remaining immobile, is alone always fixed in place."[128] Tullius thus regards the earth as silent—that is, immobile. Next after the earth he assigns the lowest sound to the moon, which is closest to silence, so that the moon is the proslambanomenos, Mercury the hypate hypaton, Venus parhypate hypaton, the sun the lichanos hypaton, Mars the hypate meson, Jupiter the parhypate meson, Saturn the lichanos meson, and the highest heaven the mese.

The place at which I discuss the division of the monochord rule will be a more appropriate place to explain which of these strings are fixed, which are completely movable, and which stand between the fixed and the movable.[129]

28. *What the nature of consonance is* [220]

Although the sense of hearing recognizes consonances, reason weighs their value. When two strings, one of which is lower, are stretched and struck at the same time, and they produce, so to speak, an intermingled and sweet sound, and the two pitches coalesce into one as if linked together, then that which is called "consonance" occurs. When, on the other hand, they are struck at the same time and each desires to go its own way, and they do not bring together a sweet sound in the ear, a single sound composed of two, then this is what is called "dissonance."[130]

29. *Under what conditions consonances occur*

In these comparisons of low with high, it is necessary that the kind of consonances be found which are commensurable with themselves—that is, which are recognized as having a common denominator. Among multiple ratios, for example, that part which is the difference between the two terms measures the duple; between 2 and 4, for example, 2 measures both. Between 2 and 6, a triple ratio, 2 measures both. Between 9 and 8, it is unity itself which measures both. Among superparticular ratios, if the ratio is

128. Cicero *De re publica* 6.18; this "Latin" order is found also in Pliny *Naturalis historia* 2.22(20).84 and Censorinus *De die natali* 13.

129. See 4.13; the threefold division of strings into those that are immobile, those that are movable, and those in between is an important thread linking books 1 and 4; it is also found in Nicomachus *Enchiridion* 12 (JanS. 263). See Bower, "Sources," pp. 26–27.

130. Compare this definition of consonance (and dissonance) with Nicomachus *Enchiridion* 12 (JanS. 262.1–6); an important element in these definitions and those found in Nicomachus is the phrase "struck at the same time" (*simul pulsae,* a translation of the Greek ἅμα κρουσθέντες). Compare this definition with the discussion of consonance in André Barbera, "The Consonant Eleventh and the Expansion of the Musical Tetractys: A Study of Ancient Pythagoreanism," *Journal of Music Theory* 28 (1984), esp. pp. 192–93, and p. 217, n. 3.

sesquialter, such as 4:6, 2 measures both, which is also the difference between them. If the ratio is sesquitertian, such as 8:6, 2 also measures both.

This does not occur in other classes of inequalities which we discussed above, such as the superpartient, for if we couple 5 with 3, 2 (which is their difference) measures neither. For if 2 is set against 3, 2 is smaller, and [221] doubled, it is larger. Likewise if 2 is set against 5, 2 is smaller; in fact, it is surpassed by 3. For this reason the superpartient is the first class of inequality logically separated from the nature of consonance.

Further, in the kind of terms which form consonances, many things are similar; in the other kind, very little is similar. This is proved in this manner: the duple is nothing other than a simple number twice; the triple nothing other than a simple number three times; the quadruple is nothing other than a simple number four times; the sesquialter is twice the half; and the sesquitertian is three times the third part.[131] This similarity is not found easily in other classes of inequality.

30. *How Plato says consonance is made*

Plato says that consonance is produced in the ear in the following manner. A higher sound, he says, is necessarily faster. Since it has thus sped ahead of the low sound, it enters into the ear swiftly, and, after encountering the innermost part of the ear, it turns around as though impelled with renewed motion; but now it moves more slowly and not as fast as when emitted by the original impulse, and, therefore, it is lower. When the lowered sound, now returning, first runs into the approaching low sound, it is similar, is blended with it, and, as Plato says, mixes in a consonance.[132]

31. *What Nicomachus holds against Plato's theory*

Nicomachus does not judge this to be accurately stated, for consonance is not of similar sounds, but rather of dissimilar, each coming into one and the same concord. Indeed, if a low sound is mixed with a low sound, it produces no consonance, for similitude does not produce concord of mu[222] sical utterance, but dissimilitude. While concord differs in individual pitches, it is united in intermingled ones.

Nicomachus holds that consonance is made in this way: it is not, he says, only one pulsation which emits a simple measure of sound; rather a string, struck only one time, makes many sounds, striking the air again and again. But since its velocity of percussion is such that one sound encom-

131. This explanation of superparticular ratios remains something of an enigma. The sesquialter, as 3:2, could be described as three halves related to two halves, and the sesquitertian, as 4:3, as four thirds related to three thirds. Such descriptions would be more consistent with 1.6.
132. See Plato *Timaeus* 80A–B.

passes the other, no interval of silence is perceived, and it comes to the ears as if one pitch. If, therefore, the percussions of the low sounds are commensurable with the percussions of the high sounds, as in the ratios which we discussed above, then there is no doubt that this very commensuration blends together and makes one consonance of pitches.[133]

32. *Which consonances precede others in merit*

Judgment should be exercised with respect to all these consonances which we have discussed; one ought to decide by the reason, as well as by the ear, which of them is the more pleasing. For as the ear is affected by sound or the eye by a visible form, in the same way the judgment of the mind is affected by numbers or continuous quantity.

Given a line or a number, nothing is easier to contemplate, with either the eye or the intellect, than its double. After this judgment concerning the double follows that of the half; after that of the half, that of the triple; after that of the triple, that of the third. Thus, since it is easier to represent the double, Nicomachus considers the diapason to be the optimum consonance; after this the diapente, which contains the half; then the diapason-plus-diapente, which contains the triple. The others he ranks according to the same method and plan.[134] Ptolemy, however, whose every opinion I shall explain later, does not treat them in this same manner.[135]

33. *How the things thus far said are to be taken*

All the things that are to be explained more fully later, we are now [223] trying to explain cursorily and briefly, so that, for the present, they might accustom the mind of the reader to what might be called the surface of the subject; the mind will plunge into deeper knowledge in the subsequent treatment. Now this has been in the manner of the Pythagoreans: when something was said by the master Pythagoras, no one thereafter dared challenge the reasoning; rather, the explanation of the one teaching was authority for them. This continued until the time that the mind of the one learning—itself made stronger through more steadfast doctrine—came to discover the rationale of these same things, even without a teacher.

In this way we also commend what we have set forth to the belief of the reader. He should think that the diapason consists of the duple ratio,

133. This theory of consonance is not found in Nicomachus's extant works but is consistent with the theory of sound and ratio expressed in books 1–4 of the present work, esp. passages such as 1.3, 2.20, and 4.1.

134. See 2.20 for a complete treatment of the ranking of consonances according to Nicomachus.

135. See 5.7–12. The concluding sentence of this chapter is rather clear evidence that Boethius intended to translate the whole of Ptolemy's musical treatise.

the diapente of the sesquialter, the diatessaron of the sesquitertian, the diapason-plus-diapente of the triple, and the bis-diapason of the quadruple. In subsequent discussion we will explain very carefully both the theory of these consonances and the means by which musical consonances should be reckoned through the judgment of the ears. Fuller treatment will disclose all the other things which were discussed above: that the sesquioctave ratio produces the tone, and that it cannot be divided into two equal parts, any more than any other ratio of that class (the superparticular); that the consonance of the diatessaron consists of two tones and a semitone; that there are two semitones, one major and one minor; that the diapente is comprised of three tones and a minor semitone; and that the diapason is made up of five tones and two minor semitones and in no way adds up to six tones. All these things I shall prove both through mathematical reasoning and aural judgment.[136] Enough of this for the time being.

34. *What a musician is*

Now one should bear in mind that every art and also every discipline considers reason inherently more honorable than a skill which is practiced [224] by the hand and the labor of an artisan. For it is much better and nobler to know about what someone else fashions than to execute that about which someone else knows; in fact, physical skill serves as a slave, while reason rules like a mistress. Unless the hand acts according to the will of reason, it acts in vain. How much nobler, then, is the study of music as a rational discipline than as composition and performance![137] It is as much nobler as the mind is superior to the body; for devoid of reason, one remains in servitude. Reason exercises authority and leads to what is right; for unless the authority is obeyed, an act, lacking a rational basis, will falter.

It follows, then, that rational speculation is not dependent on the act of making, whereas manual works are nothing unless they are guided by reason. Just how great the splendor and merit of reason are can be perceived from the fact that those people—the so-called men of physical skill—take their names not from a discipline, but rather from instruments; for instance, the kitharist is named after the kithara, the aulete after the

136. The present chapter, like 1.19, is pedagogical in purpose: it calls again for belief on the part of the reader, restates the basic tenets of Pythagorean theory, and promises theoretical treatment of each.

137. "As composition and performance" is a translation of *in opere efficiendi atque actu*—literally, "at the work of making and performance." Boethius is developing a threefold classification of people concerned with music in this chapter, in which "performer" and "composer" describe the first two classes, both of which, because of the servile nature of their work, are subservient to the third. There is no necessary correspondence between performer and composer in antiquity and musicians of these classes today.

aulos,[138] and the others after the names of their instruments. But a musician is one who has gained knowledge of making music by weighing with the reason, not through the servitude of work, but through the sovereignty of speculation.

We see this, of course, in the building of monuments and the waging of wars—that is, in the contrary ascription of titles; for monuments are inscribed and triumphs are celebrated with the names of those by whose authority and reason they were ordained, not with the names of those by whose labor and slavery they were completed.

Thus, there are three classes of those who are engaged in the musical art. The first class consists of those who perform on instruments, the second of those who compose songs, and the third of those who judge instrumental performance and song.

But those of the class which is dependent upon instruments and who spend their entire effort there—such as kitharists and those who prove their skill on the organ and other musical instruments—are excluded from com- [225] prehension of musical knowledge, since, as was said, they act as slaves. None of them makes use of reason; rather, they are totally lacking in thought.

The second class of those practicing music is that of the poets, a class led to song not so much by thought and reason as by a certain natural instinct. For this reason this class, too, is separated from music.

The third class is that which acquires an ability for judging, so that it can carefully weigh rhythms and melodies and the composition as whole. This class, since it is totally grounded in reason and thought, will rightly be esteemed as musical. That person is a musician who exhibits the faculty of forming judgments according to speculation or reason relative and appropriate to music concerning modes and rhythms, the genera of songs, consonances,[139] and all the things which are to be explained subsequently, as well as concerning the songs of the poets.

138. The text at this point, *auloedus ex tibia,* is peculiar; the derivation of *auloedus* from *tibia* is by no means obvious, and the implication that it is strictly parallel to that of *citharoedus* from *cithara* does not help. Since there is a word in Latin for tibia-player—viz., *tibicen*—it is something of a puzzle why Boethius did not use it for the parallel construction. Perhaps he was being ostentatious with his knowledge of the Latin technical terms used by Cicero, for Cicero uses the term *auloedus* in *Pro Murena* 29.

139. *Permixtio,* a word which is clearly associated with consonance, is used by Boethius one other time—viz., in 2.20 [253.9]: *consonantia [est] duarum vocum rata permixtio* ("consonance is an appropriate mixture of two pitches").

BOOK 2

1. *Introduction*

The preceding book laid out all the things which I now propose to demonstrate very carefully. But before I come to these things which should be taught in terms of their own particular properties, I should add a few comments. In this way the more enlightened mind of the student should be prepared to understand the things which are to be spoken of.[1]

2. *What Pythagoras established as philosophy*[2]

Pythagoras was the first person to call the study of wisdom "philosophy." He held that philosophy was the knowledge and study of whatever may properly and truly be said "to be." Moreover, he considered these things to be those that neither increase under tension nor decrease under pressure, things not changed by any chance occurrences. These things are

---

1. This brief chapter establishes the order of the second book: chaps. 2–17 contain the material whereby the student will become enlightened; of these, 2–5 review elements of arithmetic, while 6–17 present "axioms" (see last paragraph of 2.5). Following an excursion into the nature and merit of consonances (18–20), the classes of ratios and the specific ratios of consonances are demonstrated (21–27), along with the ratios of the tone, the major and minor semitone, and the comma (28–31). These ratios are the "things" that are to be "taught in terms of their own particular properties."

2. A fundamental dependence on the *De institutione arithmetica* is exhibited throughout the first 3 books of *Fundamentals of Music*. The dependence is ultimately on Nicomachus's *Eisagoge arithmetica,* since Boethius's treatise is a translation of Nicomachus's. In chaps. 2–5 of Book 2 Boethius rebuilds the philosophical and mathematical underpinnings of music as the discipline treating related quantity. Parallel passages are noted.

52

forms, magnitudes, qualities, relations,[3] and other things which, considered in themselves, are immutable, but which, joined to material substances, suffer radical change and are altered in many ways because of their relationship with a changeable thing.[4] [228]

3. Concerning different kinds of quantity, and the discipline with which each is associated

According to Pythagoras all quantity is either continuous or discrete. That which is continuous is called "magnitude," whereas that which is discrete is called "multitude." The properties of these are different and even opposite.

Multitude, beginning from a finite quantity and increasing to an infinite quantity, proceeds in such a way that there is no limit to increasing. Multitude is limited with regard to the smallest term, but unlimited with regard to the larger; its origin is unity, and there is nothing smaller than unity. Multitude increases through numbers and is extended to infinity; there is no number that places a limit on its increasing.

Magnitude, on the other hand, likewise assumes a finite quantity as its measure, but it is infinitely divisible. For if there is a line one foot long, or any other length for that matter, it can be divided into two equal parts, and its half can be divided in half, and this half again divided into another half, so that there will never be any limit to dividing magnitude.

Magnitude is thus limited insofar as the larger measure is concerned, but it is infinite when it begins to divide. Number (that is, multitude), to the contrary, is limited with regard to the smallest measure but begins to be infinite when it multiplies. Although these things are in a sense infinite, nevertheless, philosophy investigates them as finite things; philosophy discovers something discrete in infinite things and, concerning discrete things, can rightly summon the acuity of its own system of thought.

Some magnitudes are fixed, such as squares, triangles, or circles, whereas others are movable, such as the sphere of the universe and what- [229] ever is turned within it at a prescribed speed. Some quantities are discrete in themselves, such as three or four or other numbers, whereas others are discrete in relation to something, such as double, triple, and others that

3. This is the first occurrence of the word *habitudo* in the *Fundamentals of Music*, Boethius's translation of the Greek σχέσις. This term, which will here be translated "relation," is used in a general sense for any relation between two numbers and is often used as an equivalent of "ratio" (*proportio*, or λόγος). Nicomachus frequently uses σχεσις in his *Eisagoge arithmetica*, and consequently *habitudo* appears often in Boethius's *Arith.* That *habitudo* occurs only in Books 2 and 3 of *Fundamentals of Music* is an indication of just how dependent these two books are on the arithmetical treatise. For a definition and discussion of *habitudo*, see Nicomachus of Gerasa, *Introduction to Arithmetic*, pp. 307–08.

4. Concerning philosophy as the study of that which can truly be said "to be," see *Arith.* 1.1 [7.20–8.15] (Nicomachus *Eisagoge arithmetica* 1.1).

arise from comparison. Geometry speculates about fixed magnitude, while astronomy pursues knowledge of movable magnitude; arithmetic is the authority concerning quantity that is discrete in itself, whereas music is clearly expert concerning quantities related to other quantities.[5]

4. *Concerning different kinds of relative quantity*

We discussed sufficiently that quantity which is discrete in itself in the arithmetic books.[6] There are three simple classes of quantity in which one quantity is related to another: the first is multiple, the second superparticular, and the third superpartient. When the multiple is mixed with the superparticular or the superpartient, two other classes result: the multiple-superparticular and the multiple-superpartient.[7] The rule for all of these is as follows.

If you wish to compare unity with all other quantities in natural numerical series,[8] a fixed sequence of multiples should be formed. For two to one is duple, three to one is triple, four is quadruple, and so on in the same manner, as the following diagram [Fig. B.1] illustrates.

1	1	1	1	1	1
2	3	4	5	6	7

If you should seek a superparticular ratio, compare the quantities in a natural numerical series with each other (with unity removed, of course).

5. Concerning the subdivision of quantity and the derivation and characters of the four mathematical disciplines, see *Arith.* 1.1 [8.15–10.7] (Nicomachus *Eisagoge arithmetica* 1.3).

6. Boethius makes reference to his treatise on arithmetic only once by its title, at 1.4 [192.19]. His more usual way of referring to it is simply *in arithmeticis,* "in the arithmetic [books]."

7. Concerning "quantity related to another" (*quantitas ad aliquid relata*), see *Arith.* 1.21 (Nicomachus *Eisagoge arithmetica* 1.17). The subdivision of related quantity is somewhat more developed in *Arith.;* there are two basic genera, equal and unequal related quantity. Unequal related quantity is further divided into "major" and "minor," depending on whether the larger or the smaller term appears first in the ratio: if the larger appears first—e.g., 3:2— it is major; if the smaller appears first—e.g., 2:3—it is minor. A ratio of the minor unequal related quantity species is denoted with the verbal prefix *sub*—e.g., subsuperparticular (*Arith.* 1.22); by analogy, a ratio of the major species would be denoted with the prefix *super,* which accounts for the appearance of such terminology in the musical treatise.

8. Boethius never defines the term *numerus naturalis,* although he uses it in a technical sense throughout Book 2 (and in *Arith.*), usually in conjunction with some form of *dispono* (*dispositio, dispositus*). From the context one can determine that one "natural number" is whole—that is, an integer. But in the present context, as well as several others, *naturalis numerus* refers to more than a single number; it implies a series of numbers generated from unity, and hence it has been translated as "a natural numerical series." See also 2.5 [230.23], 2.6 [231.18], 2.8 [236.24], 2.9 [239.27–28], 2.18 [250.4], and *Arith.* 1.23 [46.23–47.1].

For example: three to two, which is sesquialter; four to three, which is sesquitertian; five to four, which is sesquiquartan; and the others in the [230] same manner, as the following diagram demonstrates [Fig. B.2].

SESQUIALTER		SESQUIQUARTAN		SESQUISEPTIMAL	
2	3	4	5	6	7
	SESQUITERTIAN		SESQUIQUINTAN		

You will find superpartient ratios in this way: You should arrange the natural numerical series beginning from three. If you skip one number, you will see a superbipartient produced; if two, a supertripartient; if three, a superquadripartient, and likewise for subsequent numbers [Fig. B.3].

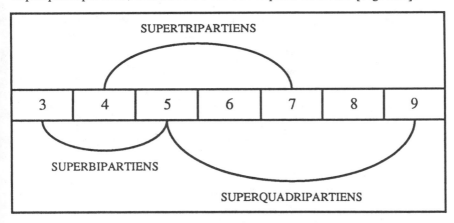

Directing attention to this same procedure, the careful reader will also see by observation the ratios put together from multiple and superparticular or multiple and superpartient. But all these things were discussed more fully in the arithmetic books.[9]

5. *Why multiplicity is superior to others*

In these matters it should be borne in mind that the multiple class of inequality seems far superior to the remaining two. For the formation of a natural numerical series is set out in multiples of unity, and unity is prior in the comparison.[10] Now the superparticular class is not made by compar-

9. Concerning classes of inequality, see *Arith.* 1.22 (Nicomachus *Eisagoge arithmetica* 1.17).
10. Concerning the formation and nature of multiples, see *Arith.* 1.23 (Nicomachus *Eisagoge arithmetica* 1.18).

ison with unity, but by comparison of those numbers which are set out after unity (for example, 3:2, 4:3, and so on in subsequent numbers).[11] The formation of the superpartient class is quite backwards. It is set down neither in continuous numbers—but rather by skipping over numbers—not always with an equal skip—but rather at one time over one, at another over two, at another over three, at another over four, and in this way it increases to infinity.[12] Further, multiplicity begins from unity, superparticularity from two, the superpartient from three. But this should suffice for now.

At this time it will be necessary to set out certain things which the Greeks describe as "axioms,"[13] the applicability of which will become clear when we treat individual matters through demonstration.

6. *What square numbers are: a reflection concerning them*[14]

A square number is one that grows by multiplying a measure by itself—for example, twice two, thrice three, four times four, five times five, six times six, of which this is a diagram [Fig. B.4]:

2	3	4	5	6	7	8	9	10
4	9	16	25	36	49	64	81	100

The natural numerical series set out in the upper row is thus the root of the square numbers presented in the lower; the squares, which follow one another in the lower row, are by nature continuous, for example, 4, 9, 16, and so on.

If I subtract a smaller square from a larger square that is continuous with it, what remains is the quantity that is the sum of the roots (or sides) of these same squares. For example, if I subtract 4 from 9, 5 remains, which is composed by joining 2 and 3—that is, the roots of both the squares. Likewise if I subtract 9 from 16, then 7 remains, which of course

11. Concerning the formation and nature of superparticulars, see *Arith.* 1.24 (Nichomachus *Eisagoge arithmetica* 1.19).

12. Concerning the formation and nature of superpartients, see *Arith.* 1.28 (Nicomachus *Eisagoge arithmetica* 1.20).

13. The axioms are presented in chaps. 6–17.

14. This axiom concerning square numbers seems to have no direct relevance to the subsequent axioms or to the musical proofs that follow. Perhaps the author thought it would serve as a fitting orientation to the arithmetical reasoning of the axioms and proofs. This chapter is clearly related to *Arith.* 2.12, although the latter is concerned primarily with the generation of squares from a natural numerical series, whereas the passage here seems more concerned with the "harmony" of differences between squares and their sides.

[231]

[232]

is composed by joining 3 and 4, which are the roots of the aforementioned squares. The same occurs with other square numbers.

If the square numbers are not continuous, but one between two others is omitted, then half the difference between these two will be that which is made from their roots. For example, if I subtract 4 from the square 16, 12 remains; half of this is the number that converges from the roots of both squares. The roots of the two are 2 and 4, which produce 6 when joined together. And in other squares the measure is the same.

If two squares are skipped over, a third of their difference will be the number which is made by joining together their roots. For example, if I subtract 4 from 25, two squares having been omitted, then 21 remains; the roots of these squares are 2 and 5, which produce 7, and 7 is a third part of 21.

This then is the rule: if three square numbers are skipped, then a fourth part of that which remains when the smaller square is subtracted from the larger is that which is made from the roots; if four are skipped over, then a fifth part. And so the parts will occur with the denomination of the number one degree larger than the number of squares skipped.

7. All inequality proceeds from equality, and the proof thereof

As unity is the origin of plurality and number, so equality is the origin of ratios. As we said in *Arithmetic,* once three terms have been assumed, we produce multiple ratios from equality.[15] We generate superparticular relations, on the other hand, from reversed multiples. Likewise, we make superpartient comparisons from reversed[16] superparticular ratios. For instance, let three unities be set out, or three twos or three threes or any three equal terms; then let a first term (in a subsequent row, of course) be [233] made equal to the first, a second equal to the first plus the second, and a third equal to the first plus twice the second plus the third. The duple, the first ratio of multiplicity, is thereby made through numerical progression, as this diagram shows [Fig. B.5].

1	1	1
1	2	4

In this case the unity of the lower series is made equal to the unity placed

15. See *Arith.* 1.32 (Nicomachus *Eisagoge arithmetica* 1.23).

16. "Reversed" is a translation of *conversus.* Boethius means a transposition of order: the multiple (duples) 1:2:4 is reversed to produce the superparticular (sesquialters). See *Arith.* 1.32 [68.21–69.1, 70.3–8].

at first in the upper; likewise the two is equal to the first unity plus the second unity of the upper row, and similarly the four is equal to the first unity plus twice the second unity plus the third unity of the upper row, and 1, 2, 4 are in the duple ratio. If you work in the same manner from these, the triple ratio will be generated, and from the triple the quadruple, from the quadruple the quintuple, and the generation of relations continues, proceeding in this manner.[17]

If the same three numbers are taken up again, superparticular ratios may be made, as we demonstrate with one example. We now reverse them and place the larger number first: 4, 2, 1. A first term is then set down equal to the first (that is, 4), a second equal to the first plus the second (that is, 6), and a third equal to the first plus twice the second plus the third (that is, 9). When these are set out, the ratio is seen to be sesquialter [Fig. B.6].

4	2	1
4	6	9

If this procedure is performed with triple terms, then the sesquitertian is made; if with quadruple, then the sesquiquartan. Thus with similar designations on either side, superparticular proportion[18] is born from multiplicity.

The superpartient relation is put together from reversed superparticular ratios. Let the sesquialter comparison be set out in reverse order: 9, [234] 6, 4; then a first term should be set down equal to the first (that is, 9), a second equal to the first plus the second (that is, 15), and a third equal to the first plus twice the second plus the third (that is, 25). Let these be arranged in the lower row in this manner [Fig. B.7]:

9	6	4
9	15	25

Thus the superbipartient relation has been produced from reversed sesquialters. If a careful student applies this process of reckoning, he produces

17. From the duple series: 1; 1 + 2 = 3; 1 + (2 × 2) + 4 = 9. Thus, from 1:2:4 the triples 1:3:9 are produced, and triples treated similarly produce quadruples, and so on.

18. This represents the first use of the word "proportion" (*proportionalitas*) in Boethius's treatise. For the distinction between "proportion" (*proportionalitas*) and "ratio" (*proportio*), see 2.12 and n. 34 below.

the supertripartient ratio from reversed sesquitertians, and he will be surprised to produce all superpartient species from superparticularity using the corresponding opposites with parallel designations.

Multiple-superparticular ratios have to be created not from reversed superparticular ratios, but rather from superparticular ratios remaining just as they were created from the multiple. From superpartient ratios remaining just as they were produced from superparticular ratios, none other than multiple-superpartient ratios will be generated. But this is enough concerning these things, for this comparison has been discussed more thoroughly in the arithmetic books.[19]

8. *Rules for finding any continuous superparticular ratios*

It often happens that someone discussing music might seek three, four, or some other number of equal ratios of superparticulars. But lest some error should entangle the process in difficulties through chance or through ignorance, we will produce any number of equal superparticular ratios from multiplicity by means of this rule: Any single multiple ratio, computed from unity, comes before as many superparticular relations (with comparable names in the opposite class, of course), as the multiple itself departs from unity;[20] in this way the duple ratio precedes a sesquialter, the triple a sesquitertian, the quadruple a sesquiquartan, and so on in this manner. Thus [235] a diagram of duple terms [Fig. B.8] may be set out.

1	2	4	8	16
	3	6	12	24
		9	18	36
			27	54
				81

In the above diagram, the first multiple (2) has one term related to it (3) which can make a sesquialter ratio. There is nothing related to the 3, however, which could make a sesquialter with it, for it has no half. The second duple is 4; this precedes two sesquialters, 6 and 9. Nine has no half, and for this reason, nothing is related to it by a sesquialter relation. The same occurs in subsequent numbers. Triple ratios create sesquitertian ratios in the same manner. Here is a similar diagram for the triple ratio [Fig. B.9].

19. See *Arith.* 1.29 (Nicomachus *Eisagoge arithmetica* 1.22) for multiple-superparticular; *Arith.* 1.31 (Nicomachus *Eisagoge arithmetica* 1.23) for multiple-superpartient.

20. Concerning the production of continuous ratios of the superparticular class, see also *Arith.* 2.2 (Nicomachus *Eisagoge arithmetica* 2.3).

1	3	9	27	81
	4	12	36	108
		16	48	144
			64	192
				246

In the above diagram we see sesquitertian ratios born in such a way that the first triple precedes one sesquitertian, the second two, the third three, and in the final number, division by a third part is always shut off by a kind of natural limit.

If you form a quadruple row, you will discover sesquiquartan ratios in the same way, or if a quintuple row, then sesquiquintan ratios, and so on. Multiple ratios of a single denomination precede as many superparticulars as they themselves depart from unity at a given place. We will give only one such disposition in quadruple ratio [Fig. B.10], so that in it, as well as in the others, a careful reader may exercise the sharpness of his mind.

[236]

1	4	16	64	256
	5	20	80	320
		25	100	400
			125	500
				625

This process of reckoning seems to have been discovered for this purpose: no matter how many (four or five or even more) continuous ratios (whether sesquialter, sesquitertian, sesquioctave, or any other ratios) someone is seeking, he will not get tripped up by any error; moreover, he will not try to fit such ratios to a first number which cannot precede or have behind it as many numbers as have been proposed. According to this method he will rather set out multiples and consider how many superparticular ratios are required, then work from that multiple which departs from unity the required number of times. Thus, if he were to seek three sesquialter ratios in the above diagrams,[21] he should not begin his search at 4, for this number, since it is the second duple, precedes only two sesquialter ratios, and a third cannot be fitted to it. Rather he should try to add the half of 8, for

21. That is, in the above diagrams of continuous ratios, he should seek out the diagram containing continuous sesquialter ratios—viz. Fig. B.8.

this number, since it is third, will yield the three sesquialter ratios which he seeks. The rule is similar in the others.

There is also another way of forming ratios in this manner. The smallest ratios in these comparisons are called "roots" of ratios. Let a natural numerical series be set out, derived from unity:[22]

$$2 \quad 3 \quad 4 \quad 5 \quad 6 \quad 7$$

The smallest ratios then are the sesquialter (3:2), the sesquitertian (4:3), the sesquiquartan (5:4), and, similarly to infinity, all other ratios which follow after unity. Thus let the proposition be to produce two sesquialter ratios in continuous comparison. I take the root sesquialter ratio and arrange it 2 then 3. Then I multiply 2 times 2, which makes 4; likewise 3 times 2, which makes 6; we multiply the three again by itself, which makes 9. Let these be arranged in the following manner [Fig. B.11].

[237]

We will thus find the two proposed sesquialter ratios: 6:4 and 9:6.

Now let the proposition be to find three. I take the same numbers which I set out above in searching out two sesquialter relations, the very same sesquialter ratios. I multiply the 4 by 2, which makes 8; likewise the 6 by 2, which makes 12, also the 9 by 2, which makes 18, the 9 again by 3, which makes 27. Let these be arranged as follows [Fig. B.12].

The method will also be the same for other ratios. If you wish to extend

22. In the course of Book 2, many such numerical series are "set out." It is often difficult to determine whether such series were intended to be independent diagrams or were merely part of the text. Manuscript traditions of the twelfth and thirteenth centuries tend to display any set of numbers as a diagram, whereas the earliest manuscripts seem to minimize the use of valuable parchment for such displays. In the present translation, the numerical series will not be given the status of diagrams unless they were so treated in the earlier manuscripts or unless a diagram is termed *descriptio* in the text; nevertheless, for the sake of clarity they will be displayed on a separate line.

sesquitertian ratios, you should set out the roots of the sesquitertian, which are 4 and 3, in relation to each other; then you multiply these in the same manner.[23] But if you set out the roots of sesquiquartan ratios, you will extend any number of sesquiquartan ratios using the same multiplication. Just how useful these observations are to us will be shown in what follows.[24]

9. Concerning the ratio of numbers which are measured by others[25]

[238]   If the difference of two numbers exactly measures them without a remainder, the numbers (the ones measured by their difference) are in the same ratio as those numbers by which their difference has measured them.[26] Take the numbers 50 and 55. These are related according to the sesquidecimal relation; their difference is 5, which is a tenth part of the number 50. Therefore, this measures the number 50 ten times and 55 eleven times. Thus their own difference, 5, exactly measures the numbers 55 and 50 by 11 and 10, and 11 and 10 are brought into relation by the sesquidecimal comparison. Thus the numbers—those which their difference measured exactly without remainder—are in the same ratio as the ones by which their difference has measured them.

If a difference measures those numbers (of which it is the difference) to an extent that a plurality remains after measurement of the numbers, and likewise the excess is the same in both numbers, and the measuring of

23. Arrange roots 3 then 4. Multiply 3 by 3, making 9, 3 by 4, making 12, 4 by 4, making 16, and thereby produce the second row: 9:12:16. For the third row, multiply 9 by 3, which makes 27, 12 by 3, which makes 36, 16 by 3, which makes 48, and 16 again by 4, making 64. The arrangement of sesquitertians becomes:

$$3 \quad 4$$
$$9 \quad 12 \quad 16$$
$$27 \quad 36 \quad 48 \quad 64$$

24. For application of the principles set forth in this chapter, see esp. 2.28, 29, and 31.

25. This chapter exhibits very strong parallels with Iamblicus *In Nicomachi arithmeticam introductionem*, 74–76 (Pistelli ed. [Leipzig, 1894], pp. 52–55). Iamblicus attributes this theory to the *Eisagoge musica* of Nicomachus.

26. The concept of one number measuring another arises from the Pythagorean notion of composite and noncomposite number (*Arith.* 1.14–16). A "measuring number" functions as a kind of common denominator that marks off discrete parts of a larger plurality. The process of measurement is described as follows in *Arith.* 1.14 [30.4–7]: "One number is a measure of another number as often as, either alone or doubled or multiplied by three, or however often that number is compared to another, its sum, neither smaller nor larger, comes exactly to the amount of the number it is compared with" (Masi trans., p. 90). This description functions well with respect to the first type of measurement described in this passage, but the notion of measurement is expanded for the second and third types of measurement; in those two instances the measurement does not "come exactly to the amount of the number."

the difference is a quantity less than the plurality of the numbers,[27] then the numbers will contain a larger ratio if the remainder is subtracted from them—that is, the numbers will contain a ratio larger than those whole numbers before their own difference measured them. Take the two numbers 53 and 58. Let 5, which is their difference, measure them. Five measures the number 53 ten times up to 50, and 3 remains. Likewise, it measures the number 58 eleven times up to 55, and again 3 is left over. Thus, if 3 is subtracted from both numbers, 50 and 55 will remain, which may be set out in this manner [Fig. B.13].

53	58
50	55

Here then, it is evident that 50 and 55 form a larger ratio than 53 and 58. [239] A larger ratio is always found in smaller numbers (which we will demonstrate a little later).[28]

If that measurement of a difference exceeds the quantity of both of two numbers by the same numerical plurality,[29] then the numbers measured will form a smaller ratio with the addition of the sums by which the measurement surpassed both—that is, smaller than they were before their own difference measured them. Take the numbers 48 and 53. Their difference is 5. If 5 measured the number 48 ten times, it would make 50; the number 50 surpasses the number 48 by 2. Likewise if it measured 53 eleven times, it would make 55, which again surpasses the number 53 by the same 2. Let the 2 be added to both and arranged in this manner [Fig. B.14].

48	53
50	55

Thus 50:55, derived by the addition of the 2 by which the measurement of

27. This second case of measurement presents three conditions: first, that the measurement is not complete—i.e., it does not "come exactly to the amount of the numbers" (compare this with n. 26); second, that the remainder is the same when both numbers have been measured; and third, that the numbers into which the measuring difference fits exactly are smaller than the original numbers.

28. See last paragraph of this chapter.

29. This third case of measurement again requires three conditions: first, that the measurement is not exact; second, that the remainder is the same when both numbers have been measured; and third, that the two numbers into which the measuring difference fits exactly are larger than the original numbers.

the difference went beyond them, will be a smaller ratio than 48:53, which the same difference of 5 had measured.

Indeed, larger and smaller ratios are recognized in this manner: a half is larger than a third part, a third part is larger than a fourth, a fourth part is larger than a fifth, and so on. It follows that a sesquialter ratio is larger than a sesquitertian, and a sesquitertian surpasses a sesquiquartan, and so on. From this it is evident that a ratio of superparticular numbers is always observed to be larger in smaller numbers. This is obvious in a natural numerical series. Let a natural numerical series be set out:

$$1 \quad 2 \quad 3 \quad 4 \quad 5$$

[240]   Now 2 is the duple of unity, 3 the sesquialter of 2, and 4 the sesquitertian of 3. The larger numbers are 3 and 4, and the smaller 3, 2, and unity. Therefore, the smaller ratio is contained in the larger numbers, and the larger in the smaller numbers. From this it is obvious that whenever an equal plurality is added to any numbers containing a superparticular ratio, the ratio is larger before the addition of the equal plurality than after the equal plurality has been added to them.

10. *What is produced from multiplied multiple and superparticular ratios*[30]

It seems that something that will be demonstrated shortly should be anticipated in this place.[31] If a multiple interval is multiplied by 2, that which arises from the multiplication is multiple. But if the product of multiplication by 2 is not multiple, then that which was multiplied by 2 was not multiple.

Likewise, if a superparticular ratio is multiplied by 2, that which is produced is neither superparticular nor multiple. But if the product of a multiplication by 2 is neither multiple nor superparticular, then what was multiplied by 2 was either superparticular or from another class, but was surely not multiple.[32]

11. *Which superparticulars produce which multiples*[33]

To this should be added that the first two superparticular ratios make [241]   the first multiple ratio. Thus, if a sesquialter and a sesquitertian are joined together, they create a duple. Take the numbers 2, 3, and 4: 3:2 is ses-

---

30. Parallels exist between this chapter and Iamblicus, *In Nicomachi arithmeticam introductionem* 77 (Pistelli ed., p. 55).

31. See 4.2, second proposition.

32. For example, the double of the sesquialter proportion 6:4 is 9:4. As 6 is to 4, so 9 is to 6, and 9:4 is neither multiple nor superparticular.

33. See also *Arith.* 2.3 (Nicomachus *Eisagoge arithmetica* 2.5).

quialter, 4:3 sesquitertian, and 4:2 duple. Likewise, the first multiple added to the first superparticular creates the second multiple. Take the numbers 2, 4, and 6: 4:2 is duple, the first multiple; 6:4 is sesquialter, which is the first superparticular; and 6:2 is triple, which is the second multiple. But if you add a triple to a sesquitertian, a quadruple will be produced; if you add a quadruple to a sesquiquartan, a quintuple will be produced. In this manner, by joining ratios of the multiple and superparticular classes, multiples are generated infinitely.

12. *Concerning the arithmetic, the geometric, and the harmonic mean*

Since we have discussed the matters concerning ratios which had to be considered, we should now discuss means. A ratio is a certain comparison of two terms measured against themselves. By *terms* I mean numerical wholes. A proportion is a collection of equal ratios. A proportion consists of at least three terms, for when a first term related to a second holds the same ratio as the second to the third, then this is called a "proportion," and the "mean" among these three terms is that which is second.[34]

There is, then, a threefold classification of middle terms joining these ratios together. Either the difference between the lesser term and the mean term is equal to that of the mean and the largest, but the ratio is not equal— in the numbers 1:2:3, for example, unity alone is the difference between 1 and 2 as well as 2 and 3, but the ratio is not equal (2:1 forms a duple [242] whereas 3:2 forms a sesquialter)—or an equal ratio is established between both pairs, but not an equal difference—in the numbers 1:2:4, for example, 2:1 is duple, as is 4:2, but the difference between 4 and 2 is 2, whereas that between 2 and unity is 1. There is a third class of mean which is characterized by neither the same ratios nor the same differences, but is derived in such a way that the largest term is related to the smallest in the same way that the difference between the larger terms is related to the difference between the lesser terms—in the numbers 3:4:6, for example, 6:3 is duple, and 2 stands between 6 and 4, while unity stands between 4 and 3, but 2 compared to unity is again duple. Therefore as the largest

---

34. There is a certain ambiguity in ancient arithmetic between "proportion" and the theory of means. Strictly speaking (as made clear in the definition and in the text that follows), only two or more equal ratios can form a proportion. But since two other classes of division of ratios were crucial to music theory, all three divisions (and by extension even more) came to be called "proportion," and language concerning "means" and "proportion" became equivocal. Boethius's definitions of proportion and ratio in this context seem even clearer than those in *Arith.* 2.40 [137.10–16] (Nicomachus *Eisagoge arithmetica* 2.21). A verbal relationship between the words *proportio* and *ratio* in Latin and Greek is unfortunately lost in English; *proportio* (λόγος) must be translated "ratio," and *proportionalitas* (ἀναλογία) "proportion." A clear exposition of Nicomachus's (Boethius's by extension) theory of proportion is found in d'Ooge's translation of Nicomachus *Eisagoge arithmetica*, pp. 60–65, esp. p. 264, n. 2.

term is related to the smallest, so the difference between the larger terms is related to the difference between the lesser terms.

That mean in which the differences are equal is called "arithmetic," that in which the ratios are equal "geometric," and that which we described third "harmonic."[35] We submit the following examples of them [Fig. B.15].

ARITHMETIC GEOMETRIC HARMONIC

| 1 | 2 | 3 |

| 1 | 2 | 4 |

| 3 | 4 | 6 |

We are not unaware that there are also other means of ratios, which we discussed in the arithmetic books.[36] But only these three are necessary for the present discussion. Yet among these three means, only the geometric is strictly and properly called a "proportion," since it is the only one totally constructed according to equal ratios. Nevertheless, we use the same word indiscriminately, calling the others "proportions" as well.

[243] 13. *Concerning continuous and disjunct means*[37]

Apropos of these things, some proportion is continuous, and some disjunct. Continuous proportion is that discussed above, for one and the same mean number is placed after the larger number and, at the same time, before the smaller number. On the other hand, when there are two means, then we call the proportion "disjunct," as in a geometric series of this kind: 1:2, 3:6. In this example, just as 2 is related to unity, so 6 is related to 3, and this is called "disjunct proportion." Hence it can be recognized that continuous proportion is acquired in at least three terms, disjunct, on the other hand, in four. However, proportion can be continuous in four or more terms if it occurs in this manner: 1:2:4:8:16. In this example there are not two ratios, but many, and always one fewer than there are terms given.

35. These three means—geometric, arithmetic, and harmonic—probably date back to the time of Pythagoras himself, and they occupy an important place in traditional musical speculation. Their invention and definition have been attributed to Hippasus, Philolaus, and Archytas; see Hermann Diels, *Die Fragmente der Vorsokratiker,* 11th ed., ed. Walther Kranz (Zurich and Berlin, 1964), I.18.15, p. 110 (Hippasus); I.44.A24, pp. 404–05 (Philolaus); I.47.B2, pp. 435–36 (Archytas).

36. *Arith.* 2.51–52 (Nicomachus *Eisagoge arithmetica* 2.28). See also *Arith.* 2.41 (Nicomachus *Eisagoge arithmetica* 2.22) concerning the development of ten types of proportion among the ancients.

37. Concerning continuous and disjunct means, see *Arith.* 2.40 (Nicomachus *Eisagoge arithmetica* 2.21).

14. *Why the means enumerated above are named as they are*

Of these means, one is named "arithmetic," because the difference between the terms is equal according to number. A second is called "geometric," because it is characterized by similarity of ratio. The "harmonic" is so named, because it is fitted together in such a way that equality of ratios is observed between differences and between extreme terms. A more thorough exposition of these things was given in the arithmetic books,[38] whereas now we run through them quickly merely to call them to mind.

15. *How the means discussed above arise from equality*

It is necessary to discuss briefly how these proportions are generated [244] from equality. It has been established that just as unity governs number, so equality governs ratios; just as unity is the origin of number, so equality is the beginning of ratio.[39] Consequently the arithmetic mean arises from equality in the following manner.

Once three equal terms are given, there are two ways of producing this proportion.

A first term is set out equal to the first, a second equal to the first plus the second, and a third equal to the first plus the second plus the third. This is shown in this example: Take three unities (upper row), and let a first term of the lower row then be set down equal to the first unity (that is, 1); a second equal to the first plus the second (that is, 2); and a third equal to the first plus the second plus the third, that is, 3. This diagram [Fig. B.16] results:

1	1	1
1	2	3

Likewise, let three twos be set out in equality: 2 2 2 (upper row). A first term of the lower row should be made equal to the first (that is, 2), a second equal to the first plus the second (that is, 4), and a third equal to the first plus the second plus the third (that is, 6). This diagram [Fig. B.17] results:

38. The second book of *Arith.* concludes with a very thorough discussion of means and proportion (2.40–53, Masi trans., pp. 163–88; and Nicomachus *Eisagoge arithmetica* 2.21–29).

39. See above, 2.7; see also *Arith.* 1.32.

2	2	2
2	4	6

And likewise with 3 [Fig. B.18].

3	3	3
3	6	9

But in relation to these, it should be observed that if unity has been set down as the foundation of equality, unity will likewise be found in the differences of the numbers, and these particular numbers allow nothing to come between them. But if 2 represents equality, 2 is the difference, and one number always falls between the terms. If 3 represents equality, it is likewise the difference, and two numbers in the natural numerical succession are skipped over between the numbers, and so on in this manner.

[245] There is a second way of producing arithmetic proportion. Again take three equal terms in the upper row, and let the first in the lower row be made equal to the first plus the second, the second equal to the first plus twice the second, the third equal to the first plus twice the second plus the third. Assuming three unities, then the first of the lower row is equal to the first plus the second (that is, 2), the second equal to the first plus twice the second (that is, 3), and the third equal to the first plus twice the second plus the third (that is, 4) [Fig. B.19].

1	1	1
2	3	4

Here, then, unity is the difference between the terms, for unity falls between 2 and 1 and between 3 and 2; indeed, no natural number can intervene, for immediately following unity, 2 is set down in series, and after 2, 3.

The same may be accomplished with 2, so take three twos, and let the first term be equal to the first plus the second (that is, 4), the second equal to the first plus twice the second (that is 6), and the third equal to the first plus twice the second plus the third (that is, 8) [Fig. B.20].

2	2	2
4	6	8

Here 2 likewise holds the difference between the terms, and one number naturally falls between them, for 5 naturally occurs between 4 and 6, and 7 between 6 and 8.

But if 3 is the foundation of equality, 3 will constitute the difference, with one less than this number always skipped between the terms; the same is observed with 4 and 5. The careful reader, with these same rules, will discover for himself the things about which we now remain silent for the sake of brevity.

We showed how geometric proportion can be obtained from equality [246] when we were demonstrating how all inequality flows from equality.[40] Nevertheless, unless it is bothersome, it should now be repeated again briefly. When three equal terms have been set out as an upper row, the first of the lower row is made equal to the first, the second equal to the first plus the second, and the third equal to the first plus twice the second plus the third. The same procedure may be continued. In this way, geometric proportion takes its first principle from equality. We discussed the properties of these ratios very thoroughly in the arithmetic books,[41] so if the reader instructed in these matters approaches this, he will not be disturbed by any error of doubt.

The harmonic mean, which should now be discussed a little more fully, is generated according to this reasoning.[42] It should be created, if we desire to produce duple proportion, through setting out three equal terms in the upper row, and then making the first of the lower row equal to the first plus twice the second, the second equal to twice the first plus twice the second, and the third equal to the first plus twice the second plus three times the third. Take three unities in this way [Fig. B.21].

1	1	1

The first term should be made equal to the first plus twice the second (that is, 3), the second equal to twice the first plus twice the second (that is, 4),

40. See above, 2.7.

41. See *Arith.* 2.44 concerning the properties of geometric proportion.

42. This method of setting forth the harmonic mean shows strong parallels with a text presented in Iamblicus *In Nicomachi arithmeticam introductionem* 157 (Pistelli ed., pp. 111–12). For a discussion of the relationship between Boethius, Nicomachus, and Iamblicus (in particular with regard to 2.9, 15, and 16), see Pizzani, "Fonti," pp. 66–78.

and the third equal to the first plus twice the second plus three times the third (that is, 6). If the equality is established with 2, or with 3, the same calculation of the mean appears, with the terms and their differences being spaced according to the duple, as the following diagrams show [Fig. B.22].

1	1	1
2	4	6

2	2	2
6	8	12

3	3	3
9	12	18

[247] But if it is required that there be a triple ratio between the extreme terms, set out three equal terms in the upper row, and make the first of the lower row from the first plus the second, the second from the first plus twice the second, and the third from the first plus twice the second plus three times the third, as the following diagram shows [Fig. B.23].

1	1	1
2	3	6

2	2	2
4	6	12

3	3	3
6	9	18

16. *Concerning the harmonic mean: a much fuller investigation of it*[43]

Since we have embarked upon a discussion of harmony, I do not believe we should tacitly pass over things which can be discussed more thoroughly. Thus, a harmonic proportion should be set out in a lower row, and the differences between its terms placed between them in an upper row, as in this diagram [Fig. B.24].

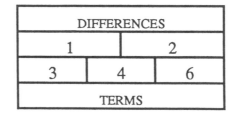

DIFFERENCES		
1		2
3	4	6
TERMS		

Do you not see then that 4:3 produces a consonance of the diatessaron, 6:4 yields a diapente, 6:3 mixes a consonance of the diapason, and their

43. Concerning the harmonic mean, see *Arith.* 2.48 (Nicomachus *Eisagoge arithmetica* 2.26) and Iamblicus *In Nicomachi arithmeticam introductionem* 152–54 (Pistelli ed., pp. 108–09).

differences themselves again bring forth the same consonance? For 2:1 is duple, fixed in the consonance of the diapason. When the extreme terms are multiplied by themselves, and the mean term is increased by multiplication of itself, then the numbers compared will hold the relation and concord of a tone.[44] For 3 times 6 makes 18, 4 times 4 makes 16; the number 18, of course, surpasses the smaller number 16 by an eighth part of 16. Again, if the smallest term is multiplied by itself, it will make 9; if the larger term is increased through multiplication of itself, it will make 36. The numbers 9 and 36 set in relation with each other hold the quadruple— that is, the consonance of the bis-diapason. If we inspect these numbers carefully, everything will be seen to be either multiplication of differences or of terms by themselves. For if the smallest term is multiplied by the [248] mean, it makes 12; likewise if the smallest term is multiplied by the largest, it makes 18. If the mean term is increased by the quantity of the largest, it makes 24; moreover if the smallest term is increased by itself, it makes 9, and if the mean is multiplied in the same manner, it makes 16. If 6, which is the largest, is multiplied by itself, it makes 36. Therefore these should be set out in series:

$$36 \quad 24 \quad 18 \quad 16 \quad 12 \quad 9$$

The terms sounding the consonance of a diatessaron are 24:18 and 12:9; the diapente 18:12, 24:16, and 36:24; the triple, which is the diapason-plus-diapente, 36:12; the quadruple, which is the bis-diapason, 36:9; the epogdous, which is a tone, is held in the comparison of 18 to 16.

17. How the means discussed above are each in turn placed between two terms

Two terms are likely to be presented and arranged in such a way that we sometimes place an arithmetic mean between them, sometimes a geometric mean, and sometimes a harmonic mean. We also discussed these things in the arithmetic books,[45] but we should nevertheless explain the same thing here briefly.

If the arithmetic mean is required, the difference of the given terms must be sought and then divided and added to the smaller term. Thus, let

44. The words in this passage, *toni habitudinem concordiamque,* could merely imply "ratio and sound of a tone," but *concordia* is a term Boethius uses as synonymous with *consonantia.* The tone is obviously not a consonance, however, despite the language.

45. See *Arith.* 2.50 (Nicomachus *Eisagoge arithmetica* 2.27), where the exact same processes are described and the same numbers are used. The passage in *Arith.* places the computation of means in *musical* terms—viz., the drilling of holes in a reed and the tuning of strings (Masi trans., p. 180). The principle of placing arithmetic means will be used in book 4 for the division of chromatic and enharmonic genera on the monochord (see book 4, nn. 58–59).

the terms 10 and, on the other side, 40 be set out, and let their mean be sought according to arithmetic proportion. I first consider the difference between the two, which is 30. This I divide, which makes 15. I add this to the smaller term, 10, which makes 25. Thus, if this mean is located between 40 and 10, an arithmetic proportion will be made in this manner [Fig. B.25].

[249]

Likewise if we wish to place a geometric mean between the same terms, we multiply the extremes: 10 times 40 makes 400. We take the square root of this, which makes 20, for 20 times 20 produces 400. If we place this mean, 20, between 10 and 40, the geometric mean is made, as set out in the following diagram [Fig. B.26].

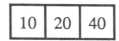

Now if we seek the harmonic mean, we add the extremes: 10 plus 40 makes 50. We multiply the difference of these terms, which is 30, by the smaller term, 10, and 10 times 30 makes 300. This we divide by the 50, which makes 6; when we add this to the smaller term, 16 is produced. If we then place this number between 10 and 40, a harmonic proportion is displayed [Fig. B.27].

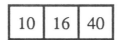

18. *Concerning the merit or measure of consonances according to Nicomachus*

Enough concerning these matters. Now we should add the justification given by the Pythagoreans for associating musical consonances with the ratios discussed above. Ptolemy appears not to have agreed with them about this; we shall speak about this later.[46]

The consonance whose property the critical faculty more easily comprehends ought to be classified as the very first and most pleasing consonance. For just as every single thing is in itself, so also is it recognized by

46. For Ptolemy's criticisms of the Pythagoreans and his classification of relative pitches, see 5.8–12.

the critical faculty.[47] Thus, if that consonance which consists of the duple ratio is easier to know than all the others, then there is no doubt that the consonance of the diapason, since it precedes the others in being known, is the first of all and surpasses the others in merit. The remaining consonances, according to the Pythagoreans, necessarily hold a rank determined by increments of multiple ratios and the reductions of superparticular relations. Now it has been demonstrated that multiple inequality should transcend superparticular ratios in priority of value.[48] Therefore let a natural numerical series be set out from unity to 4. [250]

1 2 3 4

The 2 compared to 1 makes the duple ratio and produces that consonance of the diapason which is the most excellent and, because of its simplicity, the most knowable. If 3 is related to unity, it resounds the consonance of the diapason-plus-diapente. The 4 related to unity holds the quadruple, producing, of course, the consonance of the bis-diapason. But if the 3 is placed in relation to 2, it adds the consonance of the diapente; if 4 to 3, the diatessaron. This, then, is the ranking of these when each is compared to every other. One comparison now remains: if we relate 4 to 2, they fall in the duple ratio, which 2 held in relation to unity. Sounds then are at their greatest distance in the bis-diapason, since they are separated from each other by a quadruple measure of interval. The closest sounds forming a consonance between themselves seem to occur when the higher surpasses the lower by a third part of the lower. And so the measure of consonances comes to a halt: it can neither be extended beyond the quadruple nor reduced to less than a third part. According to Nicomachus,[49] then, this is the ranking of consonances: first is the diapason; second, diapason-plus-diapente; third, bis-diapason; fourth, diapente; and fifth, diatessaron.

19. *The opinion of Eubulides and Hippasus concerning the ranking of consonances*

Eubulides[50] and Hippasus[51] maintain a different ranking of consonances, for they say that increments of multiplicity correspond to diminu-

47. "Critical faculty" is a translation of *sensus,* a word with a broad spectrum of meaning, ranging from "perception through the senses" to "understanding." Boethius, or his Pythagorean source, is obviously not arguing that "as every single thing is in itself, so it is perceived by the sense"; to do so would blatantly contradict the basic tenet of Pythagorean thought that the senses are unreliable (see, e.g., 1.9). "Critical faculty" seems the best translation for *sensus* in this context.

48. See above, 2.5.

49. The ranking of consonances is not found in any extant work of Nicomachus.

50. No works or fragments of the early Pythagorean Eubulides survive. In fact, this is probably the only specific theory that can be definitively attributed to him; see Diels, *Vorsokratiker,* I.14.8, pp. 99, 1.

tion of superparticularity in a fixed order. Accordingly, there cannot be a
[251]   duple unless a half occurs nor a triple unless a third part occurs. Thus, if
a duple occurs, from it a diapason is produced; since a half likewise occurs,
as it were, in the opposing division, from the half a sesquialter ratio is
created—that is, the diapente. If these (the diapason and the diapente) are
mixed together, a triple arises, which contains both consonances. Likewise,
from the triple a third part is divided in the opposing division, from which
arises in turn the consonance of the diatessaron. Now the triple and the
sesquitertian joined produce the quadruple comparison in ratio. It follows,
then, that from the diapason-plus-diapente (which is one consonance) and
the diatessaron, one further consonance is made, which, consisting of the
quadruple comparison, takes the name "bis-diapason." According to these
theorists, this is the ranking: diapason, diapente, diapason-plus-diapente,
diatessaron, bis-diapason.

20. *The opinion of Nicomachus regarding which consonances are placed opposite others*

But Nicomachus does not agree with these theorists regarding the
opposing positioning; rather, as unity was the first principle of increasing
and diminishing in arithmetic, so the consonance of the diapason is the first
principle of the remaining consonances, and only after it, can they be set
down in opposing division. This will be more easily known if it is first
discerned in numbers; let unity be set down, and let two sides flow from
it, one of multiple, the other of division,[52] and let this be the representation
[Fig. B.28].

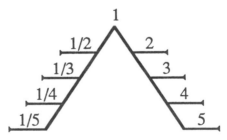

[252]   In this way, the progression is to infinity. For 2 is the duple of unity, whereas

51. Hippasus (fifth century B.C.) belongs to the very early Pythagorean school. No
complete works or fragments of his survive, but through later Greek sources he is known to
have worked in the area of musical mathematics (see above, n. 35); see Diels, *Vorsokratiker,*
I.18, pp. 107–10.

52. By "multiple" Boethius means "multitude" or "discrete quantity"; by "division"
he implies "magnitude" or "continuous quantity." See also 1.6, where multiple and superparticular ratios are specifically compared to these kinds of quantity.

the opposing side shows half of the same unity; 3 is the triple, and the opposing side the third; 4 the quadruple and the opposing side the fourth. Thus the beginning of increasing and decreasing rests in unity alone.

Now let us convert the same to consonances. The diapason, then, which is duple, will be in the highest place, at the beginning, and those which remain will be in opposing division in this manner: the sesquialter opposite the triple, and the sesquitertian opposite the quadruple. This will be proved by the following line of argument. The first sesquialter is the same number which is the first triple (of course with the first unity), for 3 unchanged is the first triple if placed in relation to unity, and the first sesquialter if placed in relation to 2. Moreover, the same 3, with the difference it makes in relation to 2 (which when placed in natural series proves to be sesquialter) is triple. Since, then, the sesquialter is rightly placed opposite the triple, the consonance of the diapente should be rationally considered positioned opposite the consonance of the diapente-plus-diapason. Again, the quadruple holds the position opposite to the sesquitertian. For that which is the first quadruple is found to be identical with the first sesquitertian in this manner: 4 is the first quadruple if it is related to unity, the first sesquitertian if related to 3. Moreover, with the difference which it holds between itself and 3, it makes the same quadruple. It follows from this that the sesquitertian ratio, which is the diatessaron, is positioned opposite the quadruple ratio, which is the bis-diapason. Since the duple has no ratio opposing it and is not itself the sesquialter of any other, and since no number exists with which 2 (which is the first duple) can be joined in a superparticular ratio, the duple is beyond any configuration of opposing ratio. And therefore, according to Nicomachus, the first principle of consonances should reside in the diapason in the following manner [Fig. B.29]. [253]

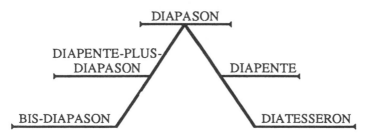

Although the whole should be related in this way, nevertheless every multiple ratio of consonances is first in sweetness, and superparticulars follow, just as we said a little earlier.[53]

53. The reference here is to 2.18; but, like the contents of that chapter, the theories presented in this chapter are not found in extant works of Nicomachus. The rationale for ordering consonances by value judgment follows logically from basic tenets expressed in Nicomachus's *Eisagoge arithmetica* and Boethius's *Arith.*, as well as tenets found earlier in this

Since consonance is an appropriate mixture of two pitches, whereas sound is an inflection of measured pitch drawn out in a single tuning; since sound is the smallest particle of modulation, and all sound consists of pulsation, and all pulsation of motion; and since some motions are equal, others unequal, and some inequalities are more unequal, others less, others moderately unequal; it follows that from inequality is derived inequality of sounds. From that inequality in which the intervals are unequal in moderate degree, the clear, first, and simpler ratios emerge; these are the multiple and superparticular: consonances of the duple, triple, quadruple, sesquialter, and sesquitertian ratios. From those that are in the other classes of ratios or are at haphazard, vague, or extremely large intervals, inequalities arise, and dissonances come into being, but no concord of sounds is created.[54]

21. What must be said by way of preface so that the diapason may be demonstrated to be in the multiple class of inequality

Now that this is clear, we should demonstrate that the consonance of the diapason, which is the most excellent of all, is found in the multiple class of inequality and in the duple relation. But first it must be demonstrated how the consonance of the diapason can be acknowledged to be in the multiple class. A certain matter must briefly precede; once this is known, the demonstration will be easier.

[254]

If you subtract a superparticular ratio from the superparticular continuous with it, the ratio subtracted naturally being smaller, then the remainder is less than the mean of the ratio that was subtracted.[55] For example, consider the sesquialter and the sesquitertian. Since the sesquialter is larger, we subtract the sesquitertian from the sesquialter; the sesquioctave ratio remains, which, doubled, does not produce a whole sesquitertian ratio but one that is smaller by the interval which is found in the semitone. Since a doubled sesquioctave comparison is not a whole sesquitertian, a single ses-

music treatise: the multiple class of inequality is the highest by nature and the superparticular class is second to it (Nicomachus *Eisagoge arithmetica* 1.18 and 19); given the primacy of number (and arithmetic) in Pythagorean doctrine, the ordering of consonances must follow the ordering of related quantities.

54. This concluding paragraph is a classic summary of Pythagorean quantification of sound and the logical extension of that quantification. For the basic language concerning sound, see 1.8; for the process of quantification, see 1.3. A similar summary, albeit not quite so elegant, is found in 4.1, based on the Euclidian *Sectio canonis*. The present summary marks a major division in Book 2; the remainder of the book is concern with demonstrations of the ratios of the primary consonances, the tone, the major and minor semitone, and the comma.

55. This theorem is found in no other music treatise from antiquity. Its sole purpose, as stated in the text, is to aid the demonstration that the diapason is not in the superparticular class but in the multiple class.

quioctave is not the full mean of a sesquitertian ratio. If I subtract a sesquiquartan from a sesquitertian, that which remains does not produce the
mean of the sesquiquartan. The same holds true with the others.

22. Demonstration through the impossible that the diapason is in the multiple class[56]

Let us now, without further delay, return to the consonance of the
diapason. If it is not in the multiple class of inequality, it will fall into the
superparticular class of inequality. Thus, let a superparticular ratio be the
consonance of the diapason. If the consonance next in position—that is,
the diapente—is subtracted from it, the diatessaron remains. Thus, twice
the diatessaron is less than one diapente, and the diatessaron itself does
not reach the mean of the consonance of the diapente, which is impossible.
For it will be demonstrated that twice a diatessaron transcends a consonance of the diapente by a tone and a semitone.[57] Thus the diapason cannot
possibly be placed in the superparticular class of inequality.[58]

23. Demonstration that the diapente, the diatessaron, and the tone are in the superparticular class [255]

Now it remains for us to demonstrate that the diapente, the diatessaron, and the tone must be placed in the superparticular class of ratios.
Although this was made very clear by a certain kind of reasoning even in
the first proof—where we demonstrated that the diapason must not be
placed in the superparticular class—we should nevertheless examine this
separately and more thoroughly.[59]

56. The demonstrations of chaps. 22–26 follow rather closely the order of propositions
10–12 of the *Sectio canonis*. Both texts set forth the logical necessity of associations of specific
consonances with specific ratios: the diapason is duple, the diapente sesquialter, the diatessaron sesquitertian, the diapason-plus-diapente triple, and the bis-diapason quadruple (and
the tone sesquioctave).

Although the order is the same, the demonstrations differ methodologically in that
Boethius's text makes no reference to specific notes in a musical system; it is as though, after
introducing the names of strings in 1.20–28, the author is striving to avoid reference to specific
pitches within a system until the whole mathematical foundation has been laid and the monochord has been divided. The demonstrations found in these chapters differ qualitatively from
those found in Book 4—which are based on the *Sectio canonis*—both in their verbosity and
in some rather loose reasoning.

57. This proposition is never demonstrated as such; perhaps the future tense refers to
the ability to give such a demonstration after mastering the axioms.

58. Compare this demonstration with that of *Sectio canonis* 10 (JanS. 158.8–18), where
the first step in establishing ratios of consonances is also a proof that the diapason is multiple.

59. Compare this proof with that of *Sectio canonis* 11 (JanS. 158.19–159.9), where the
second step is to show that the diatessaron and diapente are superparticular. The present
chapter actually presents three proofs: that neither the diapente nor the diatessaron can be

If someone says that these relations should not be placed in the superparticular, he will concede that they may be located among the multiple. The reason that they cannot be placed in the superpartient or in the other mixed classes—in my opinion—has already been explained.[60] Thus, if it can be done, let them be placed in the multiple class.

Since the consonance of the diatessaron is smaller and the diapente larger, let the diatessaron be fitted to the duple ratio, and the diapente to the triple. For it seems to be consistent with the facts that the consonance of the diatessaron is next in order to the consonance of the diapente. If the diatessaron is placed in the duple in this way, then the diapente is placed in the one continuous with the duple—that is, the triple. But the tone, since it is located in musical relations after the diatessaron, without doubt should be placed in that ratio which is less than the duple. But this cannot be found in the multiple class; thus it comes about that the tone falls into a relation of the superparticular class. So let the first superparticular—that is, the sesquialter—be the ratio of the tone.[61]

Now if we subtract the duple from the triple, that which remains is the sesquialter. If the diatessaron is duple, the diapente triple, and if a tone remains when the diatessaron is subtracted from the diapente, then there can be no doubt whatsoever that the tone should be situated in the sesquialter ratio. But two sesquialter ratios surpass one duple; just how, anyone instructed in arithmetic can ascertain for himself.[62] Therefore two tones will surpass a diatessaron, which does not make sense, for a diatessaron
[256] exceeds two tones by the interval of a semitone. Therefore it cannot follow that both the diapente and diatessaron are not located in the superparticular class of inequality.

But if someone should suggest that the tone also occurs in the multiple class, then, since the tone is smaller than the diatessaron and the diatessaron smaller than the diapente, the diapente should be placed in the quadruple, the diatessaron in the triple, and the tone in the duple. But the diapente consists of the diatessaron and a tone; thus the quadruple, according to this reasoning, will consist of the triple and the duple, which

---

in the multiple class, that the diatessaron is not in the multiple class, and that the diapente is not in the multiple class. An underlying assumption of all three is that the diapason, diapente, and diatessaron, as consonances, are "continuous"—i.e., next in order to each other, just as the duple, sesquialter, and sesquitertian are continuous.

60. See 1.5–6 and also 2.20.

61. These last two sentences do not necessarily follow. The tone need not fall into a superparticular (or multiple) ratio, for it is not a consonance. Moreover, it need not be placed in the sesquialter ratio, since it is not continuous with the diatessaron. The logic of placing it in the sesquialter—merely for argument—becomes obvious in the next sentence, and the argument works; but these two sentences would have been better left out.

62. This sentence refers not to a specific passage in *Arith.*, but to the general skill in arithmetic one would have acquired from studying the discipline. Thus, two sesquialter ratios are 4:6:9, one duple ratio is 4:8, and two sesquialters surpass one duple.

cannot follow. Likewise, if the diatessaron is in the triple and the diapente in the quadruple, when we subtract the triple from the quadruple, a sesquitertian remains. Moreover, if you subtract a diatessaron from the consonance of a diapente, the remainder is a tone. Therefore the tone, according to this reasoning, will consist of the sesquitertian ratio. But three sesquitertians are less than one triple; thus three tones will by no reasoning fill up one diatessaron. This assertion is certainly false, for two tones and a minor semitone fill up the consonance of the diatessaron. From these arguments it is demonstrated that the consonance of the diatessaron is not in the multiple class.

Moreover, I say that the consonance of the diapente cannot be placed in the multiple class either. If it is stationed there, then, since that next to it—that is, the diatessaron—is smaller, it will not be located in the smallest multiple—that is, in the duple—for that could be the place in which the consonance of the diatessaron might be fitted. But the consonance of the diatessaron is not of the multiple class; thus the diapente cannot be fitted to any multiple relation larger than the duple, which is the smallest. Therefore, let the diapente be in the smallest, the duple. Now the diatessaron, which is smaller, cannot be fitted in the multiple, for there is none smaller than the duple. Thus, let the diatessaron be the sesquialter and the tone the sesquitertian for the tone will be located in the ratio next in order.[63]   [257] But two sesquitertians are more than one sesquialter; thus two tones will surpass one consonance of the diatessaron, which no calculation will bring about.

From these arguments it is proved that the diapente and the diatessaron cannot be placed in the multiple class. Thus, they are rightly allocated to the superparticular class of inequality.

24. Demonstration that the diapente and the diatessaron are in the largest superparticular ratios

It is also necessary to add that if the diapente and the diatessaron occupy superparticular ratios, then they are placed in the largest superparticular ratios. The largest are the sesquialter and the sesquitertian. This is proved in this manner. If the consonances of the diapente and the diatessaron are located in ratios smaller than the sesquialter and the sesquitertian, there is no doubt that, just as no other superparticular ratios except the sesquialter and the sesquitertian join together to produce one duple, by the same reasoning the diapente and the diatessaron would by no means

---

63. Again the assumption is that the tone is "next in order" to, or continuous with, the diatessaron (or the sesquialter), an assumption that is very weak. The tone need not be placed in the multiple or superparticular classes, since it is not a consonance, or in the sesquitertian, for it is not next in order to the diatessaron. It might be placed in sesquiquartan, sesquiquintan, and so on.

encompass a diapason. Since the diapason has been proved to be in the duple ratio,[64] and the duple ratio is composed of the sesquialter and the sesquitertian, while the diapason is brought together from the diatessaron and the diapente, there can be no doubt that if we situate the diapason absolutely in the duple, then the diapente and the diatessaron are to be located in the sesequialter and the sesquitertian ratios. Indeed, they cannot otherwise join together to produce the consonance of the diapason (which consists of the duple ratio) unless they stand in these two ratios (that is, the sesquialter and the sesquitertian). For other superparticular ratios will by no reasoning join together in a duple.

[258] ## 25. *The diapente is in the sesquialter, the diatessaron in the sesquitertian, the tone in the sesquioctave*

I assert, then, that the diapente rightly consists of the sesquialter, the diatessaron of the sesquitertian ratio.[65] Since, of these two ratios (the sesquialter and the sesquitertian), the sesquialter is larger and the sesquitertian smaller, and since in consonances the diapente is larger, whereas the diatessaron is smaller, it appears that the larger ratio should be fitted to the larger consonance, the smaller to the smaller. Therefore the diapente is to be situated in the sesquialter and the diatessaron in the sesquitertian.

If we subtract the diatessaron from the consonance of the diapente, the interval remains which is called "tone"; if we take a sesquitertian away from a sesquialter ratio, a sesquioctave ratio is left. It follows, then, that the tone ought to be assigned to the sesquioctave ratio.[66]

26. *The diapason-plus-diapente is in the triple ratio, the bis-diapason in the duple*

Since it has been demonstrated that the diapason is duple, the diapente sesquialter, and the duple and the sesquialter joined together create the triple ratio, it is also clear that the diapason-plus-diapente is set down in the triple ratio.[67]

64. Boethius may be guilty of a sleight of hand at this point. He did indeed demonstrate that the diapason is in the multiple class of inequality (2.22) and that the diapente and the diatessaron are in the superparticular class (2.23); but he did not present a proof that the diapason is in the first multiple ratio, the duple. Missing is the proof of *Sectio canonis* 12a (JanS. 159.10–19) that the diapason is duple. In fact, Boethius has not laid the necessary foundation for the second clause of the previous hypothetical statement, that no superparticular ratios except the sesquialter and the sesquitertian join together in the duple; a proof of this can be found in a demonstration added to *Sectio canonis* by Porphyry (see Düring ed., 100.26–101.8). Perhaps a proof has been lost in the textual tradition of these chapters; if not, Boethius—or his source—is guilty of a classic paralogism.
65. See *Sectio canonis* 12b (JanS. 169.20–160.3).
66. See *Sectio canonis* 13 (JanS. 160.13–19).
67. See *Sectio canonis* 12c (JanS. 160.4–8).

If a sesquitertian ratio is joined to a triple relation, it makes a quad-ruple. Therefore if the consonance of the diatessaron is added to the con-sonance of a diapason-plus-diapente, the quadruple interval of pitches is made, which we have demonstrated above to be the bis-diapason.[68]

27. *The diatessaron-plus-diapason is not a consonance* [259] *according to the Pythagoreans*

From these things the careful reader should recognize that consonances placed over consonances have produced certain other consonances. For, as has been said, the diapente and the diatessaron joined together create the diapason. And if a consonance of the diapente is joined to this (the dia-pason), the consonance which is made is named with both words—namely, the diapason-plus-diapente. If the diatessaron is added to this, the bis-diapason is made, which holds the quadruple ratio.[69]

Now what if we join together the consonances of the diatessaron and the diapason? Will it produce any consonance according to the Pythago-reans? Not at all. For it falls into the superpartient class of inequality, and it preserves neither the order of the multiple nor the singleness of the superparticular. But enough dawdling. Let us set down the numbers by which this will be more readily confirmed. Take 3, with which 6 forms a duple, consisting, namely, of the ratio of the diapason. Let the number yielding a sesquitertian ratio, which we have already said was the diates-saron, be fitted to this—namely, 8; it holds the ratio of the diatessaron to 6. The 8 in relation to 3 contains it twice, but it is not multiple, for it contains certain of its parts besides, and they are not single parts; 8 sur-passes the double of 3 by two unities, which are third parts of the 3 which we set down as the first and smallest term. Let these, then, be the three terms: 3:6:8.

This interval is also one that falls between two consonances continuous with each other. For it is neither an integral duple, whereby it would pro-duce the consonance of the diapason, nor a triple, whereby it would make the consonance of the diapason-plus-diapente. If a tone is added to it, however, it will make the triple measure of ratio. Since a diapason joined together with a diapente makes the triple, while a diatessaron and a tone [260] unite in the consonance of a diapente, if a diatessaron is added to the consonance of a diapason, it will not make a consonance, for between the duple and the triple no naturally ordered multiple ratio can be known. But if I add a tone to it, it makes the diapason-plus-diatessaron-plus-tone, which is nothing other than a diapason-plus-diapente. For the diatessaron and tone form the diapente. Take the diapason 3 and 6, the diatessaron 6 and 8, and the tone 8 and 9. They will form a triple ratio in this way: 3:6:8:9.

68. See *Sectio canonis* 12d (JanS. 160.9–12).
69. The mathematical foundation of this principle is laid in 2.11.

Although Nicomachus said much concerning this matter,[70] we, in bringing to light in part the very things the Pythagoreans affirm and in arguing in part the same consequences, have demonstrated—inasmuch as we have been able to do so briefly—that if a diatessaron is added to the consonance of the diapason, a consonance cannot result. I will discuss later what Ptolemy thought about this.[71] But enough of this. Now the semitone must be considered.

28. Concerning the semitone: in what smallest numbers it is found

It seems that semitones were so named not because they are truly halves of tones, but because they are not complete tones.[72] The size of the interval which we now call "semitone," but which was called "limma" or "diesis" by the ancients,[73] is determined as follows: when two sesquioctave relations (which are tones) are subtracted from a sesquitertian ratio (which is a diatessaron), an interval called a "semitone" remains. Let us try to write the two tones in a continuous arrangement. As was said, since these consist of the sesquioctave ratio, and we cannot join two continuous sesquioctave ratios unless a multiple from which these can be derived is found, let unity be set out and also its first octuple, 8. From this I can derive one sesquioctave. But since I am seeking two, 8 should be multiplied by 8, making 64. This will be the second octuple, from which we can extract two sesquioctave ratios, for 8 (an eighth part of 64 unities), when added to the same, makes the total sum of 72. Similarly, let an eighth part of this be taken, which is 9, and it gives 81. And these two first continuous tones are written down in this arrangement:

[261]

$$64 : 72 : 81$$

70. Nothing concerning the consonance or dissonance of the diapason-plus-diatessaron is found in the extant works of Nicomachus. Concerning the history of the theory of this interval, see C. André Barbera, "The Consonant Eleventh and the Expansion of the Musical Tetractys: A Study of Ancient Pythagoreanism," *Journal of Music Theory* 28 (1964): 191–223.

71. See 5.9–10.

72. See 1.17.

73. *Limma* is the technical term traditionally used in Greek music theory for the interval discursively called "semitone." The traditional definition of this interval is "that which remains after two tones have been subtracted from the consonance of the diatessaron" (see the definition which follows in Boethius's text and that in Ptolemy *Harmonica* 1.10 (Düring ed., 23.2); *limma* thus means remainder—i.e., that which remains after the subtraction. The remainder after two tones have been subtracted from a diatessaron, the limma, is to be distinguished from the "remnant," that which remains after a limma has been subtracted from a tone, which is named *apotome* (see 2.30 and n. 79).

The term *diesis* is not used consistently: normally it is reserved for the very small interval (quarter-tone) found in the enharmonic genus (see, e.g., 1.21); but in Pythagorean circles it is used for the limma and the minor semitone as well (see Theon of Smyrna *Expositio* 12, ed. Dupuis, p. 87).

Now we should seek out the sesquitertian of 64 unities. But since 64 proves not to have a third part, then, if all these numbers are multiplied by 3, the third part forthwith comes into being, and all remain in the same ratio as they were before the multiplier 3 was applied to them. Thus, let 64 be multiplied by 3, which makes 192. A third of this (64) added to it produces 256. Then 256:192 is the sesquitertian ratio, which holds the consonance of the diatessaron. Now let us assemble in appropriate series the two sesquioctave ratios to 192, ratios that will be contained in two numbers: let 72 be multiplied by 3, making 216, and 81 by 3, making 243. Let these be arranged between the two terms cited above in this manner:

$$192 : 216 : 243 : 256$$

In this arrangement of ratios, the ratio of the first number to the last constitutes the consonance of the diatessaron, and those of the first to the second and the second to the third contain two identical tones. The interval that remains consists of the ratio 243:256, which constitutes in smallest integers the form of the semitone.

29. *Demonstrations that 243:256 is not half a tone* [262]

I am showing, then, that the interval of 243:256 is not the full magnitude of half a tone. The difference between 243 and 256 is contained in only 13 unities, which (13)[74] cover less than an eighteenth part of the smaller term, but more than a nineteenth part (for if you multiply 13 by 18, you will make 234, which by no means is equal to 243, and if you multiply 13 by 19, it surpasses 243). Every semitone, if it holds a full half of a tone, ought to be placed between the sixteenth part and the seventeenth—which will be demonstrated later.[75]

Now[76] it will become clear that such an interval of a semitone, if doubled, cannot complete one interval of a tone. So let us, without further

---

74. Friedlein's *qui .XIII. minus quidem quam minoris* [262.6] gave medieval scribes and scholars difficulty. Of the control manuscripts used for the present translation, none agree with Friedlein without qualifications. *M* and *R* read the same, but in both sources *xiii* has been corrected from *ccxliii*. *Q* and *T* read *qui minus quidem*, thus omitting any number; but this reading was changed from *quia ccxliii quidem* in both. In *Q*, the gloss *id est xiii* is written above *qui*, and *id est ccxliii* above *minoris;* given the alteration and the glosses, *Q* presents the clearest and most unequivocal reading. *V* follows the reading of *Q* and *T* with no alteration, omitting the gloss for *qui* but repeating the gloss for *minoris*. All other sources (*I, K, P, S*) give *qui ccxliii quidem*, a reading that makes no sense. Both numbers, 13 and 243, probably represent scribal attempts to clarify the antecedent of *qui*. The ambiguity arises because the relative pronoun for *unitates*, the actual noun which is antecedent, should be *quae* rather than *qui*.

75. See 3.1.

76. Friedlein's punctuation and capitalization are ambiguous at this point [262.13–14]: the comma at the end of line 13 should be a period; line 14 ("*Nunc illud* . . .") begins a new argument.

delay, arrange two such ratios continuous with each other that contain the same relation as 256:243, according to the rule presented above.[77] So let us multiply 256 by itself, and put the result as the largest term: 65,536; likewise 243 is increased by its own quantity, and the result is the smallest term: 59,049; again 256 is increased by the number 243, and this gives the number 62,208. Let the mean term be set down in this manner:

$$65,536 : 62,208 : 59,049$$

[263]

Therefore 256 and 243 are in the same ratio as 65,536 and 62,208, as well as 62,208 and 59,049. But the largest term of these (65,536) to the smallest (59,049) does not produce one whole tone. But if the ratio of the first to the second, which is equal to the ratio of the second to the third, should prove to be whole semitones, the two halves joined together would necessarily produce one tone. Since the ratio of the extreme terms is not sesquioctave, it is clear that these two intervals do not represent true halves of tones, for whatever is half of something, if it is doubled, makes that of which it is said to be the half. If it cannot fill that, then the part that is doubled is less than a half part; whereas if it exceeds it, it is more than a half part. Furthermore, it will be proved that 65,536 does not make a sesquioctave ratio with 59,049 unities if an eighth part of 59,049 is taken according to the rules that were given in the arithmetic books. Since this eighth part does not consist of a whole number, we leave the computing of the eighth part to the diligence of readers.[78] It is thus evident that the ratio consisting of 256:243 is not a whole half of a tone. That which is truly called "semitone" is, then, less than a half part of the tone.

30. *Concerning the larger part of the tone: in what smallest numbers it consists*

The remaining part, which is larger, is called "apotome" by the Greeks, whereas it can be called "remnant" by us.[79] For nature has so ordered things that when something is cut in such a way that it is not divided into equal parts, to the degree that the smaller part is less than half, by the same degree the larger part exceeds the half and is larger than the

77. See 2.8.
78. The reference here to "arithmetic books" is general, rather than specific. The person so instructed would have computed the difference between 65,536 and 59,049 and determined that it does not "measure" 59,049 eight times. An eighth part of 59,049 is 7,381 1/8, which added to 59,049 makes 66,430 1/8. The fraction of 1/8 is difficult to express in ancient and medieval mathematics, and one wonders if this might not be why the computation is left to the reader.
79. Boethius translates the Greek *apotome* with the Latin *decisio*—literally, "that which is cut away." No Latin treatise prior to Boethius equates the terms *apotome* and *decisio*. This "remnant" is the interval left after a *limma* (see above, n. 73) has been subtracted from a tone.

same. Therefore to the degree that the minor semitone is smaller than half a tone, to that same degree the apotome surpasses half a tone. And since we have taught that the semitone in its first instance stands in the ratio of 256 to 243, we should now prove in what smallest numbers the interval [264] called apotome consists. If 243 could admit division by an eighth part, which would allow a sesquioctave ratio to be formed with it, then the relation of 256 to the sesquioctave of the smaller number would reveal the apotome with incontrovertible reasoning. Since, however, it is known that an eighth part of it is lacking, let both numbers be multiplied by 8. From 243 multiplied by 8 we get the number 1,944. If to this we add its eighth (243), we get 2,187. Let 256 be multiplied by 8, making 2,048. This number may now be set down in the middle of the terms cited above.

$$1,944 : 2,048 : 2,187$$

Here the third term holds the ratio of a tone with the first, while the second holds that of a minor semitone with the first; the third to the second thus forms the apotome. So it appears that the ratio of the apotome consists in these smallest integers, since the interval of a semitone is contained in the smallest numbers 243 and 256. The numbers 1,944 and 2,048 are in the same ratio as 243 and 256, since they were obtained by multiplying 256 and 243 by 8. For if one number multiplies any other two numbers, those born from that multiplication will be in the same ratio as were those numbers which the first number multiplied.

31. Of what ratio the diapente and diapason consist; furthermore, the diapason does not consist of six tones

Since we have discussed the consonance of the diatessaron at some length, we should examine the consonance of the diapason and the diapente [265] briefly and, one might say, with simple numbers. The diapente consists of three tones and a semitone—that is, of a diatessaron plus a tone. Let those numbers be set out which the diagram above[80] encompassed:

$$192 : 216 : 243 : 256$$

In this disposition, the first term to the second and the second to the third hold ratios of tones, but the third to the fourth that of the minor semitone, as demonstrated above.[81] If an eighth part of the 256 is added to the same (of which it is an eighth), it will make 288, which, compared to 192, produces the interval of the sesquialter ratio. There are then three tones, if the first is related to the second, the second to the third, and the fifth to

80. These numbers are found as a diagram (*descriptio*) in 1.17, Fig. A.8. They are also found set out in the text in 2.28.
81. See 2.28.

the fourth. The comparison of the third to the fourth term holds the minor semitone.

If a diatessaron is made of two tones and a minor semitone and a diapente of three tones and a minor semitone, then, joined together, the diatessaron and the diapente would appear to produce one diapason. There will be five tones and two small intervals of semitones which do not appear to complete one tone. Therefore the diapason is not, as Aristoxenus thought,[82] a consonance consisting of six tones, which likewise becomes quite clear when set out in numbers. Let six tones be set out in order, constituted in sesquioctave ratios. Six sesquioctave ratios are created from the sixth octuple. Thus let six octuples be set out in this manner [Fig. B.30].

1	8	64	512	4,096	32,768	262,144

From this last number, six tones constituted in sesquioctave ratio are placed thus: first set out the octuple terms, then compute eighth parts at the sides of these same terms, as in the diagram of this [Fig. B.31] that follows:

[266]

OCTUPLES						SESQUIOCTAVES	8th PART
1	8	64	512	4,096	32,768	262,144	32,768
						294,912	36,864
						331,776	41,472
						373,248	46,656
						419,904	52,488
						472,392	59,049
						531,441	

The rationale of this diagram is this. The continuous row, which is called a "limit," holds octuple numbers; from the sixth octuple, sesquioctave ratios are derived. Where we have written "eighth parts," these are eighth parts of the adjacent numbers. If added to those to which they are adjacent, they create the subsequent numbers. For example, in first place is 262,144, an eighth of which is 32,768; if these numbers are joined together, they make the next number, which is 294,912. And the same process is discovered in the others. If the last number, which is 531,441, were a duple of

---

82. This theory is implicit in Aristoxenus *Harmonica* 2.56–58: the diatessaron consists of 2 1/2 tones, the diapente consists of 3 1/2 tones; thus a diapason consists of 6 tones.

the first number, which is 262,144, the diapason would appear to consist of six tones. If, however, we seek out the duple of the smallest number, that is, the first number, it will be smaller than that number which is the largest and the last. For the duple of 262,144, which of course holds the consonance of the diapason with it, is 524,288. This is smaller than that number which held the sixth tone—that is, smaller than 531,441. Therefore, the consonance of the diapason is smaller than six tones, and that interval by which six tones surpass the consonance of a diapason, I call the "comma"; it consists of the smallest numbers 524,288:531,441. [267]

I shall relate in another place what Aristoxenus,[83] who gave all judgment to the ears, thought concerning these things. But now, since I tend to avoid fastidiousness, I should bring this book to a close.

83. See 3.3 and 5.14.

BOOK 3

1. *Demonstration against Aristoxenus that a superparticular ratio cannot be divided into equal parts, and for that reason neither can the tone*

    In the above book it was demonstrated that the consonance of the diatessaron was made by joining two tones and a semitone, the diapente three tones and a semitone, but that these semitones, if treated through examination in and of themselves, cannot make an integral half of a tone, and therefore, that a diapason can by no measure extend to six tones. But the musician Aristoxenus, yielding all things to the judgment of the ears,[1] did not, following the Pythagoreans, consider these semitones to be smaller than the half. Rather, just as they are called "semi" tones, he considered that they were halves of tones.[2] Therefore, it must be argued and proved once again, albeit briefly, that no superparticular relation can be divided

[269]   into an integral half by any known number. For between two numbers comprising a superparticular ratio, whether they are the smallest integers— between which the difference is unity—or subsequent numbers, no middle number can be placed in such a way that the smallest term holds the ratio with the middle that the middle holds with the last, as in a geometric ratio. But either the middle term can produce equal differences, so that there is equality according to an arithmetic mean, or the middle term placed between these same terms will make a harmonic mean or some other mean that we mentioned in the arithmetic books.[3] But if this can be proved, the argument that a sesquioctave ratio (which is the tone) can be separated

1. Aristoxenus *Harmonica* 2.33–34.
2. Ibid., 2.46, 56–57, et al.
3. See *Arith.* 2.56–57.

into halves will not stand, since every sesquioctave ratio is located in the superparticular class of inequality.

This will be more easily proved by induction. If among individual ratios—superparticular, of course—when they are examined carefully, none is found that is divided into equal ratios by a term positioned in the middle, then there is no doubt that the superparticular comparison cannot be divided into equal parts.

Just because something seems to sound consonant to the ears when some vague pitch is compared to another pitch at a distance of two tones and an integral semitone does not mean that it is actually consonant; for inasmuch as each sense is unable to grasp things that are very small, so the sense of hearing cannot distinguish this difference that progresses beyond consonance. But perhaps the difference may come to be perceived if such particles continually increase through these same errors. For that which is scarcely discerned in the smallest thing, when placed alongside another and joined with it, is clearly perceived, for then it begins to be of some magnitude.

So from which ratio should we begin? Will we not find a shortcut in the inquiry if we begin with the one in question? That is, with whether the tone can be divided into two equal parts. So now we should thoroughly discuss the tone and demonstrate just how it cannot be divided into two equal parts. If this demonstration is applied to other superparticular com- [270] parisons, it will be similarly shown that a superparticular cannot be divided into equal parts by any integral number known.

The first numbers containing the tone are 8 and 9. But since these follow each other in natural sequence in such a way that there is no mean number between them, I multiply both these numbers by two, which, of course, is the smallest I can use. This makes 16 and 18. Between these a number, 17, falls naturally. Thus 18:16 is a tone, but 18 compared to 17 contains the latter wholly plus 1/17 part of it. Now 1/17 part is naturally smaller than 1/16 part, so the ratio contained in the numbers 16 and 17 is larger than that between 17 and 18. Let these numbers be set out in this manner: let 16 be A, 17 C, and 18 B.[4] Therefore, an integral *half* of a tone will by no means fall between C and B. For the ratio CB is smaller than the ratio CA. Thus a proportional half should be placed within the larger part. Let the half be D. Then, since the ratio DB (which is half of a tone) is larger than the ratio CB (which is the minor part of a tone), but the ratio AC (which is the larger part of a tone) is larger than the ratio AD (which

4. Some manuscripts (e.g., Munich, Bayerische Staatsbibliothek, Clm 18,478, and Clm 6,361) give Fig. C.1 at this place in the text rather than in its proper place later in the chapter. Friedlein was thus led to place the letters and numbers of this passage on a separate line, thereby creating something of an additional diagram at the beginning of book 3. The control manuscripts present these letters and numbers as text, and Fig. C.1 appears at the end of this paragraph.

is half of a tone), and since the ratio AC is 17:16 and CB is 18:17, there is no doubt that an integral half falls between 17:16 and 18:17. But this [271] will by no means be discovered in an integral number [Fig. C.1].

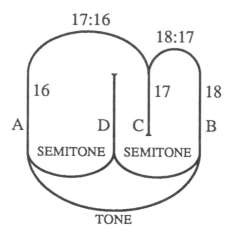

Since the number 17 compared with the number 16 creates the ratio 17:16,[5] let us work out a sixteenth part of the same number 17; that will be unity plus a sixteenth part of unity. If we join this together with the same number 17, it will make 18 and 1/16 part. But if 18 1/16 is compared with the number 16, it is seen to exceed the proper measure of a tone; for with 16 only the number 18 holds the sesquioctave ratio. Whence it follows that since the ratio 17:16 extended twice transcends a tone, it is not an integral half of a tone. For when something taken twice transcends another, the former evidently surpasses half the latter. For that reason the ratio 17:16 will not be half a tone. And because of this, no other ratio larger than the ratio 17:16 can be half a tone, since 17:16 itself is larger than an integral half of a tone.

But since the ratio 18:17 follows next after 17:16, we should see whether, multiplied by two, it will not fill a tone. The term 18 contains 17 plus one part of 17. So if we produce another number in relation to 18 with the same ratio that 18 has to 17, it will be 19 and 1/17 part. But if we produce a number situated in the sesquioctave ratio in relation to the term

5. Throughout this chapter and the next, Boethius names the ratios 17:16, 18:17, and 19:18 *sesquisextusdecimus, sesquiseptimusdecimus,* and *sesquioctavusdecimus* respectively. In the present paragraph the terms *sesquisextusdecimus* and *sesquiseptimusdecimus* are prefixed with the term *super*—e.g., *supersesquiseptimusdecimus.* No attempt is made to translate the *super,* and the terms are rendered as numerical ratios. The prefix is probably intended to specify that the larger term is to be given first position in the ratio. See also *Arith.* 1.22–24, where major and minor classes of quantity are discussed, the major class having the larger term in first position, the minor class the smaller term; ratios in the minor class use the prefix *sub* with the name of the ratio—e.g., *subsesquitertius*—and, by analogy, the major type might use the prefix *super.*

17, it will make 19 and 1/8 part. An eighth part is larger than a seventeenth [272] part, so the ratio of numbers 17 and 19 1/8 is larger than that comprised of 17 and 19 1/17 (which, of course, consists of two continuous 18:17 ratios). Thus, two continuous ratios of 18:17 are seen not to complete one tone. Therefore, 18:17 is not half a tone, since these terms, when duplicated, do not fill a whole; they do not form halves, for a half, when doubled, is always equal to that of which it is half.

2. *Half of a tone does not remain when two tones are subtracted from a sesquitertian ratio*

Now if we set out those numbers that remain after two tones are taken away from a sesquitertian ratio, we can determine whether that ratio which remains should be reckoned as the space of an integral semitone. If it were found to be that, then the consonance of the diatessaron would also be proved to be made up of two tones and an integral semitone. A first term was given above, 192, to which 256 formed the sesquitertian ratio.[6] To this first term, 216 made a tone, and moreover, to 216, the number 243 made the space of a tone. Thus what remains from the whole diatessaron ratio is that relation which consists in 243 and 256 unities. So if this proves to be half an integral tone, there can be no doubt that the diatessaron consists of two tones and a semitone.

Since it has been demonstrated that half a tone is located between the ratios 17:16 and 18:17, this comparison, 256:243, ought to be measured in [273] relation to that ratio. Lest our progress be hindered, I take an eighteenth part of 243, which is 13 1/2. If I add this to 243, it makes 256 1/2. Thus the ratio 256:243 appears to be less than the relation 19:18. But if the larger "half-tone" is in the ratio 17:16, the smaller in the ratio 18:17,[7] then, since

6. See 1.22, 2.28.
7. Friedlein's reading of the first part of this sentence [273.7–8 and apparatus] cannot be justified by manuscripts from the ninth century. It clearly represents a later textual tradition and is found in only two of the five sources he used for the chapter: Clm 14,480 (*f* in the edition) and Clm 6,361 (*h* in the edition). (Of these two, only the latter gives the reading without alterations to an earlier version.) The text for the first part of this sentence, according to Friedlein, is *Quod si dimidius tonus minor quidem est sesquisextadecima, maior vero sesquiseptimadecima proportione* ("But if the half-tone is larger than the ratio 17:16, but smaller than the ratio 18:17"). This version is correct arithmetically, and it articulates clearly the argument that Boethius is making. It may, in fact, represent a "better" version of this passage. But it does not reflect the earliest manuscripts of the treatise. The text according to *M, Q,* and *V* should read *Quod si dimidius tonus maior quidem est in sesquisextadecima, minor vero in sesquiseptimadecima proportione*. The same reading is found in *B, R, S,* and *T,* but with the *in* of each clause added above the line. *I, K,* and *P* omit the prepositions, and *maior* and *minor* are expunged in *P* and altered to give the later reading found in Friedlein. If the two ablatives (the ratios) are read as ablatives of comparison, only Friedlein's version makes sense; but they can be read as ablatives of respect, particularly given the prepositions, and the

19:18 is even smaller than 18:17, and the comparison of 256 to 243—the remainder after two tones have been subtracted from a diatessaron—is even smaller than 19:18, there is no doubt that the ratio of these two numbers is considerably smaller than a semitone.

3. *Demonstrations against Aristoxenus that the consonance of the diatessaron does not consist of two tones and a semitone or the diapason of six tones*

If, as Aristoxenus says, the consonance of the diatessaron is comprised of two tones and a *semi*tone,[8] two consonances of the diatessaron necessarily make five tones, and the diapente and diatessaron, as they unite into one diapason, joined together, equal six tones in continuous ratio. A little while ago we set out six tones,[9] the smallest of which was the number 262,144, and the highest number to this one, 531,441, held the place of six [274] tones, while 472,392 held the fifth tone. Now let these numbers be set out in this manner [Fig. C.2].

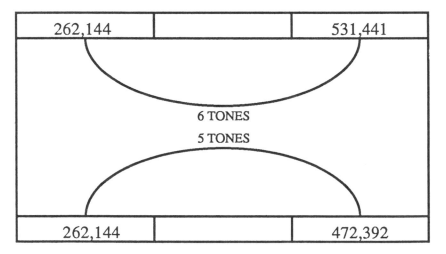

Now we should discuss the smaller numbers—that is, the five tones. If the diatessaron consists of two tones and a semitone, while the diatessaron taken twice consists of five tones, when I add—that is, ascend—a

---

original text is sufficient with no alteration.

In this passage Boethius is referring back to the major and minor partial tones of 1.16, and the argument is based on 17:16 being the major part, 18:17 the minor part, both of which some theorists might call "half-tones." The casual use of technical terms such as *semitonium* and *dimidius tonus* has obviously baffled both modern and medieval readers. (See also book 1, nn. 89 and 90.)

8. Aristoxenus *Harmonica* 2.56–57.
9. See 2.31, Fig. B.31.

diatessaron to 262,144 and subtract—that is, descend[10]—another diatessaron from 474,392, the same number should be discovered between both the addition and the subtraction. This is done in the following manner: from 262,144 I ascend a diatessaron—that is, a sesquitertian—which results in 349,525 4/12.[11] Likewise from 472,392 I descend a sesquitertian ratio,

10. This chapter presents a *locus classicus* of the Pythagorean understanding of the terms *intendo* and *remitto*. The procedures in this argument are obviously addition and subtraction, but in adding quantity, one ascends in pitch, whereas in subtracting quantity, one descends in pitch. See book 1, n. 46.

11. The abrupt shift from arithmetic to geometric reasoning in this chapter proved very difficult for medieval scribes and readers. Unity, as an arithmetical entity, is indivisible (*Arith.* 1.9), and fractions are not treated in *Arith.* In the previous chapter the simple fraction of 1/2 was employed, and this is used again later, in book 3. But in the present chapter more complex fractions occur. If a quantity is to be divided, it must be conceived as continuous (geometric) quantity, and division is accomplished by means of a theory of *minutiae,* or parts, based on the number 12, a theory that was developed and used particularly in the agrimensorial treatises of late antiquity and the Middle Ages. The parts of the unit 12, along with the notation used in *Fundamentals of Music* are as follows.

✚	assis (as)	12
S✗✓	deunx	11
S✗S	decunx (dextrans)	10
S✗✓	dodrans	9
SS	bessis (bisse)	8
✓	septunx	7
S	semis	6
✗✗✓	quincunx	5
✗✗S	triens	4
✗✓	quadrans	3
✗S	sextans	2
—	unica	1

(This set of parts is found in the margin of *M,* f. 43v, probably added in the late ninth century, and in the margin of Paris, Bibliothèque nationale, lat. 7,297, f. 72v, a codex which originated in the Loire valley in the tenth century. Such parts are often found in the margins around 3.3. of codices written in the tenth century and later.) This number with fraction should have been written *cccxlviiii.dxxv ᴹ* (or *cccxlviiii.dxxv et triens*), while the difference between this term (B) and C should have been written *iiii.dcclxviii ⩣* (or *iiii.dcclxviii et bessis*), and half of this difference *ii.ccclxxxiiii ᴹ* (or *ii.ccclxxxiiii et triens*). The scribes were confused by the fractional notation itself, but their confusion was compounded by the similarity between the symbols for *triens* (4/12), *ᴹ*, and *bessis* (8/12), *⩣*. I have transcribed fractional notation in this chapter and the next as numbers of twelfths, and fractions expressed in words (e.g., *pars*

which results in 354,294. Thus we may set out these ratios in this manner, letting the first number be A, the second B, the third C, the fourth D [Fig. C.3].

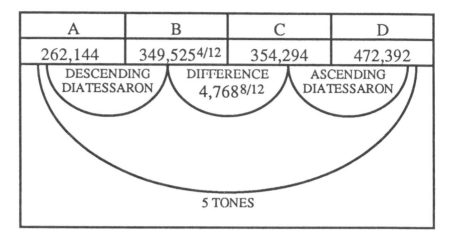

A	B	C	D
262,144	349,525 4/12	354,294	472,392

DESCENDING DIATESSARON   DIFFERENCE 4,768 8/12   ASCENDING DIATESSARON

5 TONES

Since the distance from term A to term D is five tones and the diatessaron is joined together from two tones and a semitone (as Aristoxenus believed), and since one diatessaron is placed between A and B, another between C [275] and D, then terms B and C should not be different, but one and the same, so that five tones would appear rightly to consist of two consonances of the diatessaron. But since there is a difference of 4,768 8/12, it is shown that the diatessaron is in no way joined together from two tones and a semitone.

4. Six tones exceed the consonance of the diapason by a comma, and the smallest number for the comma

Should we wish to bring together this difference using integral numbers, we should follow this procedure. Since a third part of unity added to $8/12^{12}$ produces a whole unity, and that third part is half of the same 8/12,

tertia) as their English equivalents (e.g., one-third).

    A treatise setting out clearly the theory of *minutiae* (dating probably from the ninth or tenth centuries) is found in N. Bubnov, *Gerberti postea Silvestri II papae Opera Mathematica* (Berlin, 1899), pp. 227–44.

    12. The fractions create a major problem at this point, for the symbol for 8/12 (𝕤) is omitted from the text, thus making "a third part" the subject of the dependent clause *quoniam in ea parte quae est pars tertia si addatur* in B, I, K, Q, S, and T. The word *bisse* (meaning 8/12) is added above the line after *est* in M, R, and V, thereby clarifying the meaning. Only P presents symbols resembling the fractional notation as part of the text. Friedlein [275.9 and apparatus] was mathematically correct (and wise) in basing his text at this point on only one manuscript (Munich, Clm 14,601, *l* in the apparatus), even though all other manuscripts gave the text as *quae est pars tertia*.

if we add half the total difference—which is 2,384 4/12—to the difference, the full sum of 7,153 is made. A little while ago this sum held the ratio of the comma.[13] The comma is that interval by which six tones surpass the consonance of a diapason, and it is contained in the smallest integer 7,153. Just as we added its own half to the above difference so that it might rise to 7,153, so let us also take terms A, B, C, and D and add to all of them their halves, and the ratio will be the same in all cases as above. The difference between five tones and two diatessarons will be the same as that between six tones and the consonance of the diapason—that is, 7,153 unities. It follows that five tones surpass two diatessarons and six tones surpass one diapason by the comma alone, and the smallest integer for the comma is found to be 7,153. This is made clear in the diagram [Fig. C.4] given below.

[276]

5 TONES		TWO DIATESSARONS	
262,144	349,525 4/12	354,294	472,392
HALVES OF THE ABOVE NUMBERS			
131,072	174,762 8/12	177,147	236,196
FIRST NUMBERS PLUS THEIR HALVES			
393,216	524,288	531,441	708,588
DIFFERENCE BETWEEN THE MIDDLE TERMS			
7,153			
6 TONES		DUPLE	
531,441	262,144		524,288
DIFFERENCE BETWEEN THE EXTREME TERMS			
7,153			

13. See 2.31. This sentence marks the beginning of an "error" which will appear later in book 3 (see below, n. 31). A single number obviously cannot hold a ratio, but the number 7,153—because it is the difference between numbers containing six continuous tones and numbers containing a duple ratio—takes on almost mystical significance. It will be manipulated later in this book as "the number containing the comma."

5. *How Philolaus divided the tone*

Philolaus, a Pythagorean, tried to divide the tone in another manner,[14] postulating that the tone had its origin in the number that constitutes the first cube of the first odd number—for that number was highly revered among the Pythagoreans. Since 3 is the first odd number, if you multiply 3 by 3, then this by 3, 27 necessarily arises, which stands at the distance of a tone from the number 24, the same 3 being the difference. For 3 is an eighth part of the quantity 24, and, added to the same, it gives the first [277] cube of 3, 27. From this number, 27, Philolaus made two parts, one that is more than half, which he called the "apotome," and the remainder, which is less than half, which he called the "diesis." (The diesis later came to be called the "minor semitone.") The difference between these he called the "comma."

To begin with, Philolaus thought that the diesis consisted of 13 unities, because this had been discerned to be the difference between 256 and 243, and because the same number—that is, 13—consists of 9, 3, and unity, of which unity holds the place of the point, 3 the first odd line,[15] and 9 the first odd square. Because of all this, he identified 13 as the diesis, which he called the "semitone"; the remaining part of the number 27, comprised of 14 unities, he set down to be the apotome. But since unity is the difference between 13 and 14, he said that unity ought to be considered to represent the comma. So he gave the whole tone 27 unities, for 27 is the difference between 216 and 243,[16] which stand at the interval of a tone.

6. *The tone consists of two semitones and a comma*

From all this it is easily seen that the tone consists of two minor semitones and a comma. For if the total tone consists of an apotome and a semitone, whereas a semitone differs from an apotome by a comma, an apotome is nothing other than a minor semitone and a comma. Thus, if two minor semitones are subtracted from a tone, the remainder is a comma.

7. *Demonstration that there is the difference of a comma between a tone and two semitones*

The same can also be proved in this manner. If the diapason is com-
[278]   prised of five tones and two minor semitones, and six tones exceed the

---

14. This brief chapter and also 3.8, attributed to the late fifth-century B.C. Pythagorean Philolaus, are found in no other extant source. A third fragment attributed to Philolaus is found in Nicomachus *Enchiridion* 9 (JanS. 252–53); see Diels, *Vorsokratiker,* I.44, pp. 398–415.

15. Concerning linear numbers, see *Arith.* 2.5.

16. Friedlein 277.17: *quod inter .CCXVI. ab .CCXLIII.* should read: *quod inter .CCXVI. ac .CCXLIII.*

consonance of a diapason by one comma, there is no doubt that if five tones are subtracted from the diapason, the remainder will be two minor semitones, whereas from six tones the remainder will be a tone. Moreover, this tone exceeds these remaining semitones by a comma. But if a comma is combined with the same two semitones, together they would equal a tone. Therefore one tone has as its equivalent two minor semitones and a comma; the comma is discovered to equal the first integer 7,153.

8. *Concerning intervals smaller than a semitone*

Philolaus incorporates these and intervals smaller than these in the following definitions.[17]

> The *diesis*, he says, is the interval by which a sesquitertian ratio is larger than two tones.
> The *comma* is the interval by which the sesquioctave ratio is larger than two dieses—that is, larger than two minor semitones.
> The *schisma* is half a *comma*.
> The *diaschisma* is half a *diesis*—that is, half a minor semitone.

From these definitions it can be concluded that since the tone is first divided into a semitone and an apotome, it is also divided into two semitones and a comma; whence it follows that the tone may be divided into four diaschismata and a comma. So an integral half of a tone (which is a semitone) consists of two diaschismata, which make up one minor semitone, and a schisma, which is half a comma. Since the total tone is joined together from two minor semitones and a comma, if someone wants to divide it equally, he should produce one minor semitone and half a comma. But one minor semitone is divided into two diaschismata, whereas half a comma is one schisma. Therefore it is properly said that half a tone can be properly divided into two diaschismata and one schisma; whence it follows that an integral semitone is seen to differ from a minor semitone by one schisma. An apotome, on the other hand, is different from a minor semitone by two schismata, for it is different by a comma, and two schismata make one comma. [279]

9. *Perceiving the parts of the tone by means of consonances*

But enough concerning these things. Now it seems that we should state how we can calculate intervals, on the one hand, to reach a higher pitch, and, on the other hand, a lower pitch, under the control of musical con-

17. See above, n. 14.

sonances.[18] This should be accomplished linearly, and the lines that we shall draw may be taken to represent pitch. So now let this theory unfold.

Let the goal be to perceive the space of a tone, both ascending and descending, by means of consonances. Let us start with sound B; from this I ascend to another sound, C, that stands at the interval of a diapente from B; from C, I descend a consonance of a diatessaron to D, and, since a tone is the difference between a diapente and a diatessaron, DB is found to be the interval of a tone [Fig. C.5].[19]

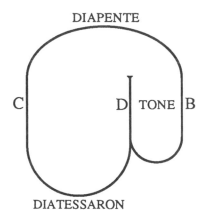

We will measure out a tone to a lower pitch in this way. From B I ascend a diatessaron to F, and from F I descend a diapente to K. Therefore, KB will be a tone. The careful reader will observe that the tone DB is produced at a higher pitch, whereas KB is produced at a lower pitch [280] [Fig. C.6].

18. Concerning the implications of the verbs *intendo* ("ascend") and *remitto* ("descend"), see above, n. 10, and book 1, n. 46. Insofar as pitch is represented geometrically in this chapter, the verbs come to be applied to continuous lines, as well as to arithmetic quantities.

19. The diagrams for this chapter, based on the earliest sources, reflect a stage of musical thought in which direction (left or right) had no implication with respect to pitch (low or high); moreover, proportions on the lines defined by letters and arches had no necessary correspondence with the relative sizes of intervals. Later sources often revise Figs. C.5, C.7, C.10, and C.12, so that high pitch is consistently placed to the right, low to the left. In later traditions the diagrams were also more to scale.

DIATESSARON

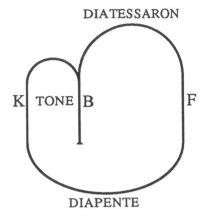

DIAPENTE

Let the goal now be to perceive the minor part of a tone by means of consonance. The minor part of a tone is that interval by which the consonance of the diatessaron exceeds two tones. Let us start with sound A; from A I ascend a diatessaron to B, and from B I ascend another diatessaron to C; from C I descend a diapente to D, so BD is a tone; from D I ascend a diatessaron to E, and from E I again descend a diapente to F, so DF is a tone. Therefore, there are two tones, BD and DF, and BA was an integral diatessaron. Then FA will be the minor part of a tone, which is named the "semitone" [Fig. C.7].

DIAPENTE   DIAPENTE

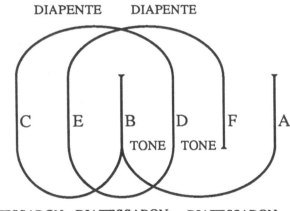

DIATESSARON DIATESSARON DIATESSARON

The semitone is measured to a lower pitch in this manner. From sound [281] A I ascend two tones to G by means of consonance,[20] and from G I descend

20. That is, the principle of consonance will be the controlling factor in deriving two tones relative to a higher pitch. One tone would be achieved by ascending a fifth then descending a fourth; the second would be achieved by repeating the same process. Note that the two tones are treated as an integral *ditone* in Fig. C.8.

a diatessaron to K. Thus KA will be that minor part, the semitone, which was required [Fig. C.8].

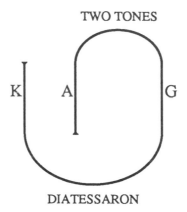

TWO TONES

DIATESSARON

If we subtract a diatessaron from three tones, the remainder is an apotome. So let there be three tones: AB, BC, and CD. From these I subtract the diatessaron AE. Thus EC will be the minor semitone, and the apotome is ED [Fig. C.9].

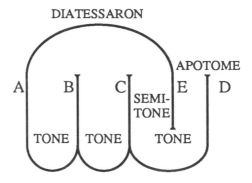

DIATESSARON

If it is of interest, let us try to perceive an apotome, first ascending. From A I ascend three tones, represented by AB, and from there I descend the consonance of a diatessaron, which is BC. The remainder, CA, forms the apotome [Fig. C.10].

[282]

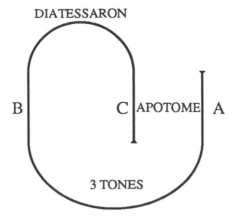

DIATESSARON

B   C APOTOME A

3 TONES

But if we wish to produce the same interval to a low sound, it is done in this manner. From A I ascend a minor semitone, AD; from D I descend the tone DE. Thus, AE will be the apotome we seek [Fig. C.11].

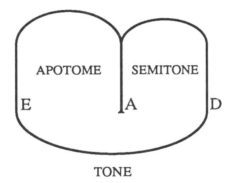

APOTOME   SEMITONE

E   A   D

TONE

Let the goal be to perceive an ascending comma. Let us start with sound A. I ascend an apotome, AB, and then descend a minor semitone, BC. Since the minor semitone is smaller than an apotome by a comma, CA will be the comma [Fig. C.12].

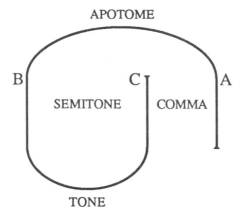

APOTOME

B   C   A

SEMITONE   COMMA

TONE

[283]   The comma is measured to a lower pitch in this manner. From sound A I ascend a minor semitone, AD, and from D I descend an apotome, DE. Thus EA will be the comma [Fig. C.13].

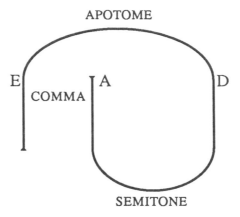

APOTOME

E   A   D

COMMA

SEMITONE

10. *Rule for perceiving the semitone*

It is necessary that we come to know these consonances through both the mind and the ears. For these things are brought together through reason and knowledge to no end unless they become known thoroughly through use and practice. What we are now undertaking concerning the fundamentals of music may not be discerned by the ears in a short period of time, for now we approach one of the more advanced matters in music; in the meantime, the faculty of reason can grasp this matter. Therefore, we shall give one example for finding the minor semitone, an interval that seems to be somewhat difficult. By this means the semitone, both ascending and descending, can become known through appropriate steps.

Take the diatessaron AB. It is necessary to work out a minor semitone

on either side of AB, both downward and upward. Thus I ascend a diatessaron, BC; I then descend a diapente, CD. BD will thus be a tone, for
the consonance of the diapente surpasses that of the diatessaron by a tone,
and the interval DC exceeds CB by the interval BD.

I again ascend a diatessaron, DE, and descend a diapente, EF. Thus
DF is a tone. But DB was a tone. Thus, AF is a minor semitone, for when
two tones are subtracted from the interval of a diatessaron—FD and BD
from AB—a semitone remains.

Next I descend a diatessaron, AG, and ascend a diapente, GH. AH [284]
will thus be a tone. But AF was a semitone; thus, FH will be an apotome.

Again I descend a diatessaron, HK, and, ascend a diapente, KL. Thus,
HL is a tone. But HA was a tone, so LB is a minor semitone. But DB was
a tone, so LD will be an apotome.

Finally, I ascend a diatessaron, FM, so BM is a semitone. I descend
a diatessaron, LN. Thus NA is a semitone.

Therefore, by means of consonances, two semitones have been perceived around the diatessaron AB: BM to a higher pitch, NA in a downward direction. The total MN is less than a diapente, for it consists of five
semitones and two identical apotomes—thus of two tones and three minor
semitones. Since two semitones cannot fill one tone, but a comma remains,
the total interval MN is less than the interval of the consonance of the
diapente by one comma, which the careful reader easily recognizes
[Fig. C.14, p. 104].

We have said very little concerning the theory of the comma, and we
should not neglect the responsibility of disclosing in what ratio the comma [285]
itself is found. For the comma is the smallest interval the sense of hearing
can grasp. Thus we must discuss the minor semitone and the major semitone with respect to the number of commas they seem to comprise, as well
as the tone with respect to the number of commas it combines. But before
we do that, we should take an appropriate first step from this place.

II. *Archytas's demonstration that a superparticular ratio cannot be divided into equal parts*

A superparticular ratio cannot be split exactly in half by a number
proportionally interposed. This will be demonstrated conclusively later.[21]
The demonstration that Archytas suggests is very weak. It is of this nature.

Let A:B be a superparticular ratio, he says. I take the smallest integers
in that same ratio, C:DE.[22] Since C:DE is the same ratio and the ratio is

21. See 4.2, proposition iii.
22. The control manuscripts are divided with respect to this proposition, two (*I* and *K*)
presenting the second term of the ratio C:DE as DE, two (*S* and *V*) simply as E (or as D, as
the text requires). Manuscripts *P, Q,* and *T* originally rendered it as DE, but the D has been
erased or expunged. Manuscripts *M* and *R*, on the other hand, originally gave C:E for the
ratio, but D has been added above the line. Given the weight of the reading as found in *I,
K,* and the original of *Q* and *M,* I follow the tradition giving C:DE.

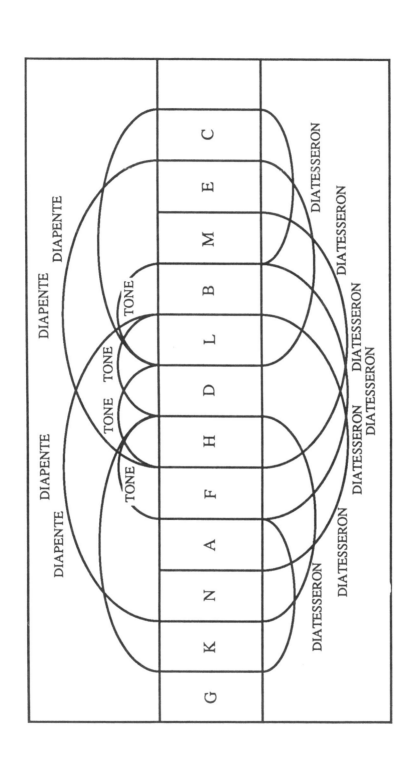

superparticular, the number DE exceeds the number C by one of its—that is, DE's—own parts. Let this part be D. I say then that D will not be a number, but unity. For if D is a number and is part of DE, the number D measures the number DE, and thus it will also measure the number E. Whence it follows that it should also measure C. Thus the number D would measure both the numbers C and DE, which is impossible. For these are the smallest integers in the same ratio as some other numbers, the first numbers so related, and they maintain the difference of unity alone. Therefore D is unity. So the number DE exceeds the number C by unity. For that reason no mean number comes between them that splits the ratio equally. It follows that between those greater numbers that maintain the same ratio as these, a mean number cannot be interposed that splits the same ratio equally [Fig. C.15].[23]

[286]

So, according to the reasoning of Archytas, no mean term falls within a superparticular ratio that divides the ratio equally, because the smallest integers in the same ratio are separated only by unity—as if, indeed, the smallest integers in multiple ratio do not also share this same difference of unity. Yet we should observe that there are many multiple ratios besides those expressed in roots between which a middle term can be placed that divides such a ratio equally; but one who has carefully read our arithmetic books[24] knows this already. So it must be added that this occurs consistently, as Archytas held, only in superparticular ratios, and must not be asserted universally.[25] Now we should turn to the following.

23. This argument attributed to Archytas (ca. 430–365 B.C.) is preserved in no other extant source. The proof is viewed by some historians of mathematics as a most significant fragment of Euclidean arithmetical thought (*Euclid's Elements*, trans. with introduction and commentary by Sir Thomas L. Heath, 2d ed. [Cambridge, 1908], vol. 2, p. 295). Porphyry *In harmonica Ptolemaei commentarius* 92 cites Archytas as author of a *De musica*. Fragments attributed to Archytas concerning the theory of sound, proportions, and harmony are found in Diels, *Vorsokratiker*, I.47.B1–3, pp. 431–38.

24. Friedlein 286.15: *arithmeticos numeros* should read *arithmeticos nostros*; Friedlein expanded the abbreviation *nros* as *numeros* rather than *nostros* (*I, Q,* etc.). It is obvious from the context that Boethius is referring to "our arithmetic books."

25. Boethius's (Nicomachus's) objection seems to be that Archytas does not notice that unity is the difference between the terms in the smallest multiple ratio—viz., the duple (2:1)—as well as between all superparticular numbers. Boethius's "refutation" is basically a slight "criticism"—viz., that Archytas should have qualified his argument and not stated the premise as universal. The proof that Boethius (Nicomachus) accepts, that of 4.2 (proposition iii) is essentially identical with this proof attributed to Archytas. André Barbera, "Placing Sectio

12. *What the ratio of the comma is; it is larger than 75:74 but smaller than 74:73*

[287]   I say, to begin with, that these numbers which contain the comma constitute a ratio larger than 75:74 but smaller than 74:73. This will now be demonstrated.

First, it must be recalled that six tones exceed a diapason by a comma. Thus, let A be 262,144, but let B, holding a consonance of the diapason with it, be set down in the duple as 524,288. Let C lie in a number at a distance of six tones from A; it should thus be 531,441, all of which have been brought together in the diagram of tones in the second book.[26] Between B and C, then, the ratio of a comma is contained. So if I subtract the number B from C, D remains, situated in the number 7,153. The number D is less than a seventy-third part of the number B, but larger than a seventy-fourth part of the same. For if I multiply the same D (7,153) by 73, I get the number E, consisting of 522,169 unities. If I multiply D by 74, I get F, 529,322. Of these, E—which came from 73—is smaller than B, but F—which came from 74—is larger than B. Thus it has properly been said that D is smaller than a seventy-third part of B, but larger than a seventy-fourth part. For this reason the number C surpasses B by a part of B smaller than a seventy-third part, but larger than a seventy-fourth. Therefore, the ratio of C to B is larger than 75:74, but smaller than 74:73.

[288]   For in the former, unity is a seventy-fourth part of the smaller term, whereas in the latter the same unity is a seventy-third part [Fig. C.16].

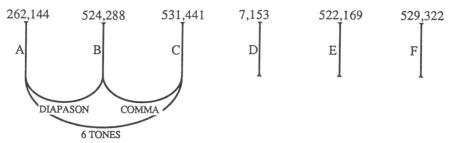

This may be explained in another manner already anticipated.[27] If the specific difference between the numbers constituting any ratio is added to both terms of the same ratio, then after the addition the ratio will be smaller than the ratio of the original numbers. Take 6 and 4, for example: if their difference, 2, is added to both, we get 8 and 6. But between 6 and 4 is a sesquialter ratio, between 8 and 6 a sesquitertian. A sesquitertian ratio is smaller than a sesquialter ratio. Now that this has been stated, let the numbers above which constituted the ratio of a comma be set out: that is,

---

Canonis in historical and philosophical contexts," *Journal of Hellenic Studies* 104 (1984): 160, briefly compares the two proofs and suggests that Archytas's version, although prolix, is not as bad as Boethius would have us believe.

26. See 2.31, Fig. B.31.

27. See 2.9, second axiom (n. 27).

531,441—let this be A—and 524,288—let this be B. Let their difference, 7,153, be C. Then let C measure the larger number, A, 75 times. If I multiply the number C 75 times, I will make D, which is 536,475. The number D, then, is larger than A by E—that is, 5,034. Again let C measure B 74 times, and let it be multiplied by 74. I then get the number F, 529,322, [289] and F is larger than B by the same number, E—that is, 5,034. Therefore D exceeds A by E, but B exceeds F by the same E. So if we add the E to A, we get D, whereas if we add the same E to B, we get F. But the number D came from 75—that is, through multiplication by C—whereas 74 brought about F through multiplication by C. Thus D and F contain between themselves the same ratio as 75:74. But D and F are A and B with one E added to them. Therefore, it is necessary that the ratio contained between A and B be larger than that between D and F. For D and F were made by the addition of one E to the numbers A and B. Thus the ratio between D and F is smaller than that between A and B. But there is the same ratio between D and F as between 75 and 74. Thus the ratio between A and B is larger than that between 75 and 74. A and B contain the comma. Therefore, the ratio of a comma is larger than 75:74 [Fig. C.17].

531,441   524,288   7,153   536,475   5,034   529,322

A| B| C| D| E| F|

Since we have shown that the ratio of a comma is larger than 75:74, [290] we must now show how the numbers constituting the interval of a comma comprise a ratio smaller than 74:73. This will be demonstrated in this manner. First, what we discussed in the second book when we spoke concerning measurement of a difference must be recalled.[28] If we subtract from the terms of any ratio the difference between them, the remainders will be in a larger ratio than those numbers that existed before they were decreased by the difference. Take 8 and 6. From these I subtract their specific difference, 2, and make 6 and 4. But the sesquitertian ratio is obtained between the first numbers, a sesquialter between the latter. A sesquialter ratio is indeed larger than a sesquitertian ratio.

Now take the same A and B as before and their difference, C. I multiply the difference, C, by 74, and I produce F—that is, 529,322— which A exceeds by G—that is, 2,119. Let the same C be multiplied again by 73; it will produce the number K—that is, 522,169—which B exceeds by the same G, 2,119. Thus if G is subtracted from A and B, K and F are made. Therefore A and B constitute a ratio smaller than F and K. But F and K are in the same ratio as 74:73, for they were produced through multiplication by C. Therefore, the ratio of the numbers A and B, those containing the comma, is smaller than 74:73. But a little earlier it was [291]

28. See 2.9, third axiom (n. 29).

demonstrated that the same ratio of the comma is larger than 74:75.[29] Therefore it is clear that the numbers which contain the comma are in a ratio larger than 75:74 but smaller than 74:73, which is what we set out to prove [Fig. C.18].

531,441   524,288   7,153   529,322   2,119   522,169

A   B   C   F   K   G

13. *The minor semitone is larger than 20:19 but smaller than 19 1/2:18 1/2*

If this kind of theorizing is directed toward the minor semitone, we shall discover quite easily the ratio that obtains between 256 and 243. Let 256 be A, 243 B, and the difference between these, 13, be C. I say that A:B is a ratio smaller than 19 1/2:18 1/2. Let C measure A 19 1/2 times— that is, let C be multiplied by 19 1/2, which makes 253 1/2. Let this be D, [292] which compared with A, exceeds it by 2 1/2. Let this difference be F. Again, let the difference C measure the number B 18 1/2 times—that is, let it be multiplied by 18 1/2, which makes 240 1/2; let this be E. Then E exceeds B by the same F (2 1/2). Therefore, D is smaller than A and E than B by the same difference, F. So if F is subtracted from A and B, D and E are produced. Therefore D and E are in a ratio smaller than A and B. But D and E are in the same ratio as 19 1/2:18 1/2. Therefore A:B is a ratio smaller than 19 1/2:18 1/2, which is what we set out to prove [Fig. C.19].

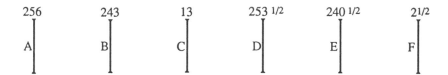

256   243   13   253 1/2   240 1/2   2 1/2

A   B   C   D   E   F

It seems, nevertheless, that the same ratio, 256:243, is larger than 20:19. Take the same A, B, and C as above. Now let the difference C measure the term A 20 times; that makes 260, which is D. When this is compared with A, it exceeds A by 4. Let this be F. Let the same C measure B 19 times, which makes 247. Let this be E. When this is compared to B, it exceeds B by the same F. Thus, D exceeds A and E exceeds B by the same F. So if F is added to A and B, D and E are produced. Therefore, the ratio of A and B is larger than that of D and E. But C multiplied by [293] 20 and 19 is what made D and E. Thus the ratio of A and B, which constitutes the semitone, is larger than 20:19 [Fig. C.20].

29. That is, earlier in this same chapter.

256	243	13	260	247	4
A	B	C	D	E	F

Therefore the semitone has been demonstrated to be a ratio larger than 20:19 but smaller than 19 1/2:18 1/2. Now we should compare the minor semitone to the comma, because the interval coming under this heading is the smallest interval heard and is the smallest ratio in size.

14. *The minor semitone is larger than three commas, but smaller than four*

We propose to demonstrate, then, that the minor semitone is larger than three commas but smaller than four. You should be able to recognize this quite easily in this way. Three numbers should be set out in such a way that they contain among themselves the ratio of a diapason and that interval which is called six tones. So let A be 262,144. From A ascend five continuous tones to B; thus B should be 472,392. The consonance of the diapason should be traced to C; thus C is 524,288. Now ascend six tones to D; thus D is 531,441. With these terms so positioned and arranged, it is clear that the comma is set down between C and D, the difference between which is 7,153. Let this difference be K.

Now descend two tones from B to E; thus, E is 373,248. Again from E I ascend a diatessaron to F, 497,664. So, since there are two tones between E and B and a diatessaron between E and F, a minor semitone thus occurs between B and F. For when two tones are taken away from the [294] consonance of the diatessaron, the remainder is a minor semitone, which, as I have said, consists of the smallest integers 256:243. If you multiply these same numbers by 1,944, you unfold the numbers B and F. B and F necessarily contain the same ratio as those mentioned above, for they both grew through multiplication by one and the same number—that is, 1,944.

Again I ascend a diatessaron from F to G; thus G is 663,552. And again I descend from the same G two tones to P; thus P is 524,288. It is necessary that this P give off the same sound as the number C, for it has progressed to equality with it through such a line of reasoning as follows. The fact is that the consonance of the diapason AC, which consists of five tones and two minor semitones,[30] falls short of six tones by a comma. Now the number P was derived from the term A by subtracting five tones and two semitones in this way: clearly five tones are collected together from A to B, but a minor semitone is observed from B to F, and F and P encompass

30. Friedlein 294.14–15: *constat tonis ac duobus semitoniis* should read *constat v tonis ac duobus semitoniis.*

the same minor semitone. Thus A to P produces five tones and two minor semitones, so A and C are rightly written together in the same number. But since there is a minor semitone between F and C, let us see what the difference is (so that we can compare it with the comma). Their difference is 26,624; let this be M. Thus, K is the difference of a comma, M that of a minor semitone. If I multiply the number K by 3, I get 21,459; let this [295] be L. If you wish to multiply the same number K by 4, you will get 28,612; let this be N. Thus M is larger than L, but the same M is smaller than N. But N arose from the comma multiplied by 4, while L arose from the comma multiplied by 3, and M holds the difference of a minor semitone. Therefore, it is correctly stated that the minor semitone is smaller than four commas, but larger than three [Fig. C.21].[31]

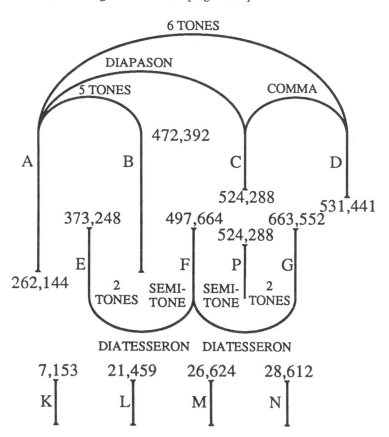

31. Boethius (Nicomachus) here and in the next two chapters makes the mistake for which he criticizes Aristoxenus; he takes a difference, 7,153, and multiplies it to determine the "space" of an interval. See André Barbera, "Interpreting an Arithmetical Error in Boethius's *De Institutione Musica* (iii.14–16)," *Académie internationale d'histoire des sciences* 106 (1981): 26–41. Although Boethius's arithmetic exhibits inconsistency in method, what he

15. *The apotome is larger than four commas but smaller than five; the tone is larger than eight commas but smaller than nine*

Through this same line of reasoning we can also discover how many commas are in a major semitone, to which, above, we assigned the name "apotome,"[32] as in the following.

[296]

Let A be 262,144, and let B be 472,392, at a distance of five tones; at the distance of six tones from A, let D be 531,441. Thus, between B and D there is a tone, while B should stand at the distance of a minor semitone from C; let C be 497,664. Thus the ratio of an apotome remains between C and D. Since BD is a tone, if you subtract the minor semitone BC from it, the larger CD is left, which was assigned above to the apotome. The difference between D and C is 33,777; let this be E. But the difference of a comma was 7,153; let this be F. So if I multiply F, the comma, by 5, I get 35,765; let this be G. If I multiply the same F by 4, it makes the number K, which is 28,612. So G is larger than E but smaller than K. But G is the comma multiplied by 5, K the comma multiplied by 4, while E is the difference of the apotome. Therefore it is correctly stated that the apotome is smaller than five commas but larger than four.

This also proves that the tone is larger than eight commas but smaller than nine. For if the minor semitone is larger than three commas but smaller than four, and the apotome is larger than four commas but smaller than five, then when the minor semitone is joined with the major—which is the apotome—the whole will be larger than eight commas but smaller than nine. But the apotome and the minor semitone produce one tone, so

---

claims is true: the semitone is in fact larger than three commas but smaller than four, the apotome is larger than four commas but smaller than five, and the tone is larger than eight commas but smaller than nine.

32. See 2.30.

the tone is indeed larger than eight commas but smaller than nine
[297]   [Fig. C.22].

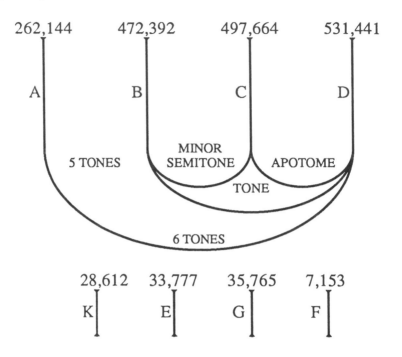

16. *Proof through numbers of the things discussed above*

This method of calculating has demonstrated how the tone is composed with respect to commas. Nevertheless we should not, like lazy musicologists, tire before demonstrating independently that the tone itself maintains a degree of comparison with respect to commas. So let A be 262,144, and B, at a distance of five tones from it, be 472,392; let C, containing the consonance of the diapason with A, be the number 524,288, and let D, which is distant from A by six whole tones, be 531,441. Thus D stands at a distance of a comma from C and at a distance of six tones from the consonance of the diapason. Let that comma be E, 7,153. But D stands at the distance of a clearly integral tone from B—namely, five tones subtracted from six tones; let that difference, 59,049, be F. If I multiply E by 9, I get [298]   H, 64,377. If I multiply it by 8, I get 57,224; let that be G. But H is greater than F, whereas G is smaller than F. Term F is the difference of a tone, H the comma multiplied by nine, and G the comma multiplied by 8. Thus it has been demonstrated that the tone is smaller than nine commas but larger than eight of the same commas [Fig. C.23].

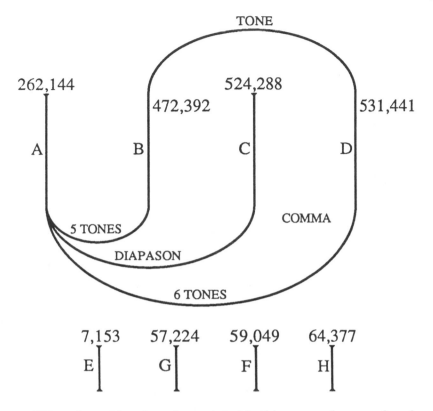

TONE

262,144

524,288

472,392

531,441

A B C D

5 TONES

DIAPASON

COMMA

6 TONES

7,153   57,224   59,049   64,377

E   G   F   H

When these things have been stated in this manner by way of preface, it has been demonstrated that the major semitone stands at the distance of a comma from the minor semitone. Nevertheless, the same matter will be proved using the numbers at hand through the following line of reasoning. Let A be 497,664, and B the number a minor semitone away from it, as written above, 524,288. This number an apotome away from A amounts to 531,441 unities; let it be C. Whereas AB is a minor semitone, and AC a major semitone, the difference between B and C should be sought. That difference is 7,153; let this be D. But this number just now was demon- [299] strated to represent the comma. Therefore the comma makes the difference between the major and the minor semitone [Fig. C.24].

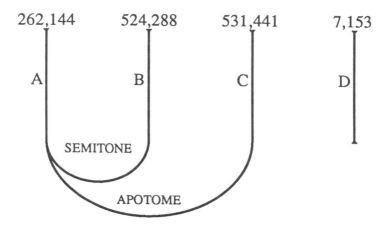

Now I propose to demonstrate that the tone is only one comma larger than two minor semitones. Let the number 472,392 be A, from which I rise a tone to 531,441; let this be D. I ascend a minor semitone from A to B, and let this be 497,664. I ascend another minor semitone from B to C, and let this be 524,288. Since AD is a tone, whereas AC contains two minor semitones, let us see what the difference is between the numbers C and D. It is, of course, E, 7,153 unities. Thus it has been demonstrated that the tone is larger than two minor semitones by a comma [Fig. C.25].

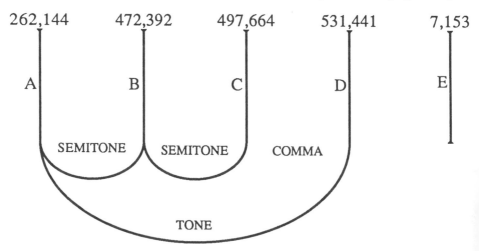

[300]   Since everything we promised to prove has been demonstrated through appropriate argument, the division of the monochord ruler is all that is left for us to do in this account of the fundamentals of music. Since this topic requires rather extended treatment, we have decided to give the matter independent discussion in the next book.

BOOK 4

1. *Differences in pitches consist in quantity*

Even though we have digested all the things which had to be demonstrated in the discussion of the last book, it will do no harm to present the same things again briefly, with some variety of treatment, to refresh our memories. With these things reinforced in the memory, we should approach the subject toward which our whole effort has been directed, the division of the monochord rule.[1]

If all things were at rest, no sound would strike the hearing; such would be the case, because, with the cessation of all motion, objects would effect no pulsation[2] among themselves.

For pitch to exist, then, pulsation is needed. For pulsation to exist, motion must come first. Therefore, for pitch to exist, motion is necessary.

Every motion is at one time fast, at another slow. If the striking motion is slow, a low sound is produced, for as slowness is close to motionlessness, so lowness is near to silence. But if the motion is fast, a high sound is present.

1. The brief recapitulation found in the first two chapters of this book is a slightly expanded translation of the Euclidian *Sectio canonis* (JanS. 148–58). For a translation of the treatise, see Thomas J. Mathiesen, "An annotated translation of Euclid's Division of a Monochord," *Journal of Music Theory* 19 (1975): 236–57. For a discussion of the treatise, see André Barbera, "Placing Sectio Canonis in Historical and Philosophical Contexts," pp. 157–61. Compare the present summary of Pythagorean premises with the summaries found in 1.1 and 2.20.

2. Friedlein 301.14: *nullum inter se res pulsum cierent* should probably read *nullae inter se res pulsum cierent*. I, K, M, P, T, and V read *nullae*, while Q and S read *nullum*. R also reads *nullum* in the text, but *nullae* has been added above the line. The present translation assumes that *nullae* is correct.

Moreover, by increasing tension, that which is low rises to proper pitch, while by decreasing tension, that which is high sinks to proper pitch.[3]

Whence it follows that every sound seems to be composed, as it were, of certain parts;[4] every association of parts is brought together through a certain ratio. Therefore, association of sounds is governed by ratios.

Ratios are studied principally through numbers. A simple ratio of numbers is found in multiple, superparticular, or superpartient classes of ratios. Indeed, consonant or dissonant pitches are discerned according to multiple or superparticular ratios.[5]

[302]   Consonant pitches are those which when struck at the same time[6] sound pleasant and intermingled with each other; dissonant pitches are those which when struck at the same time do not yield intermingled sound.

With these matters thus set forth, we should speak a little concerning ratios.

2. *Different speculations concerning intervals*[7]

i. If a multiple interval is multiplied by two, that which is produced from the multiplication will be a multiple interval. Consider the multiple interval BC, where B is a multiple of C. Arrange it so that as C is to B, B is to D. Then, since B is a multiple of C, the term C measures B, either twice or

---

3. The Latin, which pairs such terms as *intensio* and *cresco, remissio* and *decresco,* and uses these pairs in conjunction with the phrase *ad medium* ("to proper pitch"), strikes a more quantitative note than does the English translation. See book 1, n. 46.

4. That is, "parts," or quantities, of motion. Boethius's *velox* and *tardus* ("fast" and "slow") do not capture the meaning of the Greek terms πυκνός and ἀραιός (*densus* or *frequens* and *rarus,* "dense" and "sparse"), and the logic of the text as found in *Sectio canonis* is obscured.

5. Boethius omits the final sentence of the discussion in *Sectio canonis* of the superior value of multiple and superparticular ratios (JanS. 149.14–16): "Of these, the multiple and the superparticular are ordered one to another by one term" (Mathiesen trans., p. 239). Boethius's omission may support the view of Edward A. Lippman (*Musical Thought in Ancient Greece* [New York, 1964], p. 154) that this passage refers to the fact that ratios of the multiple and superparticular classes can be expressed by single words in Greek, whereas ratios of the superpartient class cannot. Since in Latin, ratios of the superpartient class can also be expressed by one word (e.g., superbipartient), the argument from "one term" would carry no weight. See Mathiesen trans., p. 254, n. 12.

6. *Simul pulsae* is added to these definitions by Boethius or his source. The phrase is probably a translation of the Greek ἅμα κρουσθέντες. Compare this definition with that found in 1.28 (see also book 1, n. 130).

7. The present chapter presents propositions 1–9 of *Sectio canonis.* Of the control manuscripts, *K, Q, R, S, T,* and *V* number the proofs with Roman numerals in the margins. The numbers in the present text (not found in Friedlein) follow these manuscripts and facilitate comparison with the numbered propositions of *Sectio canonis* (JanS. 150–58). Note that, in this recension of *Sectio canonis,* an arithmetic version of each proof (except for v) follows the geometric proposition.

three times or some other number of times. But as C is to B, B is to D. Therefore the term B measures D. For this reason the term C measures D as well as B.[8] Therefore D is a multiple of C, and the interval DC is made by bringing together and uniting the interval BC twice with itself or multiplying it by two.

The same can likewise be demonstrated in numbers: let B and C be duple, such as 2:1; and as C is to B, let B be to D; thus D will be 4. B:C is a multiple—that is, 2:1. Therefore D, 4, is a multiple with C, 1. For 4:1 is a quadruple, or its half—the interval BC—multiplied by two [Fig. D.1].

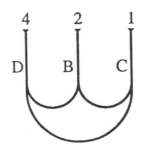

ii. If an interval multiplied by two produces a multiple, that interval itself will also be multiple. Take the interval BC and arrange it so that C is to B as B is to D, and make D to C a multiple. I say that B is a multiple of C; since D is a multiple of C, C measures D. It is known that if numbers are proportional and the first is related to the last in a numerical series, then if the last measures the first, it likewise measures the middle.[9] Thus C measures B; so B is a multiple of C. [303]

Likewise in numbers: let C be unity; let D be 4, from the doubling of the ratio B:C; then D is a multiple of C, for it is the quadruple. Thus, since this quadruple is generated from the doubling of the ratio B:C, the ratio B:C will be its half. Therefore the ratio B:C is a duple ratio. But a duple ratio is multiple. Thus the ratio B:C is multiple [Fig. D.2].

8. Friedlein [302.9–10]: *Quocirca etiam .C. terminus id, quod est .D., metietur* ("For this reason term C will also measure D") is mathematically elegant but not supported by the earliest manuscripts. Most of the control manuscripts (*K, P,* and *R; S* and *T* before emendation; and *I* with the verb as *metietur*) read *quocirca etiam C terminus id quod est D metitur B,* a text which does not lend itself to an intelligible reading. *Q* and *V,* however, give a text satisfactory as Latin and convincing in the proposition: *Quocirca etiam C terminus id quod est D et metitur B,* and the text in *S* and *T* is emended to follow *Q* and *V* by adding *et* above the line. (*M* is no help to the proposition or the text with its *Quocirca etiam C terminus id quod est B metietur.*) The version of *Q* and *V* serves as the basis for this translation.

9. See Euclid *Elementa* 8.7.

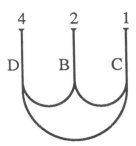

iii. In the case of a superparticular interval, neither one mean number nor several mean numbers will fit in proportionally. Take the superparticular ratio B:C, and let DF and G be the smallest terms in the same ratio. Since DF and G are the smallest terms in this ratio, they are the first integers in it; thus unity alone measures them. Then if G is subtracted from DF, D remains, and it is the common denominator of both terms. This will therefore be unity. For this reason no number that is less than DF or greater than G will fall between DF and G. Unity alone occurs between them. Now, however, many means fall proportionally between the smallest terms of some ratio in the superparticular class, just as many also fall between others in this same ratio.[10] But nothing can come between DF and G, the smallest terms of this ratio, and thus nothing falls proportionally between B and C.

[304]

Now in numbers: let there be any superparticular ratio—for example, the sesquialter. Let the terms be 10 and 15. The smallest terms in the same ratio are 2 and 3. I subtract 2 from 3; the remainder is unity, and it measures both terms. Thus there will be no number between 2 and 3 which is larger than 2 but smaller than 3, unless unity is divided—which is inconsistent. Hence, no number will come between 10 and 15 which preserves the same ratio to 10 that 15 holds to it [Fig. D.3].

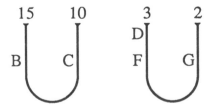

iv. If a nonmultiple interval is multiplied by 2, the result is neither multiple nor superparticular. Let B:C be a nonmultiple interval, arranged so that C is to B as B is to D. I say that D is neither a multiple nor a superparticular of C. But first, if it can be done, let D be a multiple of C. Since it is known that if an interval is multiplied by 2 and a multiple interval is produced,

10. See Euclid *Elementa* 8.8.

that which has been multiplied by 2 is a multiple interval,[11] then BC will [305] be multiple. But such was not asserted, so D will not be a multiple of C. Neither is it a superparticular, for no mean term fits proportionally into a superparticular ratio.[12] But a term is set down proportionally between D and C—that is, B—for C is to B as B is to D. Thus it will be impossible for D to be either a multiple or a superparticular of C, which is what we set out to prove.

Now in numbers: take the nonmultiple interval 6:4, and as 4 is related to 6, place 6 in relation to another number. This number will be 9, which is neither a multiple nor a superparticular of 4 [Fig. D.4].

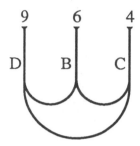

v. If an interval is multiplied by 2, and that which is created from this multiplication is not multiple, then that interval itself is not multiple. Take the interval B:C and arrange it so that C is to B as B is to D, and let D not be a multiple of C. I say that B is not a multiple of C. For if it is, D is also a multiple of C.[13] But such is not the case. Therefore, B will not be a multiple of C [Fig. D.5].

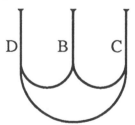

vi. The duple interval is made up of the two largest superparticular intervals, the sesquialter and the sesquitertian. Thus, let A be the sesquialter of B, and B the sesquitertian of C. I say that A is the duple of C. Since A is the sesquialter of B, then A contains the whole of B plus one of its halves. Therefore two As are equal to three Bs. Moreover, since B is the [306]

11. See proposition i above.
12. See proposition iii above.
13. See proposition i above.

sesquitertian of C, then B contains C plus a third part of it. Thus three Bs are equal to four Cs. However, three Bs were equal to two As; thus two As are equal to four Cs. Therefore one A equals two Cs. Therefore A is the duple of C.[14]

Now in numbers: let the sesquialter be 6:4, the sesquitertian 4:3; then 6:3 forms the duple ratio[15] [Fig. D.6].

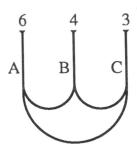

vii. The triple interval is born from the duple interval plus the sesquialter. Let A be the duple of B, and B the sesquialter of C. I say that A is the triple of C. Since A is the duple of B, A is equal to two Bs. Moreover, since B is the sesquialter of C, B contains the whole of C plus half of it. Thus, two Bs are equal to three Cs, but two Bs were equal to one A. Thus one A is equal to three Cs. Therefore, A is the triple of C.

Now in numbers: let the duple be 6:3, the sesquialter 3:2; then 6:2 is the triple ratio [Fig. D.7].

14. *Sectio canonis* (JanS. 154–55) presents two demonstrations of this proposition, only the second of which is found here.

15. There is little doubt that the prevalent reading of this text in the early ninth century was *Sit enim sesqualter .iii. ad .ii., sesquitertius vero .iiii. ad .iii.; ergo .iiii. ad .ii. duplices sunt* (compare Friedlein 306.6–8). Of the control manuscripts, *I, K,* and *R,* present 3:2 as the sesquialter, 4:3 as the sesquitertian, and 4:2 as the duple, and *M, T, S,* and *V* did the same before emendations. The problem with this sequence of numbers is that, given terms A, B, and C of the above proof, the sesquitertian ratio should be between the first and second terms (A:B), and the sesquialter between the second and third (B:C). With the terms 4:3:2 the sequence of ratios is reversed. *P* and *Q* and *S* after emendation present the consistent reading: *Sit enim sesqualter .vi. ad .iiii., sesquitertius vero .iiii. ad .iii.; ergo .vi. ad .iii. duplices sunt.* This reading serves as basis for the present translation. In *M* and *V* the ratios 12:8, 8:6, and 12:6 have been added above the ratios 3:2, 4:3, and 4:2, whereas *T* emends the text to proceed with those same numbers. This last tradition is that followed by Friedlein. It is impossible to determine whether the original version gave ratios consistent with the geometric proof but subsequently became corrupted, or whether the original version merely presented an inconsistent arithmetic version of the proof and was emended to give a consistent reading.

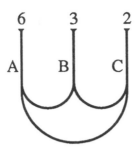

viii. If a sesquitertian interval is subtracted from a sesquialter interval, that which remains will be a sesquioctave. Let A be the sesquialter of B, and [307] C the sesquitertian of B. I say that A is the sesquioctave of C. Since A is the sesquialter of B, A contains B plus one half of it. Thus eight As are equal to twelve Bs. Moreover, since C is the sesquitertian of B, C contains B plus one-third of it. Thus nine Cs are equal to twelve Bs. However, twelve Bs were equal to eight As. Thus eight As are also equal to nine Cs. Therefore A is equal to C plus an eighth part of it. Hence A is the sesquioctave of C.

Now in numbers: Let the sesquialter interval be 9:6, and the sesquitertian 8:6. Then 9:8 is the sesquioctave ratio [Fig. D.8].

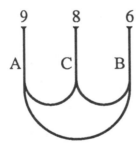

ix. Six sesquioctave ratios are more than one duple interval. Take the number A, of which B is the sesquioctave, of which C is the sesquioctave, of which D is the sesquioctave, of which F is the sesquioctave, of which G is the sesquioctave, of which K is the sesquioctave. Describe this in an arithmetical manner, and let A, B, C, D, F, G, and K be numbers. Thus, let A be 262,144, the sesquioctave of which is B, 294,912, the sesquioctave of which is C, 331,776, the sesquioctave of which is D, 373,248, the ses- [308] quioctave of which is F, 419,904, the sesquioctave of which is G, 472,392, the sesquioctave of which is K, 531,441. And 531,441, which is K, is larger than the duple of 262,144, which is A.[16] Therefore six sesquioctave ratios are larger than one duple interval [Fig. D.9].

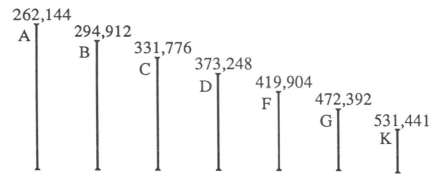

3. *The naming of musical notes in Greek and Latin scholarship*[17]

Since we are left with the task of dividing a string by means of a rule (according to the consonances just discussed), and since this same partition will display the requisite sounds through three genera of melody, at this point we must set out musical notes; in this way, when we inscribe the divided line[18] with these same written symbols,[19] the name of each individual note will be recognized very easily.

16. The duple of 262,144 is 524,288 (see 2.31).

17. This chapter recapitulates the collection of pitches forming the Greek tonal system and introduces Greek notation. The names of the notes play an essential part in unfolding the division of the monochord, and their reintroduction at this point is necessary because they have not been treated since chaps. 20–27 of book 1. The text gives the names of the notes, first using the Greek terms found in book 1, then the complete Latin names for the first time. The Latin names closely parallel those found in Martianus Capella *De nuptiis* 9.931 and probably represent the norm in Latin musical scholarship (for exceptions, see below, nn. 30 and 33).

The explication of Greek notation does not seem as important to the division of the monochord as the text that follows would lead one to believe. The notation is used in the first (incomplete) division of the diatonic genus (4.5) but does not appear in the integrated division of all three genera (4.6–12). The notational system used here would not, in fact, function in the integrated division, since there the pitch of the third notes of tetrachords in the chromatic and enharmonic genera—the parhypatai and the tritai—are different. The notational system used in this chapter, which is consistent with the system of 28 pitches found in 1.22 and 4.13, presents parhypatai and tritai as the same pitch. The notational system will play a crucial role in the explanation of the modal system (see 4.15–17).

18. The approach in these chapters is abstract and geometric, but the line, of course, represents a string. A single string (monochord) stopped at a position corresponding exactly to a point on the line would yield the pitches and intervals determined by the ratios.

19. In this sentence Boethius introduces the terms *nota* and *notula,* the former to refer to the musical notes themselves, the latter in reference to the written signs. *Nota* is here translated as "note," *notula* as "written symbol."

Ancient musicians, for the sake of an abbreviation—lest it always be [309] necessary to write out complete names of notes—devised certain written symbols whereby the designations of the strings might be notated, and they distributed them throughout the genera and the modes. At the same time, using such abbreviations, they were striving to reach the point where a musician who wanted to write down some melody over a verse, set out in the rhythmic structure of some meter, could add these written symbols for the sounds. Through this remarkable means, then, they discovered that not only the words of songs—conveyed through letters—but also the very melodies themselves—expressed in these written symbols—could be preserved in the memory and for posterity.

For the present, let us take just one of the modes, the Lydian, and arrange its written symbols through the three genera; we defer doing the same with the other modes until another time. Surely if I sketch the disposition of notes using the names of Greek letters, the reader should not be put off by anything unusual, for this whole arrangement of notes has been organized around Greek letters, which are sometimes altered and sometimes even rotated through various positions. We, of course, guard against changing anything handed down by the authority of antiquity. Thus the first, upper written symbols will be for the diction—that is, for texts— whereas the second, lower symbols will be for the playing of instruments.[20]

Proslambanomenos, which can be called *adquisitus* ("added"); an incomplete zeta and a tau lying on its side: Ζ .[21] Hypate hypaton, which is the *principalis principalium* ("principal of the principal"); a backward gamma and a normal gamma: Γ . Parhypate hypaton, which is the *subprincipalis principalium* ("subprincipal of the principal"); an incomplete beta and a supine gamma: Ϲ . Enharmonic hypaton, which is the *princi-*

20. Pizzani ("Fonti," p. 99) suggests that this chapter reflects Mutianus's translation of Gaudentius into Latin (but see Bower, "Sources," pp. 14–19). Although there are some loose parallels between Gaudentius and Boethius's text and a Latin translation of Gaudentius did exist, the differences between the two texts make it difficult to posit a direct relationship.

Systematic presentations of Greek notation are found in four sources from antiquity: Gaudentius's *Harmonica introductio* (JanS. 319–56); Bellerman's Anonymous III; Alypius's *Eisagoge* (JanS. 359–406); and Boethius. All these sources show clear parallels in their single-sentence descriptions of written symbols, and such descriptions were probably a common fund of Greek music theory. Only Alypius presents notation for the enharmonic and chromatic genera, and he does this independently of the diatonic genus. Boethius is the only source that integrates descriptions of the notes in the three genera into a single narrative.

The most problematic descriptions and notes in Boethius's text are those for the enharmonic and chromatic genera, particularly the chromatic. Inasmuch as only one source exists for comparison of these notes (i.e., Alypius *Eisagoge*), judgment concerning their accuracy and source is difficult.

21. The notational symbols found in this translation are derived from the descriptions given by Boethius (and Alypius) and from the symbols found in the control manuscripts. A critical study of these signs, comparing Greek and Latin theoretical sources, is needed. See Appendix 3 at D.20 and D.21.

[310]   *palium enharmonios* ("enharmonic of the principal"); a supine alpha and
a backward gamma with an obelus on the back:[22] ⼦ . Chromatic hypaton,
which is the *principalium chromatica* ("chromatic of the principal"); a supine alpha with a line[23] and a backward gamma with two lines:[24] ⼦ . Diatonic hypaton, which is the *principalium extenta* ("extended of the principal"); a Greek phi and a digamma: ⼲ . Hypate meson, which is the
principalium mediarum ("principal of the median"); a sigma and a sigma:
⼢ . Parhypate meson, which is the *subprincipalis mediarum* ("subprincipal
of the median"); a rho and a supine sigma: ⼢ . Enharmonic meson, which
is the *mediarum enharmonios* ("enharmonic of the median"); a Greek pi
and a backward sigma: ⼢ . Chromatic meson, which is the *mediarum chromatica* ("chromatic of the median"); a Greek pi with an obelus[25] and a
backwards sigma with an obelus through the middle: ⼢ . Diatonic meson,
which is the *mediarum extenta* ("extended of the median"); a Greek mu
and an incomplete Greek pi:[26] ⼢ . Mese, which is the *media* ("median");
an iota and a lambda lying on its side: ⼢ . Trite synemmenon, which is the
tertia coniunctarum ("third of the conjunct"); a theta and a supine lambda:
⼢. Enharmonic synemmenon, or *coniunctarum enharmonios* ("enharmonic
of the conjunct"); a Greek eta and a lambda lying on its side backward:[27]
⼢ . Chromatic synemmenon, which is the *coniunctarum chromatica* ("chromatic of the conjunct"); a Greek eta with an obelus[28] and a lambda lying
[311]   on its side backward with an obelus through the middle:[29] ⼢ . Diatonic

22. Alypius *Eisagoge* (JanS. 399.10) describes the instrumental enharmonic hypaton as
an "inverted digamma": ⼂ rather than ⼀ .
23. The line is placed differently in the Alypian tradition: ⼂ rather than ⼂ .
24. Alypius *Eisagoge* (JanS. 384.10–11) describes the instrumental chromatic hypaton
as an "inverted digamma with a line": ⼂ rather than ⼂ .
25. The obelus is placed differently in the Alypian tradition: ⼂ rather than ⼂.
26. The incomplete pi appears in two forms in the control manuscripts, with both forms
employed in single manuscripts: ⼂ and ⼂ . The second form predominates—viz., that with
the shortened member on the left. In the Alypian tradition the member on the right is
shortened.
27. Boethius's descriptions of the instrumental enharmonic and chromatic synemmenon
are corrupt, and because of the corruption both notational symbols are the same. Alypius
describes the enharmonic synemmenon as "a lambda lying on its side backwards" [JanS.
399.18–19], and the chromatic synemmenon as "a lambda lying on its side backward with an
obelus through the middle" [JanS. 384.20–22]. These descriptions follow the consistent pattern
for the "movable" note—viz., the note from the chromatic genera is the one consistently
marked with some form of line. Thus the phrase *per medium habens virgulam* [310.18] should
be moved to the description of the chromatic synemmenon [310.20], and this translation
follows the emendation. The symbol for the enharmonic synemmenon thus becomes ⼂ , in
conformity with the amended text, and the symbol ⼂ is used only for the chromatic synemmenon.
28. The obelus is placed differently in the Alypian tradition: ⼂ rather than ⼂ .
29. The description of the instrumental chromatic synemmenon [310.20–311.1], like that
of the instrumental enharmonic synemmenon (see above, n. 27) is corrupt. The word *iacens*
is missing from the definition; it is found in the description of the enharmonic synemmenon

synemmenon, which is the *extenta coniunctarum* ("extended of the conjunct"); a gamma and a nu: ⌐ᴎ . Nete synemmenon, which is the *ultima coniunctarum* ("last of the conjunct"); a supine square ω and a zeta: Ⴑ⊦ . Paramese, which is the *submedia*[30] ("submedian"); a zeta and a Greek pi lying on its side: ⊑⊐ . Trite diezeugmenon, which is the *tertia divisarum* ("third of the disjunct"); a square eta and a supine pi: ⊑ᴜ . Enharmonic diezeugmenon, which is the *divisarum enharmonios* ("enharmonic of the disjunct"); a delta and a Greek pi lying on its side backward: ≜ . Chromatic diezeugmenon, which is the *divisarum chromatica* ("chromatic of the disjunct"); a delta with an obelus[31] and a Greek pi lying on its side backward with an angular obelus: ≜ .[32] Diatonic diezeugmenon, which is the *divisarum diatonos*[33] ("diatonic of the disjunct"); a supine square ω and a zeta: Ⴑ⊦. Nete diezeugmenon, which is the *ultima divisarum* ("last of the disjunct"); a tilted phi and a nu turned upside down and shortened: ⌀ᴎ .[34] Trite hyperboleon, which is the *tertia excellentium* ("third of the highest"); an Υ leaning toward the right[35] and a half-alpha leaning upward toward the left: ⤳ .[36] Enharmonic hyperboleon, which is the *excllentium enharmonios* ("enharmonic of the highest"); a supine tau and a half-alpha supine toward the right: ⟂ꞎ .[37] Chromatic hyperboleon, which is the *excellentium chroma-*

---

above, in Alypius [JanS. 384.20–22], and a lambda must be put on its side before it can be reversed. Moreover, the words *per medium* should be added before *habens virgulam*. The translation is based on the amended text: *lambda iacens conversum per medium habens virgulam*. The obelus is placed differently in the Alypian tradition: ↠ rather than ↦ .

30. The paramese is translated as *prope media* by Martianus Capella *De nuptiis* (Dick ed., 496.3–4) rather than *submedia*.

31. Alypius *Eisagoge* (JanS. 384.28–29) describes the vocal chromatic diezeugmenon as "a delta with an acute accent" rather than "a delta with an obelus": Δ′ rather than ⌂ .

32. The angular obelus is placed differently in the Alypian tradition: ⇒ rather than ⟹ .

33. The diatonic diezeugmenon is the only "movable" diatonic note described as *diatonos* rather than *extenta*. The name of this note clearly represents a corruption in the text.

34. Gaudentius *Harmonica introductio* (JanS. 353.5) and Anonymous III (Najock ed., 118.1) describe the instrumental nete diezeugmenon as "an eta carelessly made," while Alypius *Eisagoge* (JanS. 369.25) describes it as "an eta carelessly made and shortened." Boethius's "nu turned upside down and shortened" describes the written symbol with equal validity, but the different description distinguishes the tradition of Boethius from the other sources.

35. The description and the symbol for the instrumental trite hyperboleon are problematic in all texts. The three Greek sources describe it as "an upsilon leaning downward" (Alypius *Eisagoge* [JanS. 369.26], Gaudentius *Harmonica introductio* [JanS. 353.24], and Anonymous III [Najock ed., 118.3]), while Boethius adds the phrase "to the right." However, the upsilon appears in all sources to be "inverted" rather than "leaning."

36. Boethius, Alypius *Eisagoge* (JanS. 369.27), and Gaudentius *Harmonica introductio* (JanS. 353.23–24) agree on the description of the instrumental trite hyperboleon, but Alypius and Gaudentius write the symbol as ⤵ rather than ⤶. Anonymous III (Najock ed., 118.3), on the other hand, describes the note as "a half-alpha inverted to the left," and writes the symbol the same way as Boethius. The half-alpha in all its forms presents problems in the codices containing the Greek notational treatises, probably because of the changing form of the letter alpha; see the Prolegomena to Alypius *Eisagoge* (JanS. 366) and the introduction to Najock, pp. 7–8.

[312] *tica* ("chromatic of the highest"); an inverted tau with a line and a half-alpha supine toward the right with a line behind: ☡ .[38] Diatonic hyperboleon, which is the *excellentium extenta* ("extended of the highest"); a Greek mu with an acute accent and an incomplete pi with an acute accent: ᚹ.ᛁ.[39] Nete hyperboleon, which is the *ultima excellentium*[40] ("last of the highest"); an iota with an acute accent and a tilted lambda with an acute accent: ꞁ.ᛁ.

4. An arrangement of the musical notes with their corresponding pitches in the three genera
[Fig. D.10, p. 127]

5. Partition of the monochord rule in the diatonic genus[41]

The time has come to turn to the partition of the monochord rule. By way of preface, this must be said concerning the subject: whether the division about to be described is considered in the measurement of a string or in numbers and their ratios, the longer length of string and the greater plurality of number will yield lower sounds, but if the length of string is shorter and the plurality of numbers is less, higher sounds must necessarily be produced. And this follows from this comparison: to the extent that one single partition represents a longer length or a larger number, whereas another represents a shorter length and is marked with a smaller number, a lower or higher pitch is found in corresponding degree. The reader should not be disturbed that we have usually designated the positions of higher

37. The vocal enharmonic hyperboleon is described in Alypius *Eisagoge* (JanS. 399.32) as "a half-alpha leaning toward the right," a description consistent with that of the instrumental trite .hyperboleon. Again, consistent with the previous description and symbol, the symbol appears as ꝳ rather than ꝵ . Boethius's description of this note as "a half-alpha inverted to the right" reflects the textual tradition of Anonymous III in describing the instrumental trite hyperboleon (see above, n. 36).

38. Alypius *Eisagoge* (JanS. 384.36–37) describes the symbols for the chromatic hyperboleon as "having lines, with an acute accent." The symbols appear in Alypius as ꞁ⸍ and ⱦrather than ☡ and ꝵ .

39. Concerning form of the incomplete pi, see above, n. 26.

40. The Latin translation for the final note of the system, *ultima excellentium,* is not found in the textual tradition of Boethius. I add it for consistency.

41. Chaps. 5–12 represent an important subdivision in Boethius's text, a discussion promised repeatedly in the earlier books (1.11 and 27, 3.16, 4.1). The arithmetic theory and music tradition developed to this point are now applied to the rule—i.e., the string—of the monochord. Two sections of the text treat the division of the monochord: chap. 5, which presents a straightforward division of the diatonic genus according to Pythagorean principles, and chaps. 6–11, in which a unique, complete division of the monochord in three genera is presented. The textual tradition of these chapters presents difficulties: one major portion of text appears to be missing at the end of chap. 5; certain letters are inconsistent or are omitted in the computations of chaps. 6–11; and finally, the diagrams crucial to these chapters present major editorial problems.

PROSLAMBANOMENOS

HYPATE HYPATON

PARHYPATE HYPATON

ENHARMONIC LICHANOS HYPATON

CHROMATIC LICHANOS HYPATON

DIATONIC LICHANOS HYPATON

HYPATE MESON

PARHYPATE MESON

ENHARMONIC LICHANOS MESON

CHROMATIC LICHANOS MESON

DIATONIC LICHANOS MESON

MESE

TRITE SYNEMMENON

ENHARMONIC PARANETE SYNEMMENON

CHROMATIC PARANETE SYNEMMENON

DIATONIC PARANETE SYNEMMENON

NETE SYNEMMENON

PARAMESE

TRITE DIEZEUGMENON

ENHARMONIC PARANETE DIEZEUGMENON

CHROMATIC PARANETE DIEZEUGMENON

DIATONIC PARANETE DIEZEUGMENON

NETE DIEZEUGMENON

TRITE HYPERBOLEON

ENHARMONIC PARANETE HYPERBOLEON

CHROMATIC PARANETE HYPERBOLEON

DIATONIC PARANETE HYPERBOLEON

NETE HYPERBOLEON

pitches in ratios having a larger number and the positions of lower pitches in those with a smaller number, because increasing causes higher sound, and decreasing lower.[42] In that context we showed only the sizes of the ratios, not bothering about the property of highness or lowness. Thus we increased tension and quantity to a higher pitch with larger numbers and decreased tension and quantity to a lower pitch with smaller numbers. But in the present context, where we are measuring the lengths of strings and the sounds, it is necessary to follow the nature of things and to assign larger numbers to longer lengths of string, from which lowness comes into being, and smaller numbers to shorter lengths, from which highness of pitch is born.[43]

Let AB represent a string under tension; let the rule that is to be divided according to the proposed partitions be equal to this string, so that when this rule is placed beside the string, the same divisions which we had marked previously on the rule might be marked on the length of the string. As we make the divisions in this way, it is as though we were partitioning the string itself rather than the rule.

Divide AB into four parts with three points: C, D, and E. Therefore the total, AB, will be the duple of DB and AD, and AD and DB will each be duples of AC, CD, DE, and EB. Thus AB will be the lowest (the proslambanomenos), and DB the mese, for it is half the total length, and as AB is double the length of DB, DB is twice as high as AB. For, as was discussed above, the relationship of length and pitch is always reversed; to the degree that a string is higher, it will be shorter. Thus, EB will be the nete hyperboleon; since EB is half the quantity of DB, it is twice as high. Moreover, since EB is a fourth part of the space AB, it will be four times higher[44] than AB. Therefore, as has been discussed, the nete hyperboleon is twice as high as the mese, whereas the mese is twice as high as the proslambanomenos. The nete hyperboleon is four times higher than the proslambanomenos. Thus the proslambanomenos to the mese will resound a consonance of the diapason, the mese to the nete hyperboleon the dia-

42. The linguistic parallelism of the Latin, which links higher pitches (*intendentes*) with increasing (*intensio*) tension and quantity, lower pitches (*remittentes*) with decreasing (*remissio*) tension and quantity is impossible to duplicate in English. Concerning *intendo* and *remitto* and the Pythagorean notion of pitch, see book 1, n. 46; book 3, nn. 10 and 18.

43. Concerning the Neoplatonic background of this discussion of quantity, length, and pitch, see Theon of Smyrna *Expositio* 2.13 bis (Dupuis ed., pp. 104–07). This passage links Boethius's monochord division, indirectly at least, with the tradition of Plato's *Timaeus* as developed in the Neoplatonic schools.

44. Boethius here introduces a new feature without warning, for he has nowhere discussed one pitch as being *x* number of times higher or lower than another; nor does he ever use such language again. In that the length of string AB is four times as long as EB, then, assuming that the tension remains the same, the frequency of EB will be four times that of AB. While this principle is valid for lengths of strings, it does not apply to weights of hammers or to proportional tension on strings as Nicomachus suggests in *Enchiridion* 6; see book 1, no. 75.

pason, and the proslambanomenos to the nete hyperboleon the bis-diapason.

Again, since AC, CD, DE, and EB are equal parts, AB equals four of these, but CB equals only three; therefore AB is the sesquitertian of CB. Moreover, since CB is made up of three equal parts, but DB is made up of only two, CB is the sesquialter of DB. Furthermore, since CB is made up of three equal parts, with EB as one of these, CB is the triple of EB. Therefore, CB will be the diatonic lichanos hypaton, and the proslambanomenos will sound a consonance of the diatessaron with the diatonic lichanos hypaton. The same diatonic lichanos hypaton will sound a consonance of the diapente with the mese, and the same diatonic lichanos will sound a diapason-plus-diapente with the nete hyperboleon.

If, on the other hand, I subtract a ninth part from the whole AB, which is AF, the other eight parts are FB; thus FB is the hypate hypaton, to which AB, the proslambanomenos, holds a sesquioctave ratio, or, in music, a tone [Fig. D.11].

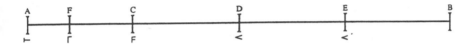

The diagram above [Fig D.11] gives signs below the line, signs from the diagram in which we assigned written symbols to the strings.[45] It would be too lengthy to write out their names.

If we likewise divide AB into three segments, AG will be one third [317] part, and GB will be two of the same. Thus, the proslambanomenos, AB, will sound a consonance of the diapente—established in the sesquialter ratio—in relation to GB, which is the hypate meson. But CB to GB will be a sesquioctave ratio and will hold the tone. This fits the sequence, for the diatonic lichanos hypaton, CB, to the hypate meson, GB, contains a tone. Moreover, the proslambanomenos, AB, to the diatonic lichanos hypaton, CB, holds the consonance of the diatessaron, whereas the proslambanomenos, AB, to the hypate meson, GB, holds the consonance of the diapente. Likewise CB to DB—the diatonic lichanos hypaton to the mese—holds the consonance of the diapente, whereas GB to DB—the hypate meson to the mese—holds the consonance of the diatessaron. The lichanos hypaton, CB, stands at the distance of a tone in relation to the hypate meson, GB.

If I take a fourth part of CB, it will be CK. Thus CB to KB will hold a sesquitertian ratio. But KB will stand at the distance of a sesquioctave from DB. Thus, KB will be the diatonic lichanos meson, and CB—the

45. See Fig. D.10 (and 4.3). Boethius here adds the term *signum* ("sign") to his other notational terms, *nota* ("note"), and *notula* ("written symbol").

diatonic lichanos hypaton—will form the consonance containing the dia-
tesaron with KB—the diatonic meson.

If I take a ninth part of DB, it will make DL for me; so LB will be
the paramese.

If I take a fourth part of DB, it will be DM; so MB will be the nete
synemmenon.

If I take a third part of DB, it will be DN; so NB will be the nete
diezeugmenon.

If KB were divided into two equal parts, it would be KX, and XB
would be the paranete hyperboleon [Fig. D.12[1]].

[If[46] CB is divided into eight parts, and the length and quantity of one
of these parts is added to CB, OB will be made, and OB will be the
parhypate hypaton, standing at the interval of a tone—according to the
sesquioctave ratio—from CB, the diatonic hypaton. The interval between
OB, the parhypate hypaton, and FB, the hypate hypaton, will be that of a
semitone, since two tones, CB:GB and OB:CB, subtracted from a diatessaron, GB:FB, leaves the remainder of a semitone.

If KB is divided into eight parts, and the length and quantity of one
of these parts is added to KB, PB will be made; PB will be the parhypate
meson, standing at the interval of a tone from KB, the diatonic meson,
and at the interval of a semitone from GB, the hypate meson. Again, if
MB is divided into eighths, and the length and quantity of one of these
parts is added to MB, RB will be made; RB will be the trite diezeugmenon,
standing at the interval of a tone from MB, the paranete diezeugmenon—
also called nete synemmenon—and at the interval of a semitone from LB,
the paramese. Finally, if XB is divided into eight parts, and the length and
quantity of one of these parts is added to XB, SB will be made; SB will
be the trite hyperboleon, standing at the interval of a tone from XB, the
paranete hyperboleon, and at the interval of a semitone from NB, the nete

46. The opening sentence of chap. 6 implies that the division of the diatonic genus has
been completed, but the text in its present state leaves out an essential component of the
diatonic division—viz., the diatonic parhypatai and tritai. Consequently, the semitones of all
the tetrachords are missing. The present edition attempts to restore a passage lost in the early
history of the Latin version of the text, or perhaps even in its original Greek version. Unlike
the notes computed up to this point, the second tones of tetrachords cannot be obtained
through simple division by 4, 3, or 9; they must be reckoned by adding an eighth part from
the higher note to create the 9:8 proportion.

diezeugmenon. Thus the division of the diatonic genus [Fig. D.12²] is completed.]

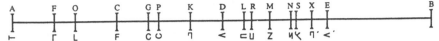

6. *Partition of the monochord of the netai hyperboleon*[47] *through three genera*

Now the diagram of the diatonic genus has been presented in that mode which is first and rather basic, the mode we call Lydian. The modes should not be discussed at this time.[48] In order that a diagram might integrate the three genera and that a specific numerical value may be given in all cases, even the numbers holding the ratios of tones and the diesis, the number that will allow all this to be accomplished has been computed. The largest number, which should be 9,216, is written down at the proslambanomenos, while the smallest number should be 2,304.[49] The ratios of the remaining sounds will be interposed between these two. We proceed from the lowest, and we designate all the notes[50] not only by words, but also by letters placed alongside. But since the partition must be made in three genera and the number of notes exceeds the number of letters, when letters give out, we double these same letters in this manner: when we get to Z we describe the remaining notes as twice A, or AA, and twice B, or BB, and twice C, or CC.

Thus let the first and largest number, which should mark the place of the proslambanomenos, be 9,216, and let the whole measure of the string be extended from this one, which is A, up to the one which is LL.[51] I divide [319]

47. In the titles of chaps. 6, 8, and 9 Boethius names the note forming the highest pitch of the tetrachord but uses the genitive plural, perhaps to express the threefold division that follows. In chaps. 10 and 11 he uses only the terms *meson* and *hypaton*, omitting the names of the top notes.

48. Concerning the modes, see 4.14–17.

49. The same numbers are used for the proslambanomenos and the nete hyperboleon in Aristides Quintilianus *De musica* 3.2. (Winnington-Ingram ed. [Leipzig, 1963], p. 97; and Mathiesen trans. [New Haven, 1983], p. 162). There the mese is assigned to number 4,608, the number that Boethius gives it in the paragraph that follows.

50. From this point on, Boethius repeatedly uses the terms *nervus* and *chorda* to denote a point on a ruler. Obviously a plurality of strings is not found on a monochord. The extension of meaning for these words comes about because the names of strings—connoting functions within the system—designate positions on the ruler. Since these terms denote specific musical functions and are defined by both names and letters, I translate them both as "note" rather than "string." (See above, n. 19, concerning Boethius's use of the terms *nota* and *notula*.)

51. The text is imprecise at this point; the string, in fact, must extend beyond, not merely up to, the note signified by LL if the pitch LL is to have any vibrating length. Since LL becomes the nete hyperboleon, it is equivalent to E of chap. 5. Thus, as in the preceding diagrams, one-fourth of the string must continue past LL.

this A, the proslambanomenos, 9,216, in half at O, so that the whole of A is the duple of O. Likewise, O should be the duple of LL. Point A will thus be the proslambanomenos, O the mese, and LL the nete hyperboleon. Point A will have the number 9,216, O half of that, or 4,608, so that the mese may be united with the proslambanomenos in the consonance of the diapason. LL will be half the mese, so that the proslambanomenos might be a quadruple ratio with the nete hyperboleon and sound the consonance of the bis-diapason with it; it should be 2,304[52] [Fig. D.13].

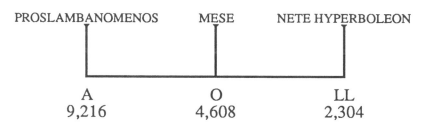

PROSLAMBANOMENOS	MESE	NETE HYPERBOLEON
A	O	LL
9,216	4,608	2,304

If I take an eighth part of 2,304, or 288, and add it to the same, I get 2,592, and this will be KK,[53] 2,592, which is the paranete hyperboleon, standing at the distance of a tone from the nete hyperboleon. Again, I take an eighth part of KK, 2,592, which is 324, and I add it to that of which it is an eighth; it will make 2,916, and I will get FF, the diatonic trite hyperboleon in the diatonic genus, 2,916, standing at the distance of a tone from the diatonic paranete (hyperboleon, but two tones from the nete hyperboleon).[54] This same FF will be the chromatic trite hyperboleon in the

[320]

52. In *Q*, a trace of Boethius's original Greek source is visible in this diagram; for written across the middle of the diagram is the Greek mathematical notation for 9,216, 4,608, and 2,304: ϲΘCIS, ΔXH, and ʙΒTΔ. This notation was not understood by subsequent scribes, so the letters became meaningless. The Greek notation that Friedlein includes as part of this diagram is not found in any of the control manuscripts and obviously does not belong with this second division of the monochord (see above, n. 17).

53. Scribes had major problems with the text of this second, more developed monochord division (chaps. 6–11). The large numbers, the notes with similar titles, and the set of 33 single and double letters presented textual elements that led to many slips of the eye and the hand. But the musical, arithmetic, and geometric elements develop so logically and consistently in this sequence of propositions that the corrupted elements can easily be restored. A significant degree of restoration took place in the manuscript traditions of the tenth to the fifteenth centuries. This translation will provide mathematical and musical consistency in these chapters, and textual discrepancies will be noted.

All the control manuscripts signify the diatonic paranete hyperboleon with the letters NN rather than KK. Friedlein [319.18] adopted KK, although all of his sources gave NN. Since the last note of the monochord (the nete hyperboleon) is LL, it is unlikely that the paranete hyperboleon would have been assigned a letter beyond LL, and KK fits the sequence of letters and notes. The application of letters is very unstable in the textual and diagrammatic tradition of these chapters (see Appendix 3), and I follow Friedlein here.

54. The text at Friedlein 320.4–6 is corrupt, and the words *hyperboleon diatonos, ditonum vero ab ea, quae est nete* should not be there. The text in its proper form—*tonum*

chromatic genus, but the enharmonic paranete hyperboleon in the enharmonic genus. One will more easily recognize why this happens once we have described the first three tetrachords of the three genera beginning from the nete hyperboleon.

Since the subtraction of two sesquioctaves from a sesquitertian ratio leaves me with a minor semitone, I take a third of LL (the nete hyperboleon); this is 768. I add this to the same and make for myself 3,072, which is DD, the nete diezeugmenon, containing a minor semitone with the trite hyperboleon. Since the nete diezeugmenon holds the consonance of a diatessaron in relation to the nete hyperboleon, whereas the trite hyperboleon stands at the distance of two tones from the nete hyperboleon, that which remains between the nete diezeugmenon and the trite hyperboleon is the interval of a minor semitone.

Now that we have carried to completion the hyperboleon tetrachord in the diatonic genus, the tetrachords of the enharmonic and chromatic genera are to be added in this manner. Since the paranete hyperboleon stands at the distance of a tone from the nete hyperboleon in the diatonic genus, but at the distance of three semitones in the chromatic and two tones in the enharmonic, if we take this distance—between the paranete hyperboleon and the nete hyperboleon of the diatonic genus—and add half of it to the paranete hyperboleon of the diatonic genus, we will get a [321] number standing at a distance of three semitones from the nete hyperboleon. This will be the paranete hyperboleon in the chromatic genus. Thus I subtract 2,304, the nete hyperboleon, from 2,592, the paranete hyperboleon of the diatonic genus, and obtain a remainder of 288; I divide this by 2, which is 144; I add this to the same 2,592 and get 2,736, HH.[55] This will be the chromatic paranete hyperboleon.

Since the trite hyperboleon, either diatonic or chromatic, stands at the distance of two tones from the nete hyperboleon, and since in the enharmonic genus the paranete hyperboleon is two tones from the nete hyperboleon, the paranete hyperboleon in the enharmonic genus will be the same as the trite hyperboleon in the diatonic and chromatic; it is notated by

---

quidem distans ab ea quae est paranete hyperboleon—is found in M (before glosses), Q, and S. The original corruption is probably that found in I and K, and also R and T before they were corrected: tonum quidem distans ab ea quae est nete hyperboleon. The mistake was leaving the prefix para off nete, for the trite (the note in question) is obviously one tone from the paranete, but two tones from the nete. R and T correct the mistake by adding para above the line. The beginning of the corruption printed in Friedlein is seen in P and V, here given from V: tonum quidem distans ab ea quae est paranete hyperboleon. di tonum vero ab ea quae est nete hiperboleon [di tonum corr ex diatonum]. Further source of the corruption is seen in the glosses of M: a first glossing hand added diatonos above paranete, thus clarifying the genus, then a second glossing hand has added above diatonos: ditono ab ea quae est nete iperboleon.

55. The letters HH are not found in any of the control manuscripts, and may not have been part of the textual tradition during the ninth century. Friedlein [321.8] is here following only one manuscript: Munich, Bayerische Staatsbibliothek, Clm 18,480.

GG.[56] But since the trite hyperboleon of the diatonic and chromatic genera stands a minor semitone from the nete diezeugmenon, and since a tetrachord of the enharmonic genus consists of two whole tones and a diesis plus a diesis, both of which are half the interval of a minor semitone, I take this distance that lies between the nete diezeugmenon and the enharmonic paranete hyperboleon. Since the nete diezeugmenon is 3,072 and the enharmonic paranete hyperboleon is 2,916, the distance between them [322] is 156. I take half of this, which is 78, and add it to 2,916, which makes 2,994. This is EE, the enharmonic trite hyperboleon.

Thus the hyperboleon tetrachord has been described according to the three genera, the scheme of which we have supplied below[57] [Fig. D.14].

7. Rationale of the diagram set out above

By such reasoning we have described three tetrachords. Each tetrachord, of course, sounds a consonance of the diatessaron. Thus, the nete

56. In two notes of the monochord division—the paranete hyperboleon and the lichanos hypaton, both of the enharmonic genus—the letters designating the point have been lost in both the text and the diagrams. Scribes of subsequent generations have altered the text and the diagrams to remedy this omission. None of the control manuscripts designate this note as GG; nor do the letters GG appear in the diagrams. In three manuscripts—Paris, Bibliothèque nationale, lat. 17,872; St. Gall, Kantonsbibliothek (Vidiana), 296; and New York, Columbia University, Plimpton 45—the words *GG literis insignita* are added to the text at this point, and this addition forms the basis of the present emendation. A number of manuscripts add GG in Fig. D.14 to designate the nete hyperboleon in the enharmonic genus (e.g., London, British Library, Arundel 77; Paris, Bibliothèque nationale, lat. 7,202, lat. 10,275, lat. 17,872; Munich, Bayerische Staatsbibliothek, Clm 6,361, Clm 14,272; Vienna, Nationalbibliothek, Cpv 2,269; and Prague, Státní knihovna, CSR XIX.C.26).

57. This diagram and the four that follow include six components: a grid representing the ruler of the monochord, the names of the notes, indications of genera, numbers representing quantitative values for each note, letters for each note, and designations of each interval. For comments on this series of diagrams and a list of abbreviations used, see Appendix 3.

hyperboleon and the nete diezeugmenon hold a consonance of the diatessaron in the three genera—diatonic, chromatic, and enharmonic. The consonance of the diatessaron consists of two tones and a minor semitone. In [323] the tetrachords written out above, the division took place as follows: in the diatonic genus, which is first, the paranete hyperboleon, 2,592, holds the distance of a tone in relation to the nete hyperboleon, 2,304. We designate this with the written symbol *T*. Likewise the trite hyperboleon of the diatonic genus, 2,916, holds the difference of a tone in relation to the paranete hyperboleon of the diatonic genus, 2,592, which we similarly designate by the written symbol *T*. But the nete diezeugmenon to the trite hyperboleon, 3,072 to 2,916, is a semitone, which we designate with the written symbol *s*. The total distance between the nete diezeugmenon and the nete hyperboleon is two tones and a semitone.

But in the chromatic genus, the same two tones and a semitone are divided according to the following scheme. The second genus, the chromatic, was described in this manner. The chromatic paranete hyperboleon, 2,736, compared to the nete hyperboleon, 2,304, holds the interval of the paranete hyperboleon of the diatonic genus to the nete hyperboleon, which is a tone—that is, two semitones, one major and one minor, plus half the space between the paranete hyperboleon of the diatonic and the nete hyperboleon. That which is a half-tone, but not a true half, was made in that way because, as amply demonstrated above, a tone cannot be divided into two equal parts. We signified this space of three semitones—a tone and a semitone—in this manner: *sss*.

Again, the chromatic paranete hyperboleon to the trite hyperboleon [324] retains a part of a tone, a semitone, that was the remainder from the two tones which were contained between the diatonic trite hyperboleon and the nete hyperboleon. Indeed, if four semitones are subtracted from the whole tetrachord, the remainder is the interval of the semitone which is contained between the nete diezeugmenon and the trite hyperboleon. Therefore, this tetrachord consists of two tones and a semitone divided into one interval of three semitones and two intervals each of which is a semitone.[58] These three intervals are held together by four notes.

It is quite easy to understand this tetrachord in the enharmonic genus. From the nete hyperboleon, 2,304, to the enharmonic paranete hyperboleon, 2,916, is the interval of two whole tones, which we have signified by *TT*. Thus there remains from this entire tetrachord—from two tones and

58. The structure of the chromatic genus is derived from the diatonic genus, and no independent rationale for the chromatic or the enharmonic genus is found in the first four books of Boethius's text. The chromatic paranete is inserted by using an arithmetic mean, computed by dividing the previous tone of the diatonic genus (2,592:2,304) in half and adding that half to the original tone. The procedure follows exactly that prescribed in 2.17 and *Arith.* 2.50. The resulting ratios are 19:16 for the interval of three semitones, 81:76 for the chromatic semitone, and 256:243 for the semitone borrowed from the diatonic genus.

a semitone—one semitone, which is contained between the nete diezeug-menon and the enharmonic paranete hyperboleon. We have divided this into two dieses by means of a note inserted in the middle, the enharmonic trite hyperboleon.[59] We signify the interval of a diesis with the sign δ.

Thus the tetrachord of the hyperboleon has been described for us. Having completed this, we should move on to the tetrachord of the die-zeugmenon. Discussions of the other tetrachords will not be drawn out to such length, since the present description can serve as an example for the others.

8. *Partition of the monochord of the netai diezeugmenon in the three genera*

[325]   If I take half of the nete diezeugmenon, 3,072, I get 1,536, and if I add this to the same, I get 4,608, the mese, which we have designated by the letter O. But if I take a third part of this same nete diezeugmenon, DD, or 3,072, I get 1,024. This added to the same makes 4,096, which is called the paramese and is signified by the letter X. Since the nete die-zeugmenon, 3,072, to the mese, 4,608, consists of a sesquialter comparison, it will unite in the consonance of the diapente. Moreover, the same nete diezeugmenon, 3,072, to the paramese, 4,096, which is related to it by the sesquitertian ratio, holds the consonance of the diatessaron. Thus if I take an eighth part of the nete diezeugmenon, 3,072, I get 384; I add this to the same, and get 3,456. This is the diatonic paranete diezeugmenon, notated with the letters CC, holding a tone in relation to the nete diezeugmenon. If I likewise take an eighth part of 3,456, which is 432, and add it to the same, I get 3,888. This is Y, the diatonic trite diezeugmenon. Now since the nete diezeugmenon held a sesquitertian ratio in relation to the par-amese, whereas the diatonic trite diezeugmenon is distant from the nete diezeugmenon by two tones, a minor semitone will be contained between the trite diezeugmenon and the paramese. Thus, the diatonic genus has also been completed in this tetrachord and pentachord in such a way that the tetrachord from the nete diezeugmenon to the paramese is a consonance
[326] of the diatessaron, whereas the pentachord from the nete diezeugmenon to the mese is the consonance of a diapente.

We will integrate the enharmonic and chromatic genera above by the

59. The structure of the enharmonic genus is likewise derived from the diatonic genus. The large interval of two tones is taken directly from the diatonic genus, and the two dieses are created by dividing the remaining semitone in half—i.e., by employing an arithmetic mean. Boethius's division of the chromatic and enharmonic genera has been criticized by Gushee, "Questions," p. 380, and Pizzani, "Fonti," pp. 117–18, who argue that Boethius's computations depart from mathematical consistency. For a clear analysis of Boethius's reck-oning, see André Barbera, "Arithmetic and Geometric Divisions of the Tetrachord," *Journal of Music Theory* 21 (1977): 308–09. For a defense of Boethius's method, see Bower, "Sources," pp. 24–26.

following rationale. I take the distance between the nete and the paranete diezeugmenon of the diatonic—3,456 and 3,072—which is 384. This I divide in half, obtaining 192. If I take this and add it to the diatonic paranete diezeugmenon, 3,456, I get 3,648. This is the chromatic paranete diezeugmenon, denoted by the double letters BB. This stands at a distance of a tone-plus-semitone—that is, three semitones—from the nete diezeugmenon. This note, the chromatic paranete diezeugmenon, holds a semitone in relation to the trite diezeugmenon, 3,888, which was diatonic a short while ago but is now chromatic; the semitone is the remainder from the tone—between the diatonic paranete diezeugmenon and the diatonic trite diezeugmenon—that was divided. There is still another semitone in this tetrachord left between the chromatic trite diezeugmenon and the paramese, and this semitone is the remainder from the consonance of the diatessaron between the nete diezeugmenon and the paramese after two tones have been subtracted; these two tones were contained between the nete diezeugmenon and the chromatic trite diezeugmenon.

Now the string that is the diatonic trite diezeugmenon in the diatonic genus, and the chromatic trite diezeugmenon in the chromatic genus is called the enharmonic paranete diezeugmenon in the enharmonic genus; it stands at a distance of two integral tones from the nete diezeugmenon and is notated AA. No note is placed between the nete diezeugmenon and the enharmonic paranete diezeugmenon, and for that reason AA is denoted with the word "paranete." But the semitone that lies between the enharmonic paranete diezeugmenon and the paramese (between AA and X), we divide according to the following rationale so as to make two dieses. I take [327] the difference between the enharmonic paranete diezeugmenon and the paramese, 3,888 and 4,096; this is 208. I divide this, obtaining 104. I add this to 3,888, which makes 3,992. This is the enharmonic trite diezeugmenon, designated by the letter Z.

I have added below the diagram of this tetrachord in the three genera. I have included the hyperboleon tetrachord discussed above, so that there is one diagram for both tetrachords, and an outline brought together from the whole disposition thus gradually begins to take shape [Fig. D.15, p. 138].

9. *Division of the monochord of the netai synemmenon through the three genera*

The above diagram of the three genera shows the arrangement of two tetrachords which are conjunct with each other but disjunct from the mese. Now we are coming to that tetrachord called "synemmenon," that which is joined to the mese.

Since we have already established that there is a consonance of the diapente between the nete diezeugmenon and the mese and, moreover, that a diapente consists of three tones and a semitone, this means that there

M	pM	DTD	DpND	ND	DTH	DpNH	NH	
O	X	Y	CC	DD	FF	KK	LL	*Diatonic*
T	*s*	*T*	*T*		*s*	*T*	*T*	
4,608	4,096	3,888	3,456		3,072	2,916	2,592	NH 2,304
	pM	CTD BB	CpND		CTH HH	CpNH		*Chromatic*
T	*s*	*s*	*sss*		*s*	*sss*		
4,608	4,096	3,888	3,648		3,072	2,916	2,736	NH 2,304
	Pm Z AA	EpND			ND EE GG	EpNH		*Enharmonic*
T	*ET* ǝ ǝ	*TT*			*ET* ǝ ǝ	*TT*		
4,608	3,992	3,888			3,072	2,994 2,916		2,304

are three tones in this pentachord: one between the nete diezeugmenon and the diatonic paranete diezeugmenon, a second between the diatonic paranete diezeugmenon and the diatonic trite diezeugmenon, and a third between the paramese and the mese. There remains a semitone between the diatonic trite diezeugmenon and the paramese. Now the tetrachord between the nete diezeugmenon and the paramese is disjunct from the mese by one tone, that between the paramese and the mese. If we subtract one tone from the pentachord between the nete diezeugmenon and the mese—the tone between the nete diezeugmenon and the diatonic paranete diezeugmenon—then we can join this other tetrachord to the mese, so that the synemmenon—that is, conjunct—tetrachord might be made. [328]

Since the diatonic paranete diezeugmenon, CC, is the number 3,456, a third part of this added to the same number will make the mese. Thus, this number notated by the letters CC in the diezeugmenon tetrachord is separated from the nete diezeugmenon by a tone in the diatonic genus, and it is called the diatonic paranete diezeugmenon; but in the synemmenon tetrachord—the conjunct tetrachord—this partition should be set as the nete synemmenon in all three genera and notated by the letter V.[60] An eighth part of this number should be taken, which is 432, and added[61] to the same; this makes 3,888, which is the diatonic paranete synemmenon, signified by the letter T.[62] An eighth part is again taken, now of the diatonic paranete diezeugmenon, 3,888, which makes 486; if this amount is added to that of which it is an eighth part, it makes 4,374, which is the diatonic trite synemmenon—that is, Q. But since the nete synemmenon to the mese (3,456 to 4,608) holds a sesquitertian ratio—that is, a diatessaron—whereas the trite synemmenon to the nete synemmenon (4,374 to 3,456) holds the ratio of two tones, the ratio of a semitone remains between the diatonic trite synemmenon and the mese, and this tetrachord is conjunct with the mese; for this reason it is called "continuous and conjunct." The [329] ratio of the diatonic genus has been completed.

60. The form of the letter V confused early scribes, and the letter is often transmitted in texts and diagrams as Y rather than V. It appears as Y in *R, S, T,* and *V.*

61. Friedlein 328.14: *adnotatur* should read *apponatur.*

62. The text is quite corrupt in these lines (Friedlein 328.14–17). The oldest textual tradition does not support Friedlein's reading. The reading of *P* seems most acceptable, but even it shows one correction: *fient iii.dccclxxxviii. ea est paranete sinemenon diatonos. quae T littera insignitur. Rursus paranetes synemmenon diatoni [diatoni ex diatonos] id est iii.dccclxxxviii. pars sumatur octava. ea quae est cccclxxxvi.* (Approximately the same reading is given in *M* after a marginal addition.) The version of *P* serves as the basis for this translation.

Three of the control manuscripts (*I, K,* and *T*) transmit the text in a very fragmentary version: *fient iii.dccclxxxviii. pars sumatur octava ea quae est cccclxxxvi.* This version of the text persists in the manuscript tradition of the treatise for the next four centuries. Other readings of the passage appear to be attempts to amend the corrupt version. *Q* reads: *fient iii.dccclxxxviii. quae est paranete synemmenon. huiusque pars sumatur octava. id est T. ea quae est cccclxxxvi. [quae . . . symmenon* added in margin]. This version, with minor variants and emendations, is also found in *R, S,* and *V.*

The division of the chromatic genus is as follows. I take the difference between the nete synemmenon and the diatonic paranete synemmenon—3,888 and 3,456—which is 432. I divide this in order to make the semitone and get 216; this I add to 3,888, so as to obtain the interval of three semitones, which is thus 4,104. This is the chromatic paranete synemmenon, to which the letter S is given. Thus, from the chromatic paranete synemmenon to the trite synemmenon, formerly diatonic but now chromatic, there is a semitone. Another semitone is found between the chromatic synemmenon and the mese.

Since there are two tones from the nete synemmenon to the diatonic or chromatic trite synemmenon, the note that is the trite synemmenon in the diatonic and chromatic genera is the enharmonic paranete synemmenon in the enharmonic genus; it holds the sum of 4,374 and is designated R. From this to the mese is a semitone. I divide this into two dieses in this manner. I take the difference between the enharmonic paranete synemmenon and the mese—4,608 and 4,374—which is 234. I divide this and get 117. This I add to the enharmonic paranete synemmenon, 4,374, making 4,491. Let this be signified by the letter P, and let it be the enharmonic trite synemmenon. The semitone contained between the enharmonic paranete synemmenon and the mese—between 4,608 and 4,374—is divided by [330] the enharmonic trite synemmenon, 4,491. Thus the scheme of this tetrachord, too, has been explained. But now a diagram [Fig. D.16, p. 141] should be set forth, combined with the others—that is, with the hyperboleon and the diezeugmenon tetrachords—so that little by little a regular progression of the disposition is taking place.

10. *Partition of the monochord of the meson through the three genera*

After all that has been said, I do not think it necessary to spend too much time on the other tetrachords, for the remaining tetrachords—the meson and the hypaton—should be integrated according to the example of these.

First we will describe the meson tetrachord of the diatonic genus in this sequence: I take a third part of the mese, designated O, 4,608 which makes 1,536. I join this to O, and the result is 6,144. This is H, the hypate meson, which makes a consonance of the diatessaron with the mese. This is divided into two tones and a semitone as follows. I take an eighth part of the mese, 4,608, which is 576. I add this to the same, making 5,184. This is the diatonic lichanos meson—that is, M. An eighth part of M is likewise taken; that is 648. I add this to the same, making 5,832. Let this be I, the diatonic parhypate meson, which stands a tone away from the diatonic lichanos meson, but two tones away from the mese. Thus there

Diatonic
Chromatic
Enharmonic

M	DTS		DpNS		NS	Diatonic
O	Q	T	T	T	V	3,456
s		4,374		3,888		
M	CTS	S	CpNS			Chromatic
s	s	4,374	4,104			3,456 NS
M	ET	P R	EpNS			Enharmonic
a	a	4,491	4,374		TT	3,456 NS

M	X pM	Y DTD	CC DpND	Diatonic
T	s	T	T	3,456
4,608		4,096	3,888	
M	pM	CTD BB	CpND	Chromatic sss
T	s	s		3,648
4,608		4,096	3,888	
M	Pm Z AA	ET EpND	Enharmonic TT
T	a	a		3,888
4,608		3,992	4,096	3,072 TT

Diatonic

ND	DTH		DpNH		NH	Diatonic
DD	FF	T	KK	T	LL	2,304
s		3,072 2,916		2,592		NH
	CTH HH	CpNH			Chromatic sss
ND	s	3,072 2,916	2,736			2,304 NH
ND ET GG	EpNH				Enharmonic
EE	a	a	2,994 2,916	TT	2,304
		3,072			

remains a semitone situated between the diatonic hypate meson and the diatonic parhypate meson—that is, between 6,144 and 5,832.

[331]   The tetrachord of the mese and the hypate meson is further divided in the chromatic genus according to the following rationale. I take the difference between the mese and the diatonic lichanos meson—4,608 to 5,184—which is 576. I divide this in half, and get 288; I add the same to the larger number, 5,184, and get 5,472, designated N, the chromatic lichanos meson. Thus two semitones remain, one between the chromatic lichanos meson and the chromatic parhypate meson—between 5,472 and 5,832—and the other between the chromatic parhypate meson and the hypate meson—between 5,832 and 6,144.

We divide the enharmonic genus as follows. Since the diatonic parhypate meson, or that which was the chromatic parhypate meson, stood at a distance of two tones from the mese and held the number 5,832, this will be the enharmonic lichanos meson in the enharmonic genus, designated by the letter L, nonetheless holding two tones in relation to the mese. We divide the semitone that remains between the enharmonic lichanos meson and the hypate meson—between 5,832 and 6,144—into two dieses in this manner. I take the difference between 5,832 and 6,144; this is 312. I divide this in half, obtaining 156. I add this to 5,832; this makes 5,988. Let this be K, the enharmonic parhypate meson. Thus there are two dieses: between the enharmonic lichanos meson and the enharmonic parhypate meson—between 5,832 and 5,988—and between the enharmonic parhypate meson and the hypate meson—between 5,988 and 6,144.

[332]   Thus the tetrachord of the meson has been divided, which should be placed in a diagram so that it can be brought together with the tetrachords described above [Fig. D.17, p. 143].

11. *The partition of the monochord of the hypaton through the three genera, and a diagram of the total disposition*

Now the hypaton tetrachord must be divided through the three genera. I take a half part of the hypate meson, 6,144, which makes 3,072. If I add this to the same, I get 9,216, which is the proslambanomenos, the note holding the consonance of the diapente in relation to the hypate meson. If I take a third part of the same hypate meson, which is 2,048, and add it to the same, I get 8,192, and this is B, the hypate hypaton. Thus, the hypate meson to the proslambanomenos is a consonance of the diapente, whereas the hypate meson to the hypate hypaton is a diatessaron.

I take an eighth part from the hypate meson, 6,144, which is 768. If this is added to the same, it makes 6,912, which is E, the diatonic lichanos hypaton, holding the ratio of a tone in relation to the hypate meson. Likewise, an eighth part of 6,912 should be taken—that is, 864. This should be joined to the same, making 7,776, which is C, the diatonic parhypate hy-

HM · DpHM · DLM · M · DTS · DpNS · NS

H · I · M · O · Q · S · T · V

Diatonic · *Diatonic*

3,456 NS

T · *T* · *T* · s · *T* · *T*

6,144 · 5,832 · 5,184 · 4,608 · 4,491 · 4,374 · 3,888

CpHM · CLM · M · CTS · CpNS

N · s · M · S · *Chromatic*

3,456 NS

s · sss · s · s · sss

6,144 · 5,832 · 5,184 · 4,608 · 4,374 · 4,374 · 4,104

Chromatic

EpHM · ELM · M · ET · P · R · EpNS

K · L · ∂ · ∂ · *Enharmonic*

∂ · ∂ · 3,456 NS

M · X · pM · Y · DTD · CC · DpND

T · *T* · s · s · *T* · *T*

5,988 · 5,832 · 4,608 · 4,096 · 3,888 · 3,456

Enharmonic

ND · DTH · DpNH · NH

DD · FF · KK · LL

Diatonic

2,304 NH

T · s · *T* · *T*

3,072 · 3,072 · 2,916 · 2,592 · 2,304

CpND · CTH · CpNH

BB · HH

Chromatic

2,304 NH

sss · s · sss

3,648 · 3,072 · 2,916 · 2,916 · 2,736

EpND · ET · EE · GG · EpNH

Pm · Z · AA · ND · ∂

∂ · ∂ · *Enharmonic*

2,304

TT · *TT* · *TT* · *TT*

4,608 · 4,096 · 3,992 · 3,888 · 3,072 · 2,994 · 2,916

	Pros	HH	DpHH	DLH	HM	DpHM	DLM
	A	B	C	E	H	I	M
Diatonic	T	s	T	T	s	T	T
	9,216	8,192	7,776	6,912	6,144	5,832	5,184
	Pros	IIII	CpHH	CLH		CpHM	CLM
			F			N	
Chromatic	T	s	s	sss	s	s	sss	4,608
	9,216	8,192	7,776	7,296	6,144	5,832	
	Pros	HH D	H G ELH		EpH K	ELM L	
Enharmonic	T	ə	ə	TT	ə	ə	TT
	9,216	8,192	7,984	7,776	5,988	5,832	

[333]

paton, which maintains the distance of a tone in relation to the diatonic lichanos hypaton, the distance of two tones in relation to the hypate meson. Thus, a semitone remains between the diatonic parhypate hypaton and the hypate hypaton—between 7,776 and 8,192. And such is the tetrachord of the hypaton in the diatonic genus.

We divide the chromatic genus according to the following scheme. I take the difference between the hypate meson and the diatonic lichanos hypaton—between 6,144 and 6,912. That difference is 768. I divide this in half, so as to make two semitones; it makes 384. I add this to 6,912 to obtain the interval of three semitones; thus I get 7,296. This is F, the chromatic lichanos hypaton, standing at a distance of three semitones from the hypate meson. Thus, two semitones remain, one between the chromatic lichanos hypaton and the chromatic parhypate hypaton—between 7,296 and 7,776—and the other between the chromatic parhypate hypaton and the hypate hypaton—between 7,776 and 8,192.

The enharmonic genus remains, the division of which corresponds to the example above. Since the parhypate hypaton, diatonic or chromatic, represented by the number 7,776, stands at the distance of two tones from the hypate meson, the same partition will be the enharmonic lichanos hypaton—which should stand at the interval of two whole tones from the hypate meson—in the enharmonic genus. It is designated by the letter G.[63]

63. No manuscript designates the lichanos hypaton of the enharmonic genus as G in the

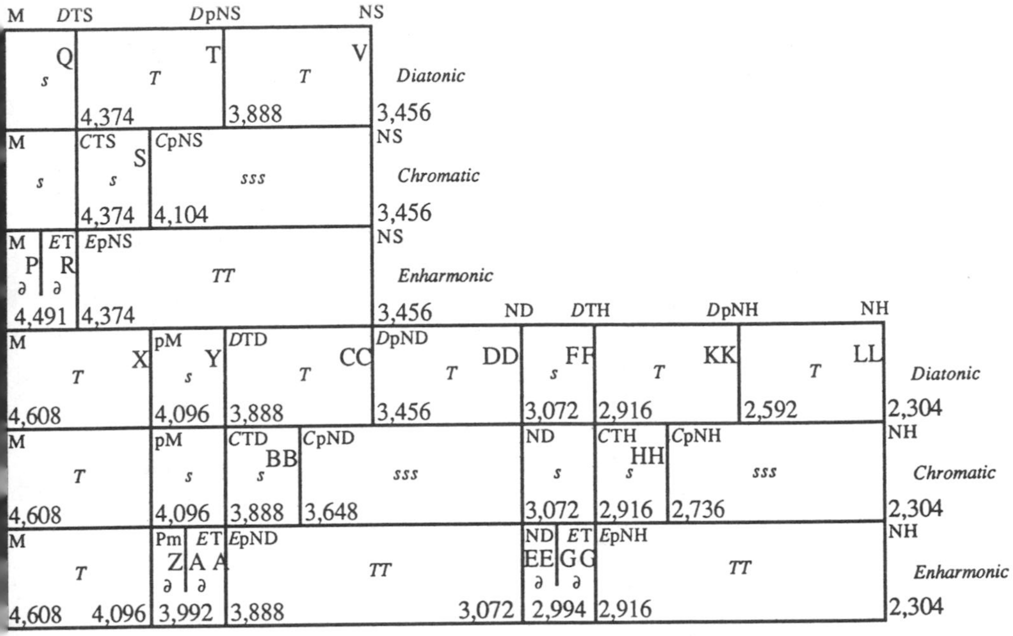
M DTS DpNS NS
Q T V
s T T
Diatonic
4,374 3,888 3,456
M CTS CpNS NS
S
s s sss
Chromatic
4,374 4,104 3,456
M ET EpNS NS
P R
∂ ∂
TT
Enharmonic
4,491 4,374 3,456
ND DTH DpNH NH
M pM DTD DpND
X Y CC DD FF KK LL
T s T T s T T
Diatonic
4,608 4,096 3,888 3,456 3,072 2,916 2,592 2,304
M pM CTD CpND ND CTH CpNH NH
BB HH
T s s sss s s sss
Chromatic
4,608 4,096 3,888 3,648 3,072 2,916 2,736 2,304
M Pm ET EpND ND ET EpNH NH
Z A A EE G G
T ∂ ∂ TT ∂ ∂ TT
Enharmonic
4,608 4,096 3,992 3,888 3,072 2,994 2,916 2,304

Thus a semitone remains from the consonance of the diatessaron; this semitone is between the enharmonic lichanos hypaton and the hypate hypaton—between 7,776 and 8,192. We divide this into two dieses in this manner. I take the difference between the enharmonic lichanos hypaton and the hypate hypaton—between 8,192 and 7,776; this is 416. I take half of this, which is 208 and add it to 7,776, thereby making 7,984, which is D, the enharmonic parhypate hypaton. Thus there are two dieses, one that is [334]
between[64] the enharmonic lichanos hypaton and the enharmonic parhypate hypaton—between 7,776 and 7,984—and the other between the enharmonic parhypate hypaton and the hypate hypaton—between 7,984 and 8,192. The final tone is contained between the hypaton and the proslambanomenos—between 9,216 and 8,192.

Thus the tetrachord of the hypaton has been divided according to the three genera, the diatonic, the chromatic, and the enharmonic. If this is added to the above tetrachords, the hyperboleon, the diezeugmenon, the synemmenon, and the meson, it will produce the complete and perfect diagram of the monochord rule divided through all genera and tetrachords [Fig. D.18, pp. 144–45].

---

text, but the following manuscripts are among those which do so in the diagram: Milan, Biblioteca Ambrosiana, Q.9 supp.; Munich, Bayerische Staatsbibliothek, Clm 6,361, Clm 14,272; Venice, Biblioteca Marciana, Z.333 (1549); Vienna, Nationalbibliothek, Cpv 51.

64. Friedlein 334.1: *quae inter lichanon* should read *quae est inter lichanon.*

12. *Rationale of the diagram set out above*

In the above figure, the proslambanomenos to the mese holds the consonance of the diapason, as does the mese to the nete hyperboleon. The proslambanomenos to the nete hyperboleon, however, holds the bis-diapason. The hypate hypaton to the hypate meson, the hypate meson to the mese, the mese to the nete synemmenon, the paramese to the nete diezeugmenon, and the nete diezeugmenon to the nete hyperboleon all preserve the consonance of the diatessaron, as do others situated so that we can account for a complete tetrachord within these consonances.

So that the complete succession of notes according to the three genera might be considered very thoroughly in this figure, notice that there are only five tetrachords: first and lowest, the hypaton, of which the hypate hypaton is the first note and the hypate meson the last; second, the meson, of which the hypate meson is the first note and the mese the last; third, the synemmenon, of which the mese is the first note and the nete synemmenon the last; fourth, the diezeugmenon, of which the first note is the paramese and the last is the nete diezeugmenon; and fifth, the hyperboleon, the first note of which is the nete diezeugmenon, and this tetrachord is terminated in the final nete hyperboleon.

[335]

13. *Concerning fixed and movable pitches*

Of all these pitches, some sound completely fixed, some completely movable, whereas others sound neither completely fixed nor completely movable.[65]

Since the following notes remain the same in all three genera, they are completely fixed: the proslambanomenos, the hypate hypaton, the hypate meson, the mese, the nete synemmenon, the paramese, the nete diezeugmenon, and the nete hyperboleon. These notes, which change according to neither place nor name, should frame a pentachord—for example, from the proslambanomenos to the hypate meson or from the mese to the nete diezeugmenon—or a tetrachord—for example, from the hypate hypaton to the hypate meson or from the hypate meson to the mese.

Those are movable which change according to individual genera, like the following: the paranete and lichanos of the diatonic and chromatic, the trite and parhypate of the enharmonic. For that which is at one time the diatonic paranete hyperboleon is at another the chromatic paranete hyperboleon and at another the enharmonic trite. The diatonic and chromatic

---

65. This classification of notes relates to that found in 1.27, a passage which specifically anticipates the present chapter. In the mainstream of Greek theory, notes are classified as either fixed or movable, and no intermediate state is given (see, e.g., Cleonides *Eisagoge* [JanS. 183–84] and Ptolemy *Harmonica* 2.5.53). The classification given here is identical with Nicomachus *Enchiridion* 12 (JanS. 263.12–15) and is closely related to the possibility of only 28 notes developed throughout the first 4 books of Boethius's treatise (see book 1, n. 122).

paranete diezeugmenon are also different, and the enharmonic trite diezeugmenon is not the same as those which are trite in the other genera.
The diatonic and chromatic paranete synemmenon are not the same, and
the enharmonic trite synemmenon is different from those which are trite
in the remaining genera. Furthermore, the diatonic lichanos meson and the [336]
chromatic lichanos meson are different, and the enharmonic parhypate meson is found to be similar to no parhypate of the other genera. The diatonic
lichanos hypaton and the chromatic lichanos hypaton do not preserve the
same places and numbers, and the enharmonic parhypate hypaton is found
dissimilar to the parhypate of the other genera.

The notes that are neither completely fixed nor completely movable
are those which remain the same in two genera—the diatonic and the
chromatic—but are made different in the enharmonic. This may be explained as follows. The diatonic trite hyperboleon and the chromatic trite
hyperboleon in the above diagram were designated by the same number,
2,916; but if we examine the enharmonic genus, we discover a different
trite, 2,994. Thus, the pitch that was common to two genera has been
changed in the third. The same is valid for the diezeugmenon tetrachord,
for the diatonic and chromatic trite diezeugmenon are one and sound the
same, but the enharmonic trite diezeugmenon is different from these. The
same applies to the synemmenon tetrachord; the diatonic and chromatic
trite synemmenon are the same, but the enharmonic trite synemmenon is
different. Moreover, the diatonic parhypate meson and the chromatic parhypate meson are notated in the same way, but in the enharmonic genus—
just as with the above trite—the parhypate is found in close proximity to
the hypate meson, and its function and acuteness of sound are different
from the other parhypatae. Furthermore, the diatonic parhypate hypaton
is the same as the chromatic parhypate hypaton, but this is not the same
if one looks in the enharmonic genus.

So that the pitches which are not completely movable may become
clearer, let us return to the hyperboleon tetrachord. In this tetrachord the [337]
trite hyperboleon of the diatonic and chromatic genera is altered in the
enharmonic genus and becomes the paranete; likewise the one named trite
diezeugmenon in either the diatonic or the chromatic genus is named paranete in the enharmonic; the trite synemmenon in the chromatic and diatonic
changes to the paranete in the enharmonic; the note considered the parhypate meson in the chromatic and the diatonic is discovered to be the
lichanos meson in the enharmonic; the one named parhypate hypaton in
the diatonic or the chromatic is named the lichanos hypaton in the
enharmonic.

Thus, the following notes are fixed: the proslambanomenos, the hypate
hypaton, the hypate meson, the mese, the nete synemmenon, the paramese,
the nete diezeugmenon, and the nete hyperboleon. The movable notes are
those designated as lichanos or paranete in the diatonic, chromatic, or

enharmonic genus. Those not completely movable or completely fixed are the ones that we designate as parhypate or trite in the diatonic and chromatic, but lichanos or paranete in the enharmonic genus.

14. *Concerning the species of consonances*[66]

The species of the primary consonances must now be discussed. The primary consonances are the diapason, the diapente, and the diatessaron.

A species is a particular segment of notes in one of the genera with a unique pattern of intervals; the segment is arranged within the terms of some ratio yielding a consonance.[67] Take the diatonic genus, for example. If we should place the diezeugmenon tetrachord between the hyperboleon tetrachord and the mese, with the synemmenon tetrachord taken away, there would be 15 notes. And if the proslambanomenos is removed, there would be 14. These may be set out in this manner. Let A be the hypate hypaton, B the parhypate hypaton, C the lichanos hypaton, D the hypate meson, E the parhypate meson, F the lichanos meson, G the mese, H the paramese, K the trite diezeugmenon, L the paranete diezeugmenon, M the nete diezeugmenon, N the trite hyperboleon, X the paranete hyperboleon, and O the nete hyperboleon.[68]

[338]

66. Chaps. 14–17 contain Boethius's exposition of the modes, one of the most difficult, misunderstood, and disputed passages of the treatise. For discussion of these chapters see Lucas Kunz, "Die Tonartenlehre des Boethius," *Kirchenmusikalisches Jahrbuch* 31 (1936): 5–24; Pizzani, "Fonti," esp. pp. 128–37; Bower "Sources," esp. pp. 27–37; and idem, "The Modes of Boethius." No extant Greek text can be posited as the single source for these chapters. As indicated in the notes that follow, Ptolemy and Nicomachus appear to be sources of much of the theory and the language of Boethius's exposition. Since these chapters are surrounded by material linked directly to Nicomachus, and since the first four books have a distinctively Pythagorean tone characteristic of Nicomachus, I have argued that this modal exposition is a translation of a lost work by Nicomachus. Such an argument implies that Nicomachus knew the work of Ptolemy (see Nicomachus *Excerpta* 4 [JanS. 275.7]) and used parts of Ptolemy's exposition or that Nicomachus and Ptolemy shared a common fund of definitions and concepts.

67. Each word in this definition [337.22–25] carries considerable weight, both grammatically and technically. Four elements are essential to the definition: the segment, the pattern, the genus, and the consonance. "Particular segment" is a translation of Boethius's *quaedam positio;* it thus represents a discrete position of some interval in a more extended sequence of notes. "With a unique pattern" (*propriam habens formam*) refers to the intervallic structure within the segment. But the intervallic structure of any segment requires that it be considered "in one of the genera" (*secundum unumquodque genus*). Finally, the segment must be bounded by pitches set in a "ratio yielding a consonance" (*in uniuscuiusque proportionis consonantiam facientis terminis constituta*). Compare this definition of species with Ptolemy *Harmonica* 2.3.49.9–10. For a discussion of species in ancient theory, see André Barbera, "Octave Species," *Journal of Musicology* 3 (1984): 229–41.

68. This alphabet consisting of alpha to omicron, representing the notes from the hypate hypaton to the nete hyperboleon, resembles Ptolemy's tracing of the species (see *Harmonica* 2.3.50). However, Ptolemy used the letters in an abstract sense—i.e., he did not equate strings or notes with them. Moreover, Ptolemy considered alpha the highest pitch, whereas Boethius

There is a consonance of a diapason between the hypate and the paramese; between the same paramese and the hypate meson a diapente, and between the mese and the hypate meson a diatessaron. Thus the diapason consists of eight strings, the diatessaron of four, and the diapente of five. Because of this the diatessaron has three species, the diapente four, and the diapason seven. There is always one fewer species than there are pitches.[69]

Beginning the enumeration of species from the mese,[70] there are three species of the consonance of the diatessaron, according to this pattern. One species will be from G to D, a second from F to C, a third from E to B.[71] The species of the diatessaron proceed up to this point, because up to this point the species contain two notes of the same diatessaron: GD contains E and D, FC contains E and D, and EB contains E and D.[72] But if I add

---

(or his source) took A as the lowest pitch. The appearance of the same alphabet in both texts is symptomatic of parallels between these passages. Friedlein follows a later textual tradition when he alters the last six letters of the Greek series (K L M N X O) to reflect the Latin alphabet (I K L M N O; see his apparatus, p. 338). All the control manuscripts present clear evidence that the series originally used in the text reflected the same Greek alphabet. (*B* and *Q*, because of their fragmentary state, do not contain the passage.)

69. This method of accounting for the number of species is markedly different from that of Ptolemy, who relates that there are as many species in an interval as there are steps within it (*Harmonica* 2.3.49).

70. With the opening words of this paragraph (*Ut enim a mese ceteras ordiamur*), Boethius consciously signals a method of enumerating species distinctly different from the traditional method of Greek theory. Normally species are traced from lower to higher pitch, and tracing begins on pitches other than those used in Boethius's first enumeration of species (see below, nn. 71–74). Boethius may have misunderstood the meaning of *mese* in this sentence (assuming that his Greek source used the term μέση), for none of the "other" (*cetera*) enumerations of species begin from the mese. The tracings of the diapente begin rather from the "middle," from the paramese, rather than at the lower end of the system.

71. This ordering of species of diatessaron produces the following intervallic sequence:

1. G-D (a-E) = t t s
2. F-C (g-D) = t s t
3. E-B (f-C) = s t t

(In this outline and those that follow, the numbers represent the ordering given by Boethius, the capital letters the notes as presented by Boethius, the letters in parentheses the modern pitches, and the lower-case letters the intervallic structure of the species.) The logic of this method is the systematic progression of the semitone from the position of lowest interval to that of highest, the same rationale for ordering the species of diatessaron found in Nicomachus *Enchiridion* 7 (JanS. 249.15–19).

72. This argument gave medieval scribes difficulties. "Contains" in this passage came to be understood in terms of each consonance, not in terms of an overlapping set of consonances unfolding different species; thus GD contained FE, FC contained ED, and EB contained DC. But this reading made nonsense out of the argument that differing species of overlapping consonances unfold to the point at which the set of consonances ceases to have at least two notes in common. For the argument to make sense, the two notes common to all three species—viz., E and D—must be named in each instance. Of the control manuscripts, none reads "... ED ... ED ... ED"; *I, K, M, R,* and *V* read "... EF ... ED ...

the diatessaron DA to these, it will have little in common with GD, for it will contain only one string of the consonance GD—that is, only D. Thus DA has gone beyond the consonance GD, and for that reason the diatessaron is said to have three species. The same occurs in the other consonances.

[339]   There are four species of diapente in this manner: one from H to D, another from G to C, another from F to B, and another from E to A.[73]

There are seven species of the consonance of the diapason in this manner: one from O to G, a second from X to F, a third from N to E, a fourth from M to D, a fifth from L to C, a sixth from K to B, and a seventh from H to A.[74]

It is clear, then, from all that has been said that the consonance of the diatessaron is bounded only once by immovable and fixed pitches.[75] For if I begin enumeration from the hypate hypaton, it will be AD—that is, from the hypate hypaton to the hypate meson—which is first in this ordering.[76]

ED," while *P*, and *T*, like Friedlein [338.22–23], read ". . . EF . . . ED . . . CD" (*S* has been altered to read the same, although the last notes are given as DC).

73. This ordering of the species of diapente, like that of the diatessaron, produces a systematic progression of semitone from position of lowest interval to that of highest interval:

    1. H-D (b-E) = t t t s
    2. G-C (a-D) = t t s t
    3. F-B (g-C) = t s t t
    4. E-A (f-B) = s t t s

Unfortunately this uncritical systematization leads to a fourth species, of a tritone, not a diapente. A similar approach to the unfolding of species of diapente can be found in Nicomachus *Enchiridion* 7 (JanS. 249.23–250.2), but again, the systematic progression is impossible within the system at hand—in the case of *Enchiridion* 7, the Pythagorean octachord. No set of pitches exists within the Greater Perfect System which allows successive fifths to follow each other with the semitone moving in order from highest or lowest pitch to the opposite.

74. The derivation of the species of diapason follows that of the other two consonances in one important respect: it proceeds from highest pitch to lowest. (Here the capital T indicates the tone of disjunction.)

    1. O-G (a-A) = t t s t t s T
    2. X-F (g-G) = t s t t s T t
    3. N-E (f-F) = s t t s T t t
    4. M-D (e-E) = t t s T t t s
    5. L-C (d-D) = t s T t t s t
    6. K-B (c-C) = s T t t s t t
    7. H-A (b-B) = T t t s t t s

The progression of the tone of disjunction, T, from position of lowest interval to that of highest may be the principle of ordering in this enumeration of species, but no precedent for this numbering can be found in previous theory. The tone of disjunction, that between the mese and the paramese, plays an important function in the derivation of the modes from the species (see below, 4.17).

75. Discussion of species bounded by fixed pitches is likewise important to Ptolemy (*Harmonica* 2.3.49–50).

For the others, BE and CF, are not bounded by fixed pitches, for the parhypate hypaton and the parhypate meson, as well as the lichanos hypaton and the lichanos meson, have been shown to be movable. If we begin the consonance of the diatessaron from the hypate meson, DG—from the hypate meson to the mese—will be the same species bounded by fixed pitches as the first. The others, EH and FK, are not fixed, for the parhypate meson, the lichanos meson, and the trite diezeugmenon have been shown not to be fixed. Moreover, if one considers the same diatessaron beginning from the paramese, HM—from the paramese to the nete diezeugmenon—will be that species of diatessaron which is confined by fixed sounds, which is the first. The others, KN and LX, are bounded by movable sounds, for we have described the trite diezeugmenon, the paranete diezeugmenon, the trite hyperboleon, and the paranete hyperboleon[77] as being movable pitches.

According to the same principle, the consonance of the diapente contains only two species that are enclosed by fixed pitches. If we begin from the hypate meson, we have DH—from the hypate meson to the paramese; this is the first species. Another is GM—from the mese to the nete diezeugmenon; this is the fourth species.[78] The remaining species, EK and FL, are not enclosed by fixed pitches at all. For the parhypate and lichanos have been shown to be unstable. The theory is similar if the species of this consonance are viewed from the nete diezeugmenon down to lower pitches. For they will be bounded by the same fixed pitches as were mentioned above. Whether we compute the consonances up from the hypate meson [340]

76. At this point Boethius introduces the traditional numbering of species of consonances, and he seems to do so with a clear awareness that it represents a different ordering. The traditional ordering of species of diatessaron is:

1. A-D (B-e) = s t t
2. B-E (C-f) = t t s
3. C-F (D-g) = t s t

Note that, in contrast to the first exposition (above, n. 71), the sequence of pitches is from low to high. (Compare, e.g., Cleonides *Eisagoge* 9 (JanS. 195–98), and Ptolemy *Harmonica* 2.3.50).

77. The text is unstable here [339.29]; nevertheless *et paranete hyperboleon* should be added to Friedlein's text following *et trite hyperboleon*. While the note is omitted in *I* and *K*, it is found in *P, S,* and *T* and is added in *M* and *T.* (A lacuna occurs at this point in *R.*) The argument also dictates that both the trite and the paranete of the hyperboleon tetrachord should be included.

78. Here Boethius presents the traditional enumeration of species of the diapente:

1. D-H (E-b) = s t t t
2. E-K (F-c) = t t t s
3. F-L (G-d) = t t s t
4. G-M (A-e) = t s t t

See above, n. 73.

or the mese,[79] or down from the paramese or the nete hyperboleon to lower pitches, there can be no disputing the two that are enclosed by fixed pitches.

Whether we begin the sequence of consonances of the diapason from the hypate hypaton to the paramese or from the nete hyperboleon to the mese, it will hold only three species that are enclosed by fixed pitches. Beginning from the hypate hypaton, AH—from the hypate hypaton to the paramese—is one species, which is the first; DM—from the hypate meson to the nete diezeugmenon—is another, which is the fourth species; and finally GO—from the mese to the nete hyperboleon—is the seventh.[80] The outermost pitches of the remaining species are by no means fixed, for the parhypate, the lichanos, the trite, and the paranete are not fixed, as was said above. Similarly, if we begin from the nete hyperboleon, the sequence [341] of species is brought together similarly through these same pitches. The diagram given below [Fig. D.19] should make all of this more intelligible.[81]

A	HYPATE HYPATON	
B	PARHYPATE HYPATON	(movable)
C	LICHANOS HYPATON	(movable)
D	HYPATE MESON	
E	PARHYPATE MESON	(movable)
F	LICHANOS MESON	(movable)
G	MESE	
H	PARAMESE	
K	TRITE DIEZEUGMENON	(movable)
L	PARANETE DIEZEUGMENON	(movable)
M	NETE DIEZEUGMENON	
N	TRITE HYPERBOLEON	(movable)
X	PARANETE HYPERBOLEON	(movable)
O	NETE HYPERBOLEON	

79. That is, to higher pitches, as in the traditional system of counting species, which Boethius gives second. This sentence again reveals the conscious application of two methods of tracing species. (See above, n. 70.)

80. This traditional ordering of species of diapason is a mirror image of Boethius's first

15. *Concerning the origins of the modes and the disposition of notational signs for individual modes and pitches*

From the species of the consonance of the diapason arise what are called "modes." They are also called "tropes" or "tones." Tropes are systems that differ according to highness or lowness throughout entire sequences of pitches.[82] A system is, as it were, an entire collection of pitches, brought together within the framework of a consonance such as the diapason, diapason-plus-diatessaron, or the bis-diapason.[83]

A system of the diapason consists of the proslambanomenos to the [342] mese, along with the other pitches counted between them, or the mese to the nete hyperboleon, with the intervening pitches, or the hypate meson to the nete diezeugmenon, with those pitches enclosed by these. The synemmenon system is that which is found between the proslambanomenos and the nete synemmenon, along with those pitches which these surround. Finally, the system of the bis-diapason is seen from the proslambanomenos to the nete hyperboleon, along with the intervening pitches.

If these entire systems were made higher or lower in accordance with the species of the consonance of the diapason discussed above, this would bring about seven modes, which are named Hypodorian, Hypophrygian, Hypolydian, Dorian, Phrygian, Lydian, and Mixolydian.

The arrangement of the modes proceeds in the following manner. Set

ordering (see above, n. 74).

1. A-H (B-b) = s t t s t t T
2. B-K (C-c) = t t s t t T s
3. C-L (D-d) = t s t t T s t
4. D-M (E-e) = s t t T s t t
5. E-N (F-f) = t t T s t t s
6. F-X (G-g) = t T s t t s t
7. G-O (A-a) = T s t t s t t

81. The purpose of Fig. D.19 seems to be twofold: first, it presents an easy reference in which all species can be traced; and second, it makes clear those species contained between fixed pitches. Although the indications for fixed and movable pitches are not part of the ninth-century textual tradition, they are given in the following diagram for the sake of clarity. (They are found only in *V,* and there added by a later hand.)

82. These opening sentences present the essential elements of Boethius's modal theory: the species and the modes are interdependent (literally, the modes "exist from" the diapason species); the word *modus* is synonymous with *tropus* and *tonus* (mode is a literal translation of τρόπος, *tropus* is a transliteration of the same, and *tonus* is a transliteration of another term, τόνος, which, like τρόπος is used in Greek theoretical literature to describe "mode"); and a mode is a transposition of a whole system, not merely a segment of a system.

83. This definition of *system* shows some similarity to that found in Ptolemy's exposition of the modes (*Harmonica* 2.4.50–51). But the similarity is superficial, for Ptolemy considers only the *systema teleion* (bis-diapason)—since it alone contains all species of the diapason—whereas Boethius includes the systems of the diapason-plus-diatessaron (synemmenon system) and the diapason itself. The lesser systems are clearly explained in the paragraph that follows, and the synemmenon system is depicted in the notational diagrams at the close of this chapter and in chap. 16.

out the succession of pitches in the diatonic genus from the proslambanomenos to the nete hyperboleon. Let this be the Hypodorian mode.[84] If one
were to raise the proslambanomenos by one tone, and further raise the
hypate hypaton by the same tone, thereby making the whole disposition
higher by a tone, then the entire succession would turn out higher than it
was before it was raised by a tone. Thus this whole system, having been
made higher, forms the Hypophrygian mode. Now if the pitches of the
Hypophrygian mode were similarly raised by a tone, the collection of
pitches for the Hypolydian mode would be born. If someone raised the
Hypolydian by a semitone, he would make the Dorian. The progression to
higher pitch is similar in the other modes.

So that the theory of these modes might be grasped by the eye as well
as the intellect, a diagram, a visual representation of the modes, handed
[343] down from ancient musicians is presented below. But since each single pitch
for the individual modes is recorded with different written symbols by
ancient musicians, it seems necessary to present a diagram of the written
symbols first [Fig. D.20, p. 155]; then, with these understood in themselves, consideration of the diagram of modes should be easy.[85]

16. *Diagram containing the disposition of and differences between the modes*

The diagram above shows the names assigned to the notes, the written
symbols ordered by positions, and additional words signifying the modes—
whether Lydian or Phrygian or Dorian. But since we said that these modes
were to be ascertained in the species of the consonance of the diapason,[86]
let us now, without further ado, depict the modes solely in the diatonic
genus. Thus put before our eyes, the disposition of these modes should be
grasped immediately[87] [Fig. D.21, p. 156].

84. The explanation is sparse. Nevertheless, the principle determining the transposition
of a system to derive a mode is clear: it is the species. See below, 4.16 and n. 87.

85. This diagram merely presents notational signs; it supplements 4.3–4 by giving the
written symbols for modes other than the Lydian. As in 4.3–4, there are significant differences
between the signs used in this text and those found in other sources. Criticism of these signs
as extremely corrupted (Pizzani, "Fonti," p. 134, n. 1) dismisses the possibility of more than
one tradition in Greek notational theory.

86. See above, chap. 16, n. 82.

87. Some explanation of this diagram is given in the next chapter, but visual perception
of species as the governing principle in modal transpositions is not explained in the text and
thus requires imagination on the part of the reader! Boethius's first species was from the nete
hyperboleon to the mese, O-G in chap. 14, Γ/N to ∾/N in this diagram's first mode, the
Hypodorian. His second species was from the paranete hyperboleon to the lichanos meson,
X-F in chap. 14, Γ/N to ∾/N in the second mode of this diagram, the Hypophrygian. His
third species was from the trite hyperboleon to the parhypate meson, N-E in chap. 14, E/ʊ
to ß/ʟ in the third mode of this diagram, the Hypolydian. Thus, between these pitches—
between Γ/N or E/ʊ and ∾/N or ß/ʟ —an intervallic matrix exists, structured according to

HYPERMIXOLYDIAN	MIXOLYDIAN or HYPERDORIAN	LYDIAN	PHRYGIAN	DORIAN	HYPOLYDIAN	HYPOPHRYGIAN	HYPODORIAN	
ω / И	∇ / ⊤	Ɔ / ⊢	∠ / E	И / Я	Ϙ / H	Ɛ / Ɛ	⊸ / ∘	PROSOLAMBANOMENOS
Φ / F	ω / И	˥ / Γ	Ɔ / ⊢	∠ / E	W / H	Ϙ / H	Ɛ / Ɛ	HYPATE HYPATON
Υ / ⊔	Ψ / И	R / L	F / ⊥	∧ / ш	V / I	⋔ / H	♭ / ш	PARHYPATE HYPATON
Π / Ϲ	T / ᴎ	Φ / F	ω / И	∇ / ⊤	Ɔ / ⊢	∠ / E	И / Я	LICHANOS HYPATON
M / ᴎ	Π / Ϲ	C / C	Φ / F	ω / И	˥ / Γ	Ɔ / ⊢	∠ / E	HYPATE MESON
Λ / ∨	O / K	P / ʊ	Υ / ⊔	Ψ / И	R / L	F / ⊥	∧ / ш	PARHYPATE MESON
H / >	K / ᴎ	M / ᴎ	Π / Ϲ	T / ᴎ	Φ / F	ω / И	∇ / ⊤	LICHANOS MESON
Γ / N	H / >	I / <	M / ᴎ	Π / Ϲ	C / C	Φ / F	ω / И	MESE
B / /	Z / ⊏	Θ / V	Λ / ∨	O / K	P / ʊ	Υ / ⊔	Ψ / И	TRITE SYNEMMENON
⚹ / ↙	ꝰ / \	˥ / N	II / >	K / ᴎ	M / ᴎ	Π / Ϲ	T / ᴎ	PARANETE SYNEMMENON
⊥ / ⅄	⚹ / ↙	Ц / Z	Γ / N	H / >	I / <	M / ᴎ	Π / Ϲ	NETE SYNEMMENON
Ц / Z	Γ / N	Z / ⊏	I / <	M / ᴎ	O / K	C / C	Φ / F	PARAMESE
⅄ / ⅄	B / /	E / U	Θ / V	Λ / ∨	Ƶ / ⋉	P / ʊ	Υ / ⊔	TRITE DIEZEUGMENON
⊥ / ⅄	⚹ / ↙	Ц / Z	Γ / N	H / >	I / <	M / ᴎ	Π / Ϲ	PARANETE DIEZEUGMENON
M˙ / ᴎ˙	⊥ / ⅄	θ / ч	Ц / Z	Γ / N	Z / ⊏	I / <	M / ᴎ	NETE DIEZEUGMENON
Λ˙ / ∨˙	O˙ / K˙	⋖ / ⋖	⅄ / ⅄	B / /	E / U	Θ / V	Λ / ∨	TRITE HYPERBOLEON
H˙ / >˙	K˙ / ᴎ˙	M˙ / ᴎ˙	⊥ / ⅄	⚹ / ↙	Ц / Z	Γ / N	H / >	PARANETE HYPERBOLEON
Γ˙ / N˙	H˙ / >˙	I˙ / <˙	M˙ / ᴎ˙	⊥ / ⅄	θ / ч	Ц / Z	Γ / N	NETE HYPERBOLEON

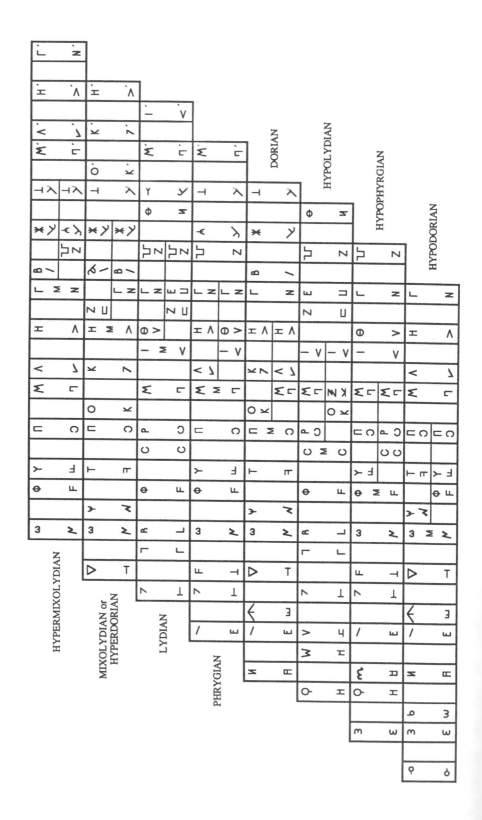

17. *Explanation of the diagram of the modes set out above*

We have said that there are seven modes, but it should not seem inconsistent that an eighth has been incorporated at the top; we will give the reason for this addition a little later.[88]

At this time we must consider the little spaces[89] created by the vertical lines. Some of these contain musical symbols, while others contain nothing at all. For example, in that mode labeled "Hypermixolydian," the first space is designated ω, the third Φ, but the second contains no written symbol. This gap shows that a tone intervenes. The note of the third space (Φ) and that of the fourth (γ) are not separated by a space, but a line created by the vertical column; this reveals that a semitone is the difference between them. This is proved in this manner. If ω is the proslambanomenos, Φ the hypate hypaton, and γ the parhypate hypaton, then the interval between the proslambanomenos (ω) and the hypate hypaton (Φ) must be a tone; but the interval between the hypate hypaton (Φ) and the parhypate hypaton (γ) is a semitone. This applies in all cases: if a full space separates the written symbols for the pitches, we should know that the interval of a tone falls between them; if a line, rather than a space, separates the written symbols, we should not fail to recognize that the interval is a semitone.

Now that I have discussed these things by way of preface, if two of the dispositions founded upon the consonance of the bis-diapason are compared to each other, how can one recognize which disposition is lower? If the proslambanomenos of one is lower than the proslambanomenos of another, or if any other pitch is notated lower than a pitch of the same relative position (set down in the same genus, of course), then it is necessary that the whole disposition be lower. This is easier to perceive from the middle pitch, which is the mese. Of two dispositions of the consonance of the bis-dispason, that one that has a lower mese will be lower in total disposition as well. For if the other pitches are compared one by one, they are found to be lower by the same degree. So if one middle pitch appears higher or

---

the species outlined in chap. 14; this matrix determines the distance between modes and the inner structure of the transposed systems.

The principle governing transportation of systems to form modes was an issue in ancient theory. Ptolemy criticizes the use of emmelic intervals (tones and semitones), arguing that only consonances should be used in determining intervals between transposed systems. Ptolemy thus sets intervallic relationships between modes by means of fourths and fifths, much as the modern tuner sets out a seven-note temperament (Ptolemy *Harmonica* 2.10.63–64). This text presents a third method: species of the consonance of the diapason form an intervallic matrix according to which the musical system is transposed, thereby creating the modes. (See Bower, "The Modes of Boethius," esp. pp. 258–62.)

88. See closing paragraph of this chapter, nn. 90–91.

89. Boethius uses two terms in describing Fig. D.21: *paginula* and *pagina*, both of which imply a column or space for writing. Only here is *paginula* translated as "little space"; all other occurrences of *paginula* or *pagina* are translated as "space." Both words clearly refer to the boxlike spaces in which the notational symbols appear or from which they are missing.

[345] lower than another middle by a tone, all strings, if they are in the same genus, will appear to be higher or lower by a tone if compared one by one.

Given four middle pitches, if the first holds the interval of a diatessaron in relation to the fourth, the first to the second differs by a tone, the second to the third differs by the same tone, then the third to the fourth will produce the difference of a semitone, as follows. Take four middle pitches: A, B, C, and D. A should hold the sesquitertian ratio—the diatessaron— in relation to D; likewise A should stand a tone away from B, and B a tone away from C. The remainder, C to D, should maintain the interval of a semitone [Fig. D.22].

A B C D

If there are five middle pitches, the same pattern ensues. For if the first is set in relation to the fifth according to the sesquialter ratio, and the first to the second, the second to the third, and the third to the fourth are set according to individual tones, the fourth to the fifth will exhibit the difference of a semitone.

Those middle pitches that come nearer to the proslambanomenoi of other modes bring about the lower modes, while those that come nearer to the netai produce the higher modes. Since the first notes, those named proslambanomenos in the figure above where the modes are represented [Fig. D.21, p. 156], occur to the reader's left, whereas the last notes, those named nete, occur to the reader's right, that mode labeled "Hypermixo-lydian" will be the highest mode of all, while that labeled "Hypodorian" will be the lowest.

[346] We will trace out the others, with respect to what difference they hold in relation to each other, beginning from the lowest mode—that is, the Hypodorian. The mese in the Hypodorian mode, ω, stands a tone away from the mese which is in the Hypophrygian. This is easily seen thus: if the written symbol Φ of the Hypophrygian is compared with the mese of the hypophrygian, ω, it is the mese of the Hypodorian, but the lichanos meson of the Hypophrygian. For Φ and ω differ by a tone, which the space placed between them demonstrates. Likewise the mese of the Hypolydian exhibits the difference of a tone from that which is the mese of the Hy-pophrygian, for C, the mese of the Hypolydian, stands at the distance of a tone from Φ, the lichanos meson in the Hypolydian but the mese in the Hypophrygian. Likewise the mese of the Hypolydian, C, stands at the distance of a semitone from the mese of the Dorian. This can be recognized because a single line, rather than a space, separates the vertical column of the mese belonging to the Hypolydian from the vertical column of the mese belonging to the Dorian. It follows that the mese of the Hypodorian stands

at the distance of a full consonance of the diatessaron from the mese of the Dorian. For ω, the mese in the Hypodorian, is the same as ω, the hypate meson in the Dorian; the mese and the hypate meson differ by the consonance of a diatessaron in any mode or genus. Likewise the mese of the Dorian, Π, stands at the distance of a tone from the mese of the Phrygian, M, for Π, the mese of the Dorian, is the same as the lichanos meson of the Phrygian. Again the mese of the Phrygian, M, stands at the distance of a tone from the mese of the Lydian, I, for M, the mese of the Phrygian, is the lichanos meson of the Lydian. Furthermore, the mese of the Lydian mode, I, stands at the distance of a semitone from the mese of [347] the Mixolydian, H, for one vertical column—that containing the mese of the Lydian—is not set off by a little space, but by a line, from the other vertical row—that containing the mese of the Mixolydian. Moreover, the mese of the Mixolydian, H, to the mese of the Hypermixolydian, Γ, makes the difference of a tone, for H, the mese of the Mixolydian, is the same as the lichanos meson of the Hypermixolydian. It follows that the mese of the Dorian stands at the distance of a consonance of the diatessaron from the mese of the Mixolydian. This is proved as follows: the mese of the Dorian, Π, is the same as the hypate meson of the Mixolydian, Π; in any mode the hypate meson holds the consonance of a diatessaron in relation to the mese. Likewise the mese of the Dorian, Π, holds the consonance of the diapente in relation to the mese of the Hypermixolydian, Γ. The mese of the Dorian, Π, is the lichanos hypaton in the Hypermixolydian disposition. In any mode, if the lichanos hypaton of the diatonic genus is compared with the mese, it stands at a consonance of the diapente.

The reason for adding an eighth mode, the Hypermixolydian, is evident because of the following. Take this consonance of the bis-diapason[90] [Fig. D.23].

A to H holds a consonance of a diapason, for it is joined together by eight

90. No indication of pitch is given in conjunction with this alphabetical series. The enumeration of species here may be seen as an abstract demonstration that, given a two-octave system, one octave segment remains after the seven species have been computed, and that this segment may become the basis of an eighth mode. If this series is taken concretely, on the other hand, letter A must represent the *highest* pitch (the nete hyperboleon). In Boethius's numbering of species and derivation of the modes, the first species of diapason, that between the nete hyperboleon and the mese, becomes the basis for the first mode. Insofar as the eighth mode is an octave higher than the Hypodorian, its species should be from the mese to the proslambanomenos (a species intervallically identical with the first species), and thus HP would represent the lower octave of the *systema teleion*. The present sequence of species cannot be construed as the traditional numbering of the species, for then the remaining octave segment would not correspond to the species of the eighth mode given in Fig. D.19.

[348]

pitches. Thus, we have said that the first species of diapason is AH, the second BI, the third CK, the fourth DL, the fifth EM, the sixth FN, and the seventh GO. There still remains then HP, which has been added so that the whole series might be filled out. This then is the eighth mode, which Ptolemy incorporated at the top.[91]

18. *How the musical consonances can be discerned by the ear beyond all doubt*

The theory of consonances can be made clear using a simple instrument, and in this way the theory can be learned beyond all doubt. Let a rule AD be carefully extended, on which two hemispheres, which the Greeks call "magadai," are mounted in such a way that a line extended from E on the curved part to B on the rule makes a right angle at that point. Likewise the line extended from F on the curved part to C on the rule should repeat the right angle at that point. These hemispheres should be uniformly finished in every detail, and others equal to these should be prepared for the same purpose. Let a string of uniform consistency be stretched over these points, A, B, C, and D.

If I wish to discover the character of the consonance of the diatessaron, I should do the following. I divide EF—the space from point E, where the string touches the hemisphere, to point F, where the string is joined to the hemisphere at the other end—into seven parts. I place a point at the fourth part of the seven, which is K. Thus EK is a sesquitertian ratio in relation to KF. I place a hemisphere equal to the above hemispheres at K and, using a plectrum prepared for this purpose, strike EK and KF. If I strike them one after the other, the interval of a diatessaron will resound, but if I strike

[349]

both at the same time, I come to know the consonance of the diatessaron.[92]

To produce the diapente, I divide the whole into five parts and assign three parts to one portion and two to the other. With the hemisphere positioned in the manner described above, I weigh consonance or dissonance.

Should I wish to test the consonance of the diapason, I divide the

91. This attribution is basically incorrect. Ptolemy indeed reports that some theorists placed an eighth mode at the top, but he argues against the validity of the eighth mode, since its species is identical with that of the Hypodorian (*Harmonica* 2.10.63.5–7). This linking of Ptolemy with an eighth mode is part of theoretical tradition, for Bryennius (*Harmonica* 1.8) stated that while Aristoxenus argued for thirteen modes, Ptolemy argued for eight. Given the placement of the mode in Fig. D.21 and the nature of the argument presented here, I suggest that Boethius (or his source) cites Ptolemy because of the placement of the mode at the top, not for the specific attribution of the eighth mode.

92. The concept of consonance as simultaneous sounds found in this passage is wholly consistent with that found earlier in the treatise—e.g., at 1.28 and 4.1. The distinction between consonance and interval, the one struck at the same time (*simul*), the other alternately (*alterutra*), is unique to this passage.

whole into three parts. When I group them into one part and two parts, and strike them at the same time or one after the other, I become acquainted with what is consonant or what is dissonant.

The triple, which is born through combining consonances, is brought about as follows. We partition the whole into four parts, so that the entire length of string is divided into three parts and one part. When the hemisphere is positioned after the third part, the dissonance or consonance of the triple ratio will be produced[93] [Fig. D.24].

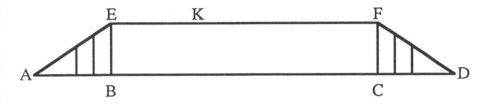

93. The strong similarity between this chapter and Ptolemy *Harmonica* 1.8 led Pizzani ("Fonti," pp. 137–38) and Gushee ("Questions," p. 379) to state that it was taken directly from Ptolemy. But several marked differences should be noted between Ptolemy and the present text. First, Ptolemy's testing of intervals is concise and abstract, whereas in Boethius's text both interval and consonance are tested. Second, the notion of striking "at the same time," like the distinction between interval and consonance, is absent from Ptolemy. Yet the *simul percussero* [348.26] and *simul pulsans* [349.7] of this closing chapter of book 4 strongly resemble the *simul pulsae* [301.3] embedded in the text of the opening chapter of book 4 (see above, n. 6). Third, Ptolemy tests all ratios of intervals he considers consonant, including 8:3 (the diapason-plus-diatessaron). Boethius (or his source) tests only the ratios 4:3, 3:2, 2:1, and 3:1. The test of 8:3 is conspicuous by its absence, for the Pythagoreans argue that this interval is not consonant. These differences link this closing chapter more tightly with the foregoing text than with the translation of Ptolemy that follows.

BOOK 5

[351] I. *Introduction*

After the division of the standard monochord I think we should discuss those matters about which ancient musical scholars express contradictory opinions.[1] Sharp discernment needs to be summoned concerning all these things, and that which is purposely omitted from this treatise must be supplemented with the aid of ordinary learning.

Another division can take place in which not only one string is brought into use and divided according to the proposed ratios, but eight. A kithara

1. This sentence signals a shift in direction. Up to this point, the orientation has been overtly Pythagorean. Theories of Aristoxenus, who disagreed with the Pythagoreans concerning basic principles as well as musical particulars, have been dismissed as fundamentally flawed (see 2.31, 3.1, and 3.3). Throughout the first four books Boethius cited only Ptolemy as an authoritative critic of Pythagorean positions: he acknowledged Ptolemy's tolerance of the multiple-superpartient ratio (1.5–6) and contrasted Ptolemy's approach to the ranking of consonances with that of the Pythagoreans (1.32); he mentioned Ptolemy's different demonstration of the link between specific ratios and consonances (2.18) and cited Ptolemy's claim that the diapason-plus-diatessaron was consonant (2.27). These points of disagreement become the basis of book 5, which is based on the first book of Ptolemy's *Harmonica*. But Boethius's fifth book is not a close translation of Ptolemy's work, and may indeed represent a translation of a textual tradition no longer extant. Passages in Ptolemy containing theory presented in the first four books are highly condensed and paraphrased with no indication that the passage is an abridgment (compare 2.27, where Nicomachus is abridged). While the basic premises of Ptolemy's thought are presented, many of the details of Ptolemy's scientific approach are deleted. Several theoretical details of Boethius's text are not found in Ptolemy. These alterations transform Ptolemy's work into a more arithmetic tract compared with the original music treatise. In the following notes, numbers in brackets following references to *Harmonica* indicate page and line numbers in the edition of Ingemar Düring, *Die Harmonielehre des Klaudio Ptolemaios*.

162

of this kind may also be made, in order that a complete theory of ratios might be discerned, set out before the eyes, as it were, in a number of strings, however many are necessary.

2. Concerning the function of harmonics as a discipline: what the instruments for judgment within harmonics are, and the extent to which the senses can be trusted

We shall speak about this a little later.[2] Now we must state the function [352] of harmonics, that discipline concerning which we have filled four books in setting out the basic fundamentals. We have deferred the exposition of its nature and function until this fifth book.

Harmonics[3] is the faculty[4] that weighs differences between high and low sounds using the sense of hearing and reason. For sense and reason are, as it were, particular instruments[5] for the faculty of harmonics. The sense perceives a thing as indistinct, yet approximate to that which it is; reason exercises judgment concerning the whole and searches out ultimate differences. So the sense discovers something confused, yet close to the truth, but it receives the whole through reason. Reason itself comes to know the whole, even though it receives an indistinct and approximate likeness of truth. For sense brings nothing whole to itself, but arrives only at an approximation. Reason makes the judgment.

If, for example, a circle is drawn by hand, the eye may judge it to be a true circle, but reason knows that it is by no means what it appears to be. This occurs because the sense is concerned with matter, and it grasps species in those things that are in flux and imperfect and that are not delimited and refined to an exact measurement, just like matter itself is. For this reason confusion accompanies the sense. But since matter does not impede the mind and reason, the species discerned by reason is observed over and above association with the particular subject.[6] Hence, wholeness

2. This postponement may refer to 5.13, but it is more likely that it refers to Ptolemy *Harmonica* 2.16. Boethius's translation of that chapter is not extant.

3. At this point Boethius takes up his paraphrase of Ptolemy, and the remainder of this chapter is based on *Harmonica* 1.1. The introduction of the word *harmonica* ("harmonics") reflects the Ptolemaic orientation of the text. The first four books treated *musica* ("music"), one of the four mathematical disciplines preparatory to the study of philosophy; here those books are described as introductory to a broader science, that of "harmonics."

4. Boethius translates Ptolemy's δύναμις [Düring 3.3] with the Latin *facultas* [352.4]. "Harmonics," unlike music, is thus not merely a discipline, but a power or capability of the mind.

5. *Instrumentum* ("instrument") is Boethius's translation of Ptolemy's κριτήριον; the English cognate "criterion" is helpful in understanding this passage, but "instrument" or "tool" reflects the Latin usage.

6. These sentences linking the senses with matter and affirming the independence of mind and reason from matter do not appear in Ptolemy's argument.

and truth attend reason; moreover, reason amends or fills out that which is either mistaken or missing from sense perception.

Perhaps what the sense, as a kind of simple appraiser, discerns incompletely, even confusedly, and as less than the truth amounts to little as a single error. But collected together, such errors are multiplied into a significant quantity, and then they come to make a considerable difference.[7] [353] If the sense judges two pitches to stand at the interval of a tone, and they do not; and further, if it estimates that a third pitch stands at the interval of a tone from one of them, and it is not the whole and true distance of a tone; and if the sense estimates the difference between the third and a fourth pitch to be the same, and it also errs in this, and it is not the difference of a tone; and if it estimates that a fifth pitch stands at the interval of a semitone from the fourth one, and it does not judge truly and correctly: then perhaps each error seems insignificant as a singular instance, but inasmuch as the sense was faulty in the first tone, and likewise in the second and the third, plus the degree to which it was mistaken in the fourth semitone, all these errors, grouped and collected, add up to a cumulative error, with the result that the first pitch does not make a consonance of a diapente with the fifth pitch—which would be the case if the sense had judged the three tones and the semitone correctly. That which seemed insignificant in individual tones has, therefore, become significant collected in a consonance.

To see how the sense gathers confused information and by no means attains the fullness of reason, let us consider the following. Given a line, it is not difficult for the sense to tell what is longer or what is shorter. But if the goal is to determine a measure some precise degree larger or smaller, the first impression of the sense will not be able to do it, but the clever skill of reason will. Or if the goal is to double a given line or to cut it in half—granted that this is a little more difficult than casually telling the longer from the shorter—perhaps this can be accomplished with the aid of sense. But if we are required to triple a proposed line or cut away a third part of it, to determine a quadruple or to cut back a fourth part, will not this be impossible for the sense unless the integrity of reason is brought into play? At this point, as the status of reason increases in importance [354] through the process, the status of the sense weakens. For if someone is told to take an eighth part of a proposed line or if he is required to produce an octuple of the same, he will be compelled to take a half of the total and a half of the half (so that a fourth occurs), then a half of the fourth (so that an eighth occurs); or he will have to double the whole, then double the duple so that there is a quadruple, then double the quadruple so that there is an octuple. Faced with such a multitude of tasks, the sense is

7. The fundamental inadequacy of the hearing in judging intervals precisely is addressed by Ptolemy [Düring 4.2–7], but the notion of multiplying mistakes, along with the detailed example, is not found in Ptolemy. Compare this passage with 3.1 above [269.19–29].

helpless; all its judgment, hasty and superficial, falls short of wholeness and perfection. For this reason the entire judgment is not to be granted to the sense of hearing; rather, reason must also play a role. Reason should guide and moderate the erring sense, inasmuch as the sense—tottering and failing—should be supported, as it were, by a walking stick.

Just as each of the arts has certain instruments, some of which, like the adze,[8] fashion something inexactly, some of which, like the compass, reveal what is whole, so also there are two parts to the function of harmonics: one grasps differences between neighboring pitches by means of the sense, the other considers the integral measure and quantity of these same differences.

3. What a harmonic rule is, or what the Pythagoreans, Aristoxenus, and Ptolemy posited as the goal[9] of harmonics[10]

An instrument of this kind—one by means of which differences between sounds are investigated using some measure of reason—is called a "harmonic rule." Among learned scholars there has been considerable difference of opinion concerning this matter. Those who have followed the teachings of the Pythagoreans have claimed that the goal of harmonics is to bring all things into conformity with reason.[11] For the sense, so to speak, plants certain seeds of knowledge, but reason nourishes them to maturity.[12]   [355]

Aristoxenus maintained, to the contrary, that reason is a partner, but a secondary one—indeed, that all things are delimited through judgment of the sense, and that the sense should determine the measure of intervals and consonance.[13]

The goal of harmonics is defined in another way by Ptolemy, so that there is nothing irreconcilable between the ears and reason. According to Ptolemy the harmonic scholar[14] directs his activity in such a way that what the sense estimates, reason weighs; accordingly, reason searches out ratios to which the sense expresses no objection. The goal of every harmonic

8. The simile of the adze is not found in Ptolemy.

9. "Goal" is a translation of Boethius's *intentio*, a translation, in turn, of Ptolemy's πρόθεσις. This usage of *intentio* stands in contrast with earlier usage, although the notion of "tuning up" resonates well with that of "goal," or "objective." (See book 1, n. 46.)

10. The present chapter is based on Ptolemy *Harmonica* 1.2.

11. See, e.g., Plutarch *De musica* 1144F.

12. This metaphor is not found in Ptolemy, but strongly recalls 1.9, where sense perception is described as an "exhortation."

13. Aristoxenus *Harmonica* 2.33–34.

14. Following Ptolemy, Boethius introduces the term *armonicus* ("harmonic scholar") rather than using *musicus* as in book 1 (see esp. 1.34).

scholar should be to blend these two faculties into a concord.[15] Hence Ptolemy is quite critical of Aristoxenus and the Pythagoreans in this matter, for Aristoxenus does not trust reason at all but only the senses, while the Pythagoreans are too little concerned with the senses and too much concerned with the ratios yielded by reason.

4. *The basis of high and low pitch according to Aristoxenus, the Pythagoreans, and Ptolemy*[16]

All agree that sound is percussion of the air.[17] The followers of Aristoxenus and the Pythagoreans account for the difference between high and low pitch by means of contrasting theories. Aristoxenus expresses the judgment that differences between sounds with respect to highness or lowness are qualitative.[18] The Pythagoreans, on the other hand, hold that these differences are quantitative.[19] Ptolemy appears to side with the Pythagoreans insofar as he also thinks that the basis for high and low pitch does not reside in quality, but rather in quantity, because he holds that more compact, thinner bodies emit high pitch, and less compact, very large bodies emit low pitch. At this moment nothing is said concerning the measure [356] of tension or slackness, although when something becomes slack, it becomes, as it were, less dense and thicker, whereas when it becomes tauter, it is restored to a more compact condition and is stretched thinner.[20]

5. *Ptolemy's opinion concerning differences between sounds*

With these matters set in order, Ptolemy divides differences between sounds in this manner. Of pitches, some are unison, while others are not. Unison pitches are those between which one sound occurs, either high or low. Pitches are not unison when one is lower, another higher. Of these non-unison pitches, some are such that their difference is not defined by a point of distinction between them, for their difference is not discrete, but

15. Boethius's general rendering of Ptolemy's "goal of harmonics" is accurate, particularly in the opening sentence of this paragraph [Düring 5.14–19]. However, this particular musical metaphor—the blending of sense and reason into a concord—is not found in Ptolemy.

16. This chapter presents a highly condensed version of Ptolemy *Harmonica* 2.3. Ptolemy does not mention Aristoxenus or the Pythagoreans in his treatment of the problem, but discusses quality of sound—e.g., tone color and loudness—and establishes that the difference between high and low sound is quantitative.

17. See, e.g., 1.3 above.

18. Although "qualitative" is the antithesis of "quantitative," it is a superficial description of Aristoxenus's theory of pitch (see Aristoxenus *Harmonica* 1.10–13). This theory of sound is ascribed to Aristoxenus by Boethius, but not by Ptolemy.

19. See, e.g., the opening of *Sectio canonis* (JanS. 148–49); compare 4.1 above.

20. This closing statement may represent a concession to Aristoxenus, who held that tension and relaxation were the "causes" of high and low "quality" of sounds (*Harmonica* 1.10–13).

is so drawn from the low to the high that it seems continuous. There are other non-unison pitches between which the difference is marked by an intervening silence.[21]

Pitches not defined by a point of distinction occur in this manner. Just as when a rainbow is observed, the colors are so close to one another that no definite line separates one color from the other—rather it changes from red to yellow, for example, in such a way that continuous mutation into the following color occurs with no clearly defined median falling between them—so also this may often occur in pitches. If someone strikes a string and—while it is sounding—tightens it, it happens that at first the pulsation is lower, whereas when it is tightened, the pitch becomes sharper, and the sounding is continuous between the low pitch and the high.[22]

6. Which pitches are appropriate for harmony[23]

Thus some non-unison pitches are continuous, others discrete. Continuous pitches are such that the difference between them is joined by a [357] continuous line, and the high pitch—or the low—does not maintain a clearly defined position. Discrete pitches, on the other hand, have their own positions, just as unmixed colors do, between which a difference is perceived by virtue of a clearly established position.

Non-unison[24] pitches that are continuous are not considered by the faculty of harmonics, for they are dissimilar from each other and yield no single entity of sound. Discrete pitches, on the other hand, are subject to the harmonic discipline, for the difference between dissimilar pitches separated by an interval can be comprehended; such pitches, which, when joined together, can make a melody are called ἐμμελής. Those that cannot make a melody when joined are called ἐκμελής.

7. What number of ratios the Pythagoreans proposed

Those pitches are called consonant that make intermingled and pleasant sounds when joined together, while those are dissonant which do not.

21. The first paragraph of this chapter is loosely related to the first part of Ptolemy *Harmonica* 1.4 [Düring 9.29–10.5].

22. This second paragraph is a slightly expanded paraphrase of the second part of Ptolemy *Harmonica* 1.4 [Düring 10.6–9]. Although Boethius elaborates on Ptolemy's comparison of continuous sound to a rainbow, he omits Ptolemy's comparisons of low sound of the continuous kind to the bellow of an ox and high sound of this kind to the howl of a wolf [Düring 10.9–11].

23. This chapter is a paraphrase of Ptolemy *Harmonica* 1.4 [Düring 10.11–25], except for the last sentence [Düring 10.25–28], which forms the beginning of the following chapter of Boethius. Concerning continuous and disjunct pitches, see above, 1.12.

24. Boethius's text here reads *non aequisonae* [257.5]; it should read *non unisonae*.

This represents the judgment of Ptolemy concerning the different kinds of sounds.

At this point it seems that we should discuss how he disagrees with others concerning the disposition of consonances.[25]

The Pythagoreans held that the consonances of the diapente and the diatessaron were simple consonances, and from these joined together they formed one consonance of the diapason. There are, moreover, the diapente-plus-diapason and the bis-dispason, the former in triple, the latter in quadruple ratio. But they did not consider the diapason-plus-diatessaron to be a consonance, on the grounds that it does not fall among superparticular or multiple comparisons, but among the multiple-superpartient. Its ratio of pitches is 8:3, for if someone were to place a 4 in the middle of these, he would make these terms: 8:4:3. Of these 8:4 yields the consonance of a diapason, 4:3 that of a diatessaron. The ratio 8:3 is situated in the multiple-superpartient class of inequality. One should know what a multiple-super-partient comparison is from the arithmetic books and the things we discussed in the second book of this work.[26]

[358]

The Pythagoreans posit consonances in the multiple and the superparticular classes, as was discussed in the second and fourth books, but they dissociate consonances from the superpartient and from the multiple-superpartient classes. One should look in the second and fourth books of this treatise on the fundamentals of music to discover how the Pythagoreans associate the diapason with the duple, the diatessaron with the sesquitertian, and the diapente with the sesquialter.[27]

8. Ptolemy's criticism of the Pythagoreans with respect to the number of ratios[28]

Ptolemy reproves the Pythagoreans and rejects the proof that we have expounded in previous books by which, through various means, they associate the diapente with the sesquialter and the diatessaron with the sesquitertian but relate no consonances whatsoever to other superparticular ratios, even though these are of the same class.

25. The remainder of this chapter is an abridgment of Ptolemy Harmonica 1.5. The Pythagorean position has been presented thoroughly in the first four books.
26. See Arith. 1.31 and above, 2.4.
27. Concerning the disposition of consonances by the Pythagoreans (Nicomachus, Eubulides, and Hippasus), see 2.18–20. Concerning the association of certain consonances with certain ratios, see 2.21–27 and 4.2.
28. In this chapter and the two that follow, Boethius reorganizes and paraphrases Ptolemy Harmonica 1.6, albeit omitting many details of Ptolemy's arguments. The present chapter is a translation of a short passage from the middle of Ptolemy's chapter [Düring 13.23–14.2].

9. *Demonstration according to Ptolemy that the diapason-plus-diatessaron is a consonance*[29]

Ptolemy proves that a particular consonance is made from the diapason-plus-diatessaron in this manner. The consonance of the diapason produces a conjunction of pitch such that the string seems to be one and the same. Even the Pythagoreans agree on this point. For this reason, if some consonance is added to the diapason, it is preserved whole and inviolate, as though the consonance added to the consonance of the diapason were [359] added to only one string.

Take the consonance of the diapason contained between the hypate meson and the nete diezeugmenon. These two combine and are united together in sound so that one pitch, as if produced from one string and not mixed from two, strikes the hearing. If we joined any consonance to this consonance of the diapason, its consonance would be preserved intact, because it would be joined as though it proceeded from only one sound and one string. If two upper diatessarons are joined, one to the hypate meson and one to the nete diezeugmenon—the nete hyperboleon to the nete diezeugmenon and the mese to the hypate meson—the two extremes will sound consonant with each other. Moreover, the mese will sound consonant with the nete diezeugmenon, as will the mese with the hypate meson; likewise, the nete hyperboleon will sound consonant with the nete diezeugmenon and also with the hypate meson. Furthermore, if the two lower consonances of the diatessaron are tuned, one between the hypate hypaton and the hypate meson, the other between the paramese and the nete diezeugmenon, the hypate hypaton will sound consonant with the hypate meson and the nete diezeugmenon, and the paramese will sound consonant with the nete diezeugmenon and the hypate meson, but in such a manner that the lower note maintains a consonance of the diatessaron with that closest to it, but a consonance of the diatessaron-plus-diapason with that farthest from it. The hypate hypaton forms the diatessaron with the hypate meson, a diatessaron-plus-diapason with the nete diezeugmenon. [360] Likewise, the nete hyperboleon makes a consonance of the diatessaron above with that closest to it, the nete diezeugmenon, but a consonance of the diatessaron-plus-diapason with the hypate meson.

10. *The property of the consonance of the diapason*[30]

Ptolemy argues that this occurs because the diapason is almost like a single pitch, and that it forms such a consonance by creating, as it were, a

29. The basic contents of this chapter follow the opening argument of Ptolemy *Harmonica* 1.6 [Düring 13.1–23], but the references to specific musical notes, however, are not found in Ptolemy.

30. This chapter is based on a brief remark of Ptolemy in *Harmonica* 1.6 comparing the diapason with the number 10 [Düring 13.6–7]. The expansion of the comparison and the recapitulation of Ptolemy's theory that concludes this chapter are not found in *Harmonica*.

single sound. It is like the number 10, which retains its character whole and inviolate if some number within it is added to it. This does not happen with other numbers, however, and so it is with this consonance. For if you add 2 to 3, you forthwith make 5, and the species of the number has been changed. But if you add the same to 10, you will make 12, and the 2 is preserved in conjunction with the 10. The same applies to the number 3 and to others.

The consonance of the diapason adds another consonance to itself in the same way. It retains its consonant quality and does not change, nor does it yield something dissonant from something consonant. So just as the consonance of a diapente, joined—in triple ratio, to be sure—to the consonance of a diapason, maintains its consonance as the diapason-plus-diapente, so too the consonance of the diatessaron joined to that of the diapason yields another consonance, and this becomes—according to Ptolemy—the addition of one further consonance, the diapason-plus-diatessaron, established in the multiple-superpartient class of inequality. Its ratio is the duple-superbipartient, 8:3, for eight contains three twice, plus two of its parts—that is, two unities.

11. *The manner in which Ptolemy set out consonances*

[361]   Ptolemy also differs from the Pythagoreans in his method for searching out ratios and numbers of consonances. This, according to Ptolemy, is their order.[31]

He holds that pitches are either unison or non-unison with respect to each other. Of non-unison pitches,[32] some are equison,[33] some are consonant, some are melodic, some are dissonant, and some are nonmelodic.

Unison pitches are those which, struck at the same time, yield one and the same sound.[34]

31. This chapter and the next constitute what in Boethius's view is the Ptolemaic reply to Nicomachus's evaluation and classification of consonances, as found in 1.32 and 2.20. The basis of these chapters is Ptolemy *Harmonica* 1.7, but Boethius also draws definitions from *Harmonica* 1.4 in setting out Ptolemy's basic definitions. Some compromise of Ptolemy's position inevitably results from Boethius's conflation of different parts of his source (see below, n. 32). The most important aspects of these chapters as far as Boethius is concerned are the rationale for associating intervals with ratios and the implicit evaluation of intervals that results. The definition and classification of pitches is a means to that end.

32. Boethius here conflates two passages by bringing the terms "unison," "dissonant," and "nonmelodic," from *Harmonica* 1.4, where Ptolemy is discussing pitches (φθόγγοι), into the definitions of *Harmonica* 1.7, where Ptolemy is working toward a classification of intervals (διαστήματα) which can be used within sets of pitches. Boethius's use of the term "pitches" to the exclusion of the term "intervals" compromises the careful distinctions made by Ptolemy.

33. "Equison" is a translation for *aequisonus,* Boethius's translation of Ptolemy's ὁμόφωνος. We have thereby created a word parallel to "unison," the English for *unisonus.*

34. Ptolemy defines unison pitches (*Harmonica* 1.4 [Düring 5.1–2]) as those which do not change with respect to tension. This definition is appropriate, since his term for unison is

Equison pitches are those which, struck at the same time,[35] yield one and an apparently simple sound from two—for example, the diapason and its double, the bis-diapason.

Consonant pitches are those that give a composite, intermingled, but nevertheless pleasant, sound—for example, the diapente and the diatessaron.[36]

Melodic pitches are any of those that are not consonant but can nevertheless be properly fitted to melody—for example, those which join consonances together.[37]

Dissonant pitches are those that do not mix sounds together and that affect the senses unpleasantly.[38]

Nonmelodic pitches are those that are not acceptable for joining consonances together.[39] (We will discuss these a little later in the division of the tetrachord.[40])

Since equison pitches are most closely associated with identical pitches, it is necessary that the numerical inequality closest to equality be brought into relation with equal numbers.[41] The duple ratio is that directly next to numerical equality, for it is the first species of the multiple class, and the larger number—insofar as it goes beyond the smaller—exceeds the smaller by a quantity equal to the smaller number itself. For example, two exceeds one by one, which is equal to unity itself. The duple ratio is therefore rightly fitted to equison pitches—that is, to the diapason, while the bis-diapason is found in twice the duple—that is, the quadruple.

ἰσότονος. The definition given by Boethius is not found in Ptolemy. It is significant that the two terms for unison and equison in Greek—ἰσότονος and ὁμόφωνος—do not share the same root (sonus) as they do in Latin—unisonus and aequisonus.

35. This definition paraphrases Ptolemy's from *Harmonica* 1.7 [Düring 15.10–12], although the phrase "struck at the same time" is not found in Ptolemy. Concerning this phrase (simul pulsae), see book 1, n. 130; book 4, n. 6; and below, n. 50.

36. Ptolemy gives only examples of consonances in *Harmonica* 1.7 [Düring 15.12–15]; the definition given here seems to be a paraphrase of *Harmonica* 1.4 [Düring 10.25–27].

37. Ptolemy's definition of melodic (ἐμμελής) pitches is found in *Harmonica* 1.4 [Düring 10.23–25]. Ptolemy gives examples of melodic intervals only in *Harmonica* 1.7 [Düring 15.14–15]. He defines these pitches as "those which, placed next to each other, please the hearing." While Boethius's definition cannot be called a translation of either passage, it is consistent with both.

38. Ptolemy's definition of dissonant pitches occurs in *Harmonica* 1.4 [Düring 10.27–28], as a negative corollary of his definition of consonant pitches. The present definition functions in the same way in relation to the definition of consonant pitches above.

39. Ptolemy's definition of nonmelodic (ἐκμελής) pitches is found in *Harmonica* 1.4 [Düring 10.15], as a negative corollary of his definition of melodic pitches, and does not include any phrase such as "acceptable for joining consonances together."

40. This reference seems to apply to the use of melodic intervals in divisions of tetrachords (because they please the ear) and the rejection of nonmelodic intervals. See, e.g., Ptolemy's criticisms of Archytas in 5.18. These intervals would have been discussed further, presumably, in chaps. 20–30.

41. The concluding section of this chapter, linking intervals with specific ratios, paraphrases Ptolemy *Harmonica* 1.7 [Düring 15.18–16.21].

[362] The ratios that divide the duple ratio—the first and largest of the superparticular class—should be assigned to those consonances that divide the equison diapason. Thus it follows that the diapente should be associated with the sesquialter ratio, the diatessaron with the sesquitertian.

These consonant intervals form other consonances when joined to equison intervals—for example, the diapente-plus-diapason in the triple ratio and the diatessaron-plus-diapason in the ratio 8:3.

Melodic pitches are those that divide the diapente and the diatessaron, like the tone and those other ratios which we shall discuss a little later in the division of tetrachords. These are the simple parts of tetrachords.

12. *Which intervals are equison, which are consonant, and which are melodic*[42]

The diapason and the bis-diapason are equison, since, by virtue of their proper mixture and blend, a sound is produced that seems single and simple. The first ratios of the superparticular class are consonant: the sesquialter and the sesquitertian, or the diapente and the diatessaron. The diapason-plus-diapente and the diapason-plus-diatessaron are consonant also; these are combined and united out of equison and consonant intervals. The remaining intervals that can be placed within these consonances are melodic; the tone, for example, is the difference between the diatessaron and the diapente.

Just as equison intervals are brought together from consonant intervals—for example, the diapason from the diatessaron and the diapente—so consonant intervals are brought together from those called melodic—for example, the diatessaron and diapente from whole tones and from other ratios that we will discuss later.[43]

But in order to grasp how the theory of all these things can be brought together, one should turn to that place at the close of the fourth book where we described a string being stretched out over hemispheres.[44] In that place [363] one discerns the equison diapason and bis-diapason, the simple consonances of the diapente and the diatessaron, the composite consonances of the diapason-plus-diapente and the diapason-plus-diatessaron, and the melodic sounds consisting of the difference of a whole tone.

42. The first two paragraphs of this chapter follow the summary found at the conclusion of Ptolemy *Harmonica* 1.7 [Düring 16.21–29].
43. This reference would apply to chaps. 20–30 of this book.
44. See above, 4.18. This reference to the closing chapter of book 4 represents, for Boethius, the theory presented in Ptolemy *Harmonica* 1.8, a chapter describing tests of intervals on an instrument identical to that described earlier by Boethius. But that chapter does not test the diapason-plus-diatessaron or the bis-diapason as Boethius's text implies.

13. *How Aristoxenus considered intervals*[45]

The opinion of Aristoxenus concerning these matters should be discussed briefly. Since he attached little value to reason but yielded to aural judgment, he does not indicate numbers for pitches as a means of obtaining their ratios. Instead, he estimates the differences between them, not to inquire into pitches per se but rather the differences between them.[46] Very incautiously he considered that he knew the differences between pitches for which he had established no magnitude or measure. Consequently he proposed that the diatessaron consists of two tones and a semitone,[47] the diapente of three tones and a semitone, and the diapason of six tones, all of which was demonstrated to be impossible in the above books.[48]

14. *Diagram of an octachord demonstrating that the diapason is less than six tones*[49]

Ptolemy teaches that the interval of a diapason falls within six tones through division of a certain octachord, as in the following.

Eight strings should be set out under tension: A, B, C, D, E, F, G, and H. Let AK form a sesquioctave ratio in relation to BL, likewise BL in relation to CM, likewise CM in relation to DN, likewise DN in relation to EX, likewise EX in relation to FO, and likewise FO in relation to GP. [364] These will, therefore represent six whole tones. Then let the string H be divided in the middle, at R, and let AK be the duple of HR. Therefore, when AK and HR are struck at the same time, they should sound the consonance of the equison diapason. If, however, GP is struck, it will always be a little higher than HR; because of this, six tones surpass the consonance of a diapason. If AK and GP, being struck together,[50] did sound the consonance of a diapason, the consonance of the diapason would consist of six whole tones. If these do not form a consonance, whereas AK and HR do, and if HR were higher than GP, then the consonance of the diapason would exceed six whole tones. But in this case, since AK and HR form the con-

45. This chapter compresses the exposition of Aristoxenian theory presented by Ptolemy *Harmonica* 1.9–10. Boethius evidently saw no need to translate these chapters at length because he had already offered similar arguments and criticisms in books 2 and 3.

46. Aristoxenus *Harmonica* 1.15.

47. By "semitone" Aristoxenus understands "half of a tone," and thus it follows that a diapason consists of six tones (see above, 3.1).

48. See above, 2.31 and 3.3. ·

49. This chapter reports the basic theory found in Ptolemy *Harmonica* 1.11, although many subtle points of Ptolemy's argument are missing in Boethius's paraphrase, as is the whole discussion of relations between thicknesses and lengths of strings and their pitches.

50. The words "struck together" (*pulsae . . . simul* [364.3]) in this sentence do not come from Ptolemy's text; rather they echo language about consonance found in 1.28 (see book 1, n. 130) and 4.1 (see book 4, n. 6); see also above, n. 35.

sonance and the same HR is discovered to be lower than GP, it is not possible that six whole tones exceed the consonance of a diapason.

In this manner it can be established, using the sense of hearing, that the consonance of the diapason falls short of six whole tones; therefore the error of Aristoxenus is incontestably demonstrated [Fig. E.1].

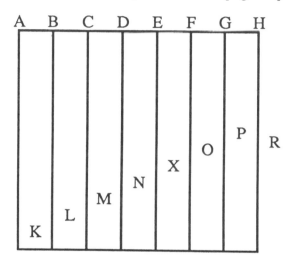

15. *The consonance of the diatessaron is contained within a tetrachord*[51]

[365]   At this time the division of tetrachords should be discussed. The consonance of the diatessaron is formed from four strings and, in fact, is called "diatessaron" for that reason. Therefore, to make a tetrachord, two outer strings sounding the consonance of a diatessaron are set in place, and two other strings are situated between them, which, in turn, form three ratios with themselves and the outermost strings.

16. *How Aristoxenus divides the tone and the genera, and a diagram of his division*[52]

Aristoxenus divides the diatessaron into three genera using the following scheme.[53] He divides the tone into two parts and calls each part a

---

51. This chapter serves as a transition to the discussion of the division of tetrachords that follows. It thus functions like the opening of Ptolemy *Harmonica* 1.12 [Düring 28.15–29.11]. But Boethius's text omits significant technical considerations found in Ptolemy's text, not least the discussion of *pyknon* in relation to the enharmonic and chromatic genera and *apyknon* in relation to the diatonic, which is a particularly unfortunate omission.

"semitone." He divides the tone into three parts and calls each third the "soft chromatic diesis." He divides the tone into four parts, and this fourth part plus its own half—that is, an eighth part of the whole—he calls the "hemiolic chromatic diesis."

Since, according to Aristoxenus, these parts of the tone are so constituted, and since, according to him, the division of genera is twofold, one being softer, the other sharper, the enharmonic genus represents the softer, while the diatonic represents the sharper. The chromatic occupies a place between these, participating in sharpness and softness. According to this sequence, then, six degrees of intermingled genera come into being: one enharmonic, three chromatic—the soft chromatic, the hemiolic chromatic, and the tonic chromatic—and two diatonic—soft and sharp. The division of all these, according to Aristoxenus, is as follows.

It has already been established that the fourth part of a tone is named "enharmonic diesis," and that Aristoxenus does not set out pitches in ratios, but rather measures the interval and the difference between pitches. Thus, according to Aristoxenus, the tone consists of 12 unities,[54] and three of these represent a fourth part of a tone, the enharmonic diesis.

Since the consonance of the diatessaron is joined together from two [366] tones and a semitone, the whole of a diatessaron will be made from twice 12 plus 6. But since, as often happens, we wish to deduce parts of tones as small as eighths, we should arrive at these eighths as discrete parts, rather than as numbers which are not whole. For this reason the whole of a diatessaron should be 60, the tone 24, the semitone 12, the fourth part of a tone, called "enharmonic diesis," 6, and the eighth part of a tone 3. When an eighth part of a tone is joined to a fourth, thereby producing the hemiolic chromatic diesis, 6 is added to 3, making 9.

Having set out the three genera—enharmonic, chromatic, and diatonic—according to these principles, Aristoxenus thought that they shared certain properties such that some were compact and others were not. Compact genera are those in which the two lower ratios do not surpass in size the one ratio positioned just above them in pitch; noncompact are those

52. Boethius's principal source for the content of this chapter is Ptolemy *Harmonica* 1.12 [Düring 29.11–30.2]. See below, n. 54.

53. The extant passages of Aristoxenus treating genera are *Harmonica* 1.21–27 and 2.46–52. For a review of these passages see R. P. Winnington-Ingram, "Aristoxenus and the Intervals of Greek Music," *Classical Quarterly* 26 (1932): 195–208.

54. The extant passages of Aristoxenus treating divisions of genera assign no specific numerical values to the tone or other intervals. In Ptolemy, the tone is immediately assigned the number 24 [Düring 29.22], and no mention is made of the number 12. The tradition of 12 as the value of the tone can be documented in chapter 7 (JanS. 192.13) of Cleonides *Eisagoge harmonica* (JanS. 179–207), a treatise in the Aristoxenian tradition. There is no evidence, however, that Boethius knew the treatise of Cleonides. This sentence in Boethius and the paragraph that follows cannot be accounted for by the extant textual tradition of Ptolemy; they may represent a gloss in Boethius's source which he incorporated into the text, or they may represent a textual tradition of Ptolemy no longer extant.

in which two ratios can surpass the one remaining. The enharmonic and chromatic are compact, the diatonic is noncompact.[55]

Accordingly, following Aristoxenus, the enharmonic genus is divided as follows: 6, 6, 48. In this way a fourth part of a tone, called the "enharmonic diesis," falls between the lowest string and that next to the lowest. This is because a tone has been established as 24 unities. Likewise the second interval, that between the second from the lowest string and the third, is the same fourth part of a tone, 6. The remainder, that which is left from 60, which forms the whole of the ratio,[56] is 48, placed between the third from the lowest string and the fourth and highest. And the two ratios found in the lowest position, 6 and 6, do not surpass the one remaining, 48, placed in the highest position.

The soft chromatic genus yields the division 8, 8, 44. In this way 8 and 8 represent thirds of tones. For the tone, as has been said, consists of 24 unities, and a third of a tone is called the "soft chromatic diesis."

[367] The diatessaron of the hemiolic chromatic genus is divided 9, 9, 42. For the hemiolic chromatic diesis is an eighth part of a tone along with a fourth—that is, 3 along with 6 parts of 24.

The partition of the tonic chromatic genus, following Aristoxenus, is as follows: 12, 12, 36. In this way it sets down two individual semitones plus that which remains in the last interval. And in all of these chromatic genera, the two ratios which are close to the lower string do not surpass in magnitude the remaining ratio, that found in the highest position. These divisions are, as has been said, compact genera. Indeed, the enharmonic and the chromatic are the compact genera.

The diatonic division itself is also twofold. The division of the soft diatonic takes place in this way: 12, 18, 30. In this way 12 represents a semitone, 18 a semitone plus a fourth part of a tone, and 30 forms the remainder. Now 18 plus 12 make 30, and thus these are not surpassed by that part which remains.

The division of the sharp diatonic genus is such that it contains a semitone plus two whole tones—that is, 12, 24, 24. Now the sum of 24 plus

55. "Compact" and "noncompact" are translations of Boethius's *spissus* and *non spissus,* which in turn translate the Greek terms πυκνός and ἄπυκνος, which are very significant in the tetrachord divisions of both Aristoxenus and Ptolemy. Ptolemy presented these terms in his chapter setting out the basic principles of tetrachord division (*Harmonica* 1.12), but Boethius failed to include this discussion in his paraphrase (see above, n. 51).

56. In the above definitions of compact and noncompact genera Ptolemy does use the word "ratio" (λόγος) when referring to the lowest two intervals of genera [Düring 29.7–8]; but thereafter, when discussing the structure of tetrachords according to Aristoxenus, he carefully uses the terms "interval" (διάστημα [Düring 29.20, 26–27, 29, 32]). It is, at best, imprecise to use the word "ratio" (*proportio* [e.g., 366.26, 27]) in reference to an interval described in Aristoxenus's terms. This "imprecision" is not Ptolemy's but Boethius's or the latter's source.

12 (36) is not surpassed by the remaining part, the one in the highest position, but rather surpasses them.

This, then, is the division of tetrachords according to Aristoxenus, which are shown in the following diagram [Fig. E.2].   [368]

48	44	42	36	30	24
6	8	9	12	18	24
6	8	9	12	12	12
60	60	60	60	60	60

| ENHARMONIC | SOFT CHROMATIC | HEMIOLIC CHROMATIC | TONIC CHROMATIC | SOFT DIATONIC | SHARP DIATONIC |

17. How Archytas divides tetrachords, and a diagram of the same[57]

Archytas, who determined all things by reason, not only neglected to use the sense of hearing in establishing the primary consonances, but even held rigidly to reason in the division of tetrachords. But he did so in such a way that he neither effectively worked out what he sought nor set forth a scheme consistent with the sense of hearing.

He held that there were three genera: the enharmonic, the chromatic, and the diatonic. In these he set down the same lowest and highest sounds, making 2,016 the lowest sound in all genera, and 1,512 the highest. He then placed 1,944 as the string next to the lowest in the three genera, 2,016 in relation to 1,944 holding the ratio 28:27.

Following this, he set out, in the enharmonic genus, the string below the highest one, the one third from the lowest. This one should be 1,890, which is joined to 1,944 by the ratio 36:35. This same 1,890 is set in the   [369] sesquiquartan ratio in relation to the highest string, 1,512.

In the diatonic genus he placed the string below the highest—the one third from the lowest—at 1,701, which is joined to 1,944 by the sesquiseptimal ratio. The same 1,701 forms a sesquioctave with the highest term, 1,512.

In the chromatic genus he placed a string third from the lowest—or second from the highest—holding the ratio 256:243 in relation to 1,701, the second string in the diatonic genus; this term is 1,792, placed second from the highest. And the note second from the highest in the diatonic

---

57. This chapter is based on Ptolemy *Harmonica* 1.13; Ptolemy's text and Boethius's paraphrase are the only extant sources of Archytas's tetrachord division.

genus, 1,701, to the note second from the highest in the chromatic genus, 1,792, contains the ratio of 256:243.

The following diagram [Fig. E.3] shows the form of these tetrachords divided according to the opinion of Archytas.

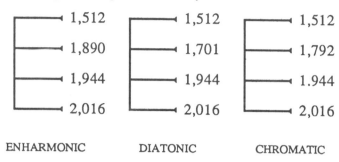

| ENHARMONIC | DIATONIC | CHROMATIC |

18. *How Ptolemy criticized the division of tetrachords by both Aristoxenus and Archytas*[58]

[370] Ptolemy criticized both of these divisions of tetrachords. He faulted Archytas first of all because the second to highest string in the chromatic genus, 1,792, forms a superparticular ratio with neither the term above it, 1,512, nor the term below it, 1,944—even though Archytas held superparticular ratios in such esteem that he accepted them as the theoretical basis of consonances. He faulted him further because the sense of hearing grasps the first ratio from the lowest string in the chromatic genus as larger than Archytas would make it; for Archytas made it the ratio 28:27 in the chromatic genus, 2,016:1,944, while it should be 22:21 according to the customary ordering of pitches in the chromatic genus.[59] Likewise that ratio in the enharmonic genus—the one that the first from the lowest maintains according to Archytas's division—is such that it should be much smaller than it is found to be in the other genera, whereas he made it equal to that in the other genera, for he placed the ratio 28:27 first from the lowest in all three genera.

Ptolemy reproached Aristoxenus for placing the first and second ratios in the soft and hemiolic chromatic genera so close to the lowest string that the sense of hearing can distinguish no difference between them. For 8 represents the first ratio in the soft chromatic division of Aristoxenus, 9 in the hemiolic chromatic genus. But 8 and 9 are separated by unity. The total

58. This chapter is based on Ptolemy *Harmonica* 1.14.

59. Although Ptolemy criticizes Archytas for making the first interval in the chromatic genus too small [Düring 32.4–7], the ratio 22:21 is not found in Ptolemy. Boethius's source for this ratio is unknown. Boethius omits Ptolemy's objection [Düring 32.7–11] that the second interval of Archytas's chromatic genus is smaller than the lowest interval and is nonmelodic.

tone consists of 24 unities according to Aristoxenus's thesis, of which unity is a 1/24 part. Therefore the first ratios from the lowest strings in the soft and hemiolic chromatic genera are separated from each other by 1/24 part [371] of a tone, which cannot possibly be perceived by the hearing because the difference is too small. Ptolemy rebuked Aristoxenus further because he made only two divisions of the diatonic genus (dividing it into soft and sharp), whereas other species of diatonic genera could also be discovered.[60]

19. *The manner in which Ptolemy said the division of tetrachords should be accomplished*[61]

Ptolemy divided tetrachords according to a different scheme.

He began with the principle that the pitches between the two outer sounds should be placed in such a way that they progress according to superparticular ratios. These ratios are nonetheless unequal, for a super-particular ratio cannot be divided equally.

Moreover, the division should be such that every ratio that is made in relation to the lowest pitch should be smaller than those associated with the other three pitches.

The divisions that we call "compact" ought to be such that the two ratios which are next to each other at the lower end should be smaller than the ratio that remains at the top. But in the "noncompact" divisions—for example, in the diatonic genera, nowhere are two ratios smaller than one.

60. Boethius does not report Ptolemy's last two criticisms of Aristoxenus [Düring 32.23–27]—viz., that Aristoxenus makes the two intervals within his *pyknon* equal, and that the lowest intervals in the sharp diatonic division and the tonic chromatic division are the same.

61. This chapter abstracts three basic principles of tetrachord division from Ptolemy *Harmonica* 1.15: viz., that all ratios in the division should be superparticular [Düring 33.5–11], that the lowest ratio should be the smallest [Düring 33.22–24], and that the highest interval in compact divisions should be larger than the sum of the two lower intervals [Düring 33.24–26], whereas no interval in a noncompact division should be larger than the two remaining intervals [Düring 33.26–27]. Nevertheless, the major portion of Ptolemy's text is not included in Boethius's paraphrase.

Chapters 20–30 of Book 5

The text of the final 11 chapters of book 5 is not extant, but the titles for these chapters have been preserved in all the control manuscripts which preserve the earlier chapters of book 5 except *P*. The contents of these chapters can be reconstructed on the basis of Boethius's extant text and the last two chapters of Ptolemy's first book. This appendix thus presents Boethius's titles for the final chapters of book 5, followed by an estimation of what each chapter would have contained. The summaries include only material which is indicated in the title; it is impossible to determine the extent to which Boethius would have included other theoretical details found in Ptolemy's closing chapters.

20. *How inequality of ratios is made from equality* [350]

Ptolemy's *Harmonica* contains no discussion of ratios proceeding from equality; the contents of this chapter may have reviewed the principles set out in 2.7 above. Multiple and superparticular ratios are the first departures from equality, and Ptolemy, like the Pythagoreans, assigns particular importance to the first two classes. But Ptolemy, unlike the Pythagoreans, carries this value into the division of tetrachords by requiring that all melodic intervals within tetrachords be based on superparticular ratios.

21. *How Ptolemy divided the diatessaron into two parts*

Ptolemy *Harmonica* 1.15 [Düring 33.27–34.4]. Ptolemy divides the ratio 4:3 into as many pairs of superparticular ratios as possible: 5:4 and 16:15; 6:5 and 10:9; and 7:6 and 8:7.

22. *Which genera are compact and which are not; and how Ptolemy adapts ratios to the division of the enharmonic genus*

Ptolemy *Harmonica* 1.15 [Düring 34.5–14]. Compact genera are those that take the larger ratios cited in 5.21 as the highest interval in each tetrachord—that is, 5:4, 6:5, and 7:6—while they derive the lowest two intervals within the smaller ratios—that is, 16:15, 10:9, and 8:7. The smaller, lower intervals are divided into three terms (just as tetrachords are divided into three), and two superparticular ratios, which are only approximately equal, are used to form the tetrachord.

Ptolemy *Harmonica* 1.15 [Düring 35.13–18]. Noncompact genera are those that use the smaller ratios from 5.21 above as the highest intervals in each tetrachord—that is, 16:15, 10:9, and 8:7. The larger ratios are distributed according to the same principles as above—that is, by dividing the larger ratios into two superparticular ratios.

Ptolemy *Harmonica* 1.15 [Düring 34.14–21]. The numbers 15 and 16 are multiplied by 3, making 45 and 48; between these fall 46 and 47, with equal differences. Since 47 does not form a superparticular ratio with both 45 and 48, it is discarded. The ratio between 48 and 46 equals 24:23. This ratio is joined with 46:45 and 5:4, and the resulting complete tetrachord is as follows: 5:4, 24:23, and 46:45.

23. *Ptolemy's division of the soft chromatic genus*

Ptolemy *Harmonica* 1.15 [Düring 34.21–27]. The numbers 9 and 10 are multiplied by 3, making 27 and 30; between these fall 28 and 29, with equal differences. Since 29 does not form a superparticular ratio with both 27 and 30, it is discarded. The ratio between 30 and 28 equals 15:14. This ratio is joined with 28:27 and 6:5, and the completed tetrachord is as follows: 6:5, 15:14, and 28:27.

24. *Ptolemy's division of the sharp chromatic genus*

Ptolemy *Harmonica* 1.15 [Düring 34.27–33]. The numbers 7 and 8 are multiplied by 3, making 21 and 24; between these fall 22 and 23, with equal differences. Since 23 does not form a superparticular ratio with both 21 and 24, it is discarded. The ratio between 24 and 22 equals 12:11. This ratio is joined with 22:21 and 7:6 and the completed tetrachord has the ratios 7:6, 12:11, and 22:21.

25. Disposition of Ptolemy's compact genera with numbers and ratios

Ptolemy *Harmonica* 1.15 [Düring 35.3–12]. Ptolemy computes the whole numbers containing the ratios for each compact division, as follows:

> Enharmonic (5:4, 24:23, and 46:45): 106, 260:132, 825:138, 600:141, 680
> Soft chromatic (6:5, 15:14, and 28:27): 106, 260:127, 512:132, 620:141, 680
> Sharp chromatic (7:6, 12:11, and 22:21): 106, 260:123, 970:135, 240:141, 680

26. Ptolemy's division of the soft diatonic genus

Ptolemy *Harmonica* 1.15 [Düring 35.18–36.6] begins the exposition of noncompact genera with the soft diatonic genus. One cannot create a noncompact division using the ratio 16:15 as the highest interval, because it cannot combine with the ratios derived from 5:4 (which would be 7:6 and 15:14) in such a way that the smallest ratio would be in the lowest position (see above, 5:19 and n. 61).

Ptolemy *Harmonica* 1.15 [Düring 36.6–13]. The numbers 6 and 7 are multiplied by 3, making 18 and 21; between these fall 19 and 20. Since 19 does not form a superparticular with both 18 and 21, it is discarded. The ratio between 20 and 18 equals 10:9. This ratio is joined with 21:20 and 8:7, and the division is completed as follows: 8:7, 10:9, and 21:20.

27. Ptolemy's division of the sharp diatonic genus

Ptolemy *Harmonica* 1.15 [Düring 36.13–20]. The numbers 5 and 6 are multiplied by 3, making 15 and 18; between these fall 16 and 17. Since 17 does not form a superparticular ratio with both 18 and 15 it is discarded. The ratio between 18 and 16 equals 9:8. This ratio is joined with 16:15 and 10:9, and tetrachord is structured as follows: 10:9, 9:8, and 16:15.

28. Ptolemy's division of the tonic diatonic genus

Ptolemy *Harmonica* 1.15 [Düring 36.19–28]. Neither of the above two divisions places the ratio 9:8 in the highest position, and, since this ratio is the difference between the first two consonant intervals, a division should occur in which the ratio 9:8 holds the highest position. No superparticular ratio will form the ratio 4:3 when combined with 9:8. The ratio 10:9 was combined with 9:8 in one of the above divisions, but not with 8:7. If the ratio 8:7 is combined with 9:8, the superparticular ratio 28:27 remains, which becomes the lowest interval, as follows: 9:8, 8:7, and 28:27.

29. *Disposition of the various noncompact genera with numbers and ratios*

Ptolemy *Harmonica* 1.15 [Düring 36.28–37.4]. Ptolemy computes the whole numbers containing the ratios for each noncompact division, as follows:

> Soft diatonic (8:7, 10:9, and 21:20): 504:576:640:672
> Tonic diatonic (9:8, 8:7, and 28:27): 504:567:648:672
> Sharp diatonic (10:9, 9:8, and 16:15): 504:560:630:672

30. *Ptolemy's division of the equal diatonic genus*

Ptolemy *Harmonica* 16 [Düring 38.17–27]. A division of the tetrachord can be obtained by multiplying the terms 4 and 3 by 3, thus making 12 and 9, and filling in the numbers between—namely, 11 and 10. The resulting division is 10:9, 11:10, and 12:11. The division sounds similar to the sharp diatonic, especially if it is expanded to a pentachord using the 9:8 tone, thus creating continuously decreasing ratios from 9:8 to 12:11.

Ptolemy *Harmonica* 16 [Düring 39.5–6]. This division is called the "equal diatonic," for its intervals are close to being equal.

Notes on the Text of the Spartan Decree

Boethius copied this text from Nicomachus, but Nicomachus's source is unknown. It is in Spartan, or Doric dialect, and, perhaps for that reason, Boethius did not attempt to translate it. Boethius's implication (1.1 [182.5–6]) that the principal problem with the text consists of changing C (sigma) to P (rho) is misleading, for it is filled with dialectical peculiarities which go far beyond the word endings with -οϱ in place of -ος. Moreover, the transmission of the decree by scribes who were for the most part ignorant of Greek multiplied problems in a text already difficult. The scribes of the earliest extant manuscripts, those dating from the ninth century, were already making mistakes, such as confusing Δ, Λ, and A, writing IO or OI for ω, confusing Γ and T, transcribing Π as TT, TI, or even P, and changing H to E and Ω to O; and these mistakes were compounded in the centuries that followed.

The earliest "critical" edition of the decree was that of Jacobus Gronovius in the *Praefatio* (last 3 unnumbered pages) to volume 5 of his *Thesaurus Graecarum Antiquitatum* (Leiden, 1699). Gronovius based his text on "a Cambridge manuscript"—probably University Library Ii.3.12, with which it accords—and reviewed all previously printed versions. The decree was next published in Oxford in 1777, edited by Bishop William Cleaver under the heading *Decretum Lacedaemoniorum contra Timotheum Milesium, e codd. msstis. oxoniensibus, cum commentario.* This text is based on Bodleian Library, Auct. F.3.13 and Seld. supra 25, Balliol College, MS 306; Corpus Christi College, MS 118; and Magdalen College, MS 19. It came in for sharp criticism in R. P. Knight's *An Analytical Essay on the Greek Alphabet* (London, 1791), a work which exists in a copy owned and annotated by Charles Burney (British Library, 624.i.8), who used it as the basis for his comments on the decree (C. Burney, *A General History of Music* [London, 1776–89], vol. 1, pp. 45, 411). Another English divine,

Bishop T. Burgess, published a defense of Cleaver and contributed additional notes on the decree in *A Vindication of Bishop Cleaver's Edition of the Decretum Lacedaemoniorum Contra Timotheum, from the Strictures of R. P. Knight, Esq.* (London, [1821]). Considerable erudition and informed reflection are found in these works, and it is unfortunate that Friedlein had access only to Gronovius's work.

Friedlein's edition of the decree is remarkably good, especially since his only access to the earliest sources was through the Parisian humanist André Laubmann. Friedlein's text became the foundation of a revised version by Ulrich von Wilamowitz-Möllendorf in Timotheos, *Der Perser* (Berlin, 1903), pp. 70–71. Wilamowitz-Möllendorf, who regarded the decree as a forgery from the first or second century B.C., emended Friedlein's text rather freely, with no reference to primary sources, but his comments (particularly p. 71, n. 1) are the most thorough, competent criticisms of the decree to date.

The rendering of the decree in this translation represents an attempt to reconstruct the best possible Greek text that could have been available to the scribes of *K, M, P,* and *Q,* the sources which preserve the decree in its most literate state. The text has been emended and corrected in these manuscripts, but the emendations appear to date from the ninth century, and, in some cases, were made by the original scribes or their near contemporaries. The emendations are not recorded in the following apparatus, although they deserve a careful, separate study. Underlining of a word in the apparatus signifies that the word does not exist as printed in any of the manuscripts; such emendations incorporate changes that seem both credible—based on the kinds of errors evident in the sources—and grammatically necessary.

The following variants are found in the four manuscripts, Friedlein (*FR*), and Wilamowitz-Möllendorf (*WM*).

1 ΕΠΕΙΔΗ] ΕΠΕΙΑΝΑ *K*
2 <u>ΠΑΡΑΓΙΝΟΜΕΝΟΡ</u>] ΠΛΑΤΙΜΕΝΟΡ *K* ΠΑΡΑΓΙΜΕΝΟΡ *M Q*
  ΠΑΡΑΤΙΝΟΜΕΝΟΡ *P* παραγενόμενορ *WM*
  ΕΤΤΑΝ] ΕΝ ΤΑΝ *FR*
  ΑΜΕΤΕΡΑΝ] ΔΜΕΤΕΡΑΝ *K*
3 ΤΑΝ] ΤΑ *P* ΤΑΜ *FR WM*
  ΠΑΛΑΙΑΝ] ΠΑΛΑΓΙΑΝ *M*
  ΜΩΑΝ] ΠΩΑΝ *P*
  ΑΤΙΜΑCΔΕ] ἀτιμάσδη *WM*
4 ΚΑΙ ΤΑΝ] ΤΑΝ *om. K*
  ΚΙΘΑΡΙΖΙΝ] ΚΙΕΑΡΙΖΙΝ *K* ΚΙΤΑΡΙΖΙΝ *P* κιθάρισιν *WM*
5 ΠΟΛΥΦΩΝΙΑΝ] ΓΟΧΥΦΩΝΙΑΝ *K* ΠΟΛΥΦΟΝΙΑΝ *M Q*
  ΕΙCΑΓΩΝ] ΕΙCΑΡΩΝ *K* ΕΙCΑΤΑΝ *P*
  ΤΩΝ] ΤΩ *P*
  ΝΕΩΝ]ΝΕΟΝ *P*
6 ΠΟΛΥΧΟΡΔΙΑΡ] ΠΟΛΙΚΟΡΔΙΑΡ *M P*

ΚΑΙ ΤΑΡ] ΚΑΙ ΓΑΡ *M Q*
ΚΕΝΟΤΑΤΟΡ] καινότατορ *WM*
ΜΕΛΕΟΡ] ΜΕΑΕΟΡ *K*
7 ΑΓΕΝΝΗ] ΑΡΕΝ *K* ΑΓΗΝΝΗ *M* ΑΓΕΝΝΕ *Q*
ΠΟΙΚΙΛΑΝ] ΠΟΙΚΙΤΑΝ *K M* ΠΟΚΙΤΑΝ *Q*
ΑΠΛΟΑΡ] ΑΠΑΟΑΡ *P*
ΤΕΤΑΓΜΕΝΑΡ] ΤΕΤΑΤΜΕΝΑΡ *K*
8 ΜΩΑΝ] ΜΟΑΝ *M*
ΕΠΙ] ΕΤΤΙ *K*
ΧΡΩΜΑΤΟΡ] ΚΡΩΜΑΤΟΡ *P*
CΥΝΕΙCΤΑΜΕΝΟΡ] ΓΥΝΕΥC ΤΑΜΕΝΟΡ *M* CΙΝΕΙCΤΑΜΕΝΟΡ *P*
συνιστάμενορ *WM*
9 ΤΑΝ] ΑΑΝ *K*
ΤΩ] ΤΟ *M*
ΔΙΑCΚΕΥΑΝ] ΔΙΑCΚΕΙΝ *M Q* ΔΙΑCΚΕΙΝΑΝ *K*
lacuna post ΕΝΑΡΜΟΝΙΩ *WM*
10 ΠΟΤΤΑΝ] ΠΟΙΤΑΝ *M* ΠΟΤΑΝ *P* ΠΟΤ ΤΑΝ *FR*
11 ΠΑΡΑΚΛΗΘΕΙC] ΠΑΡΑΚΛΕΘΙC *P*
ΕΛΕΥCΙΝΙΑΡ] ΕΛΕΙCΙΝΙΑΡ *P*
12 ΑΠΡΕΠΗ] ΑΠΡΕΠΕ *M P*
ΔΙΕCΚΕΥΑCΑΤΟ] ΔΙΕCΚΕΙCΑΤΟ *K Q* ΔΙΕSΚΕΙCΑΤΟ *M*
διεσκευακὼρ *WM*
ΤΑΝ] τᾶι *WM*
ΜΥΘΩ] ΜΥΩ *K* ΜΙΤΩ *M* ΜΥΤΩ *P*
ΔΙΑCΚΕΥΑΝ] ΔΙΑCΚΕΙΑΝ *K M Q* διασκευᾶι *WM*
13 ΤΑΡ] ΓΑΡ *K M P Q*
ΩΔΙΝΑΡ] ΩΔΑΙΝΑΡ *K* ΟΔΙΝΑΡ *M* ΟΔΥΝΑΡ *FR* ὠδῖνα *WM*
14 ΝΕΩΡ] ΝΕΟΡ *M*
ΔΙΔΑΚΚΗ] ΔΙΔΑΚΗ *K* ΔΙΔΑΚΚΕ *P* διδάσκη *WM*
15 ΔΕΔΟΧΘΑΙ] ΔΕΔΟΧΤΑΙ *P*
ΦΑ] τ(ύχαι) α(υαθᾶι) *WM*
ΤΟΥΤΩΝ] ΤΟΥΤΟΙΝ *K M P Q FR*
16 ΤΩΡ (*pr.*)] ΤΟΥC *Q*
ΤΩΡ (*sec.*)] ΤΟΡ *K M Q*
ΕΦΟΡΩΡ] ΕΦΟΡΑΡ *M* ΕΦΟΠΟΡ *P*
17 ΕΠΑΝΑΓΚΑΖΑΙ] ΕΤΙΑΝΑΤΚΑΖΔΙ *K* ΕΠΑΝΑΚΑΖΑΙ *M Q*
ἐπαναυκάσαι *WM*
ΕΝΔΕΚΑ] ΕΝΔΕΧΑ *P*
ΧΟΡΔΑΝ] ΧΟΡΛΑΝ *K* ΚΟΡΔΑΝ *P*
18 ΕΚΤΑΜΩΝ] ΕΚΤΑΜΟΝ *M P* ΕΚΤΑΜΟΝΤΑΡ *FR* ἐκταμὲν *WM*
ΓΑΡ] ΤΑΡ *K P om. WM*
ΠΕΡΙΤΤΑΡ] ΠΕΠΙΤΑΡ *M* ΠΕΡΙΤΑΡ *P*
19 ΥΠΟΛΙΠΟΜΕΝΩΝ] ΥΠΟΛΙΠΟΜΕΝΩ *K P Q* ΥΠΟΛΥΠΟΜΕΝΩ *M*
ΥΠΟΛΙΠΟΜΕΝΩΡ *FR* ὑπολειπόμενον *WM*
ΕΠΤΑ ΟΠΩΡ] *om. P*
20 ΟΠΩΡ] ΩΠΩΡ *K M om. P*
ΤΑΡ] ΓΑΡ *M*
ΠΟΛΙΟΡ] ΛΟΛΙΟΡ *P*
ΟΡΩΝ] ΟΡΙΟΝ *M* ΟΡΟΝ *P*
21 ΕΥΛΑΒΗΤΑΙ] ΕΙΛΑΒΝΤΑΙ *K* ΕΥΛΑΒΕΤΑΙ *P*
ΕΤΤΑΝ] ΕΝ ΤΑΝ *FR*

22 ΕΠΙΦΕΡΗΝ] ΕΠΙΦΕΡΝΝ *K* ΑΠΕΦΕΡΗΝ *P* ΕΠΙΦΕΡΕΙΝ *Q*
ΕΠΙΦΕΡΕΝ *FR WM*
ΤΩΜ] ΤΩ *P*
ΜΗ *om. K*
ΕΟΝΤΩΝ] ΝΕΤΩΝ *K* ΗΕΤΩΝ *M Q* ΗΤΩΝ *P*
23 ΜΗΠΟΤΕ] ΜΕΠΟΤΕ *M P* ΜΗ ΠΟΤΕ *FR*
ΤΑΡΑΡΕΤΑΙ] ΤΑΡΑΡΕΤΑΡ *K M Q* ΤΑΠΑΠΕΤΑΡ *P* ΤΑΡΑΡΡΕΤΑΙ
FR ταραττήται *WM*
ΑΓΟΝΩΝ] ΑΓΟΝΤΩΝ *K M Q* ΑΡΟΝΤΩΝ *P* ΑΓΩΝΩΝ *FR WM*

Oliver Strunk published an English translation of the decree, based on the
text of Wilamowitz-Möllendorf, in *Source Readings in Music History* (New
York: Norton, 1950), pp. 81–82. Below I give the English translation of
Bishop Burgess (1821), which, although somewhat freer than Strunk's, accurately captures the content and background of the decree:

> Whereas Timotheus, the Milesian, coming to our city, dishonours the ancient
> music, and, rejecting the melody of the seven-stringed lyre, corrupts the ears
> of our youth by introducing a variety of tones; and by the multiplicity of the
> strings, and the novelty of the melody, renders the music effeminate and com-
> plex instead of simple and uniform; composing his melody in the chromatic
> instead of the enharmonic, using the antistrophic change: and whereas being
> invited to the musical contests at the festival of Eleusianian Ceres, he com-
> posed a poem unbecoming the occasion; for he described to our youth the
> pains of Semele at the birth of Bacchus not with due reverence and decorum:
> be it therefore resolved, that the Kings and Ephori shall censure Timotheus
> for these things, and moreover shall oblige him to retrench the superfluous
> number of his eleven strings, leaving seven, that all men, seeing the grave
> severity of our city, may be deterred from introducing into Sparta any thing
> immoral, or not conducive to the honour of virtue.

Notes on the Diagrams and their Sources

The diagrams in this translation are modeled on those found in the control manuscripts. Two criteria have been used in determining what constitutes a diagram: the use of the term *descriptio* in the text immediately before or after a drawing or series of terms or an obvious drawing at a given place in all control manuscripts. The figures are numbered consecutively in each book, and the books are designated A, B, C, D, and E.

Although numerous minor inconsistencies occur in the ninth-century sources, the diagrams in nine of the ten control manuscripts exhibit an agreement remarkable for a tradition of graphic representations. Manuscripts *K, P, Q,* and *R* represent the earliest recension, and the diagrams given here are based on at least one of these codices in each case. *R* and *Q* seem to be the examplars of *S* and *T,* and *V* conforms to the same basic tradition with some later additions. *M,* although very helpful as a source for textual variants, is of little use for the diagrams; most of the drawings seem to have been altered or added at a later date, and they often show incompetence. *B,* a fragment of book 3, is an important representative of the ninth-century tradition but contains only the first fifteen diagrams of the third book. *Q* breaks off after Figure D.18, unfortunately, so this crucial source is of no help for the important notational and modal diagrams at the close of book 4.

The following notes indicate the principal sources for each diagram, as well as further comments where necessary. Insofar as most of the diagrams fall into groups, they are treated accordingly in what follows. These notes should not be construed as a critical apparatus for the diagrams. The variants in some diagrams—in particular those containing notation—are sufficient to merit a separate study.

BOOK 1

A.1–7: Exposition of Basic Ratios and Combinations of Ratios
Sources: *K, Q, S, T*
Comments: The text is written in majuscule script in the manuscripts, and the diagrams are centered on the page. These first seven drawings with their accompanying sentences are prominently displayed in all early sources.

A.8–9: Exposition of the Diatonic Diatessaron and Diapente
Source: *P*
Comments: Although both these series of numbers are designated *descriptio*, the manuscripts include them in the text, giving prominence to numbers only through size. *P* gives the numbers additional prominence by writing them in red and beginning a new line thereafter. Boxes are not found in any of the control manuscripts, but often appear in tenth-century sources.

A.10–16: The Development of Musical Systems
Sources: *I, P, Q, S, T, K, P,* and *R* for arch indicating disjunction in A.13
Comments: *R* and *V* give arches indicating tetrachordal structure for A.10 and A.13; the arches are a later addition in *R*.

A.17: The Three Genera
Sources: *P, Q, R, S, T, V*
Comments: In these representations of intervals there is no correspondence between size of interval and space allotted to it.

A.18: The 28 Notes
Sources: *I, K, P, Q*
Comments: Prominent placement of the words *Diatonic, Chromatic,* and *Enharmonic* in *P* helps to highlight the pitches that are not fixed and to perceive clearly the 28 notes. The other manuscripts give the names of the notes in the same form, but with no special attention to the variable pitches.

A.19–20: Conjunct and Disjunct Tetrachords
Sources: *K, Q, S, T*
Comments: *P* and *R* indicate the conjunction in A.19 with an arch; *I* and *V* indicate the tetrachordal structure in both diagrams with arches, although the arches appear to be a later addition in *I*.

BOOK 2

B.1–7: Classes of Ratios, Square Numbers, and Generation of Ratios
Sources: *K, P, Q, R, S, T*

B.8–12: Sieves for Continuous Superparticular Ratios
Sources: *I, K, P, Q, R, S, T; I* for boxes in B.11–B.12
Comments: The numbers in B.11 and B.12 are sometimes justified on the left, sometimes arranged as a pyramid.

B.13–14: Measurement of Ratios by their Difference
Sources: *I, K, T*
Comments: Only *I* frames the numbers with boxes. The numbers for these diagrams are written in a line in the text of *P, Q,* and *S,* whereas they are displayed in a line in *R* and *V.*

B.15–24: Classes of Proportion, Generatioan of Means, and the Harmonic Means
Sources: *I, K, P, Q, R, S, T, V*

B.25–27: Computation of Means
Sources: *P* and *R*
Comments: Although B.26 is termed *descriptio* [249.6–7], these sets of numbers are consistently given in the text. *P* displays them prominently, however, using large red numbers, and *R* creates the same effect by using boxes.

B.28–29: Relative Merits of Ratios Compared to Diapason
Sources: *I, K, P, Q, R, S, T, V*

B.30–31: Six Continous Tones compared to Diapason
Sources: *I, K, P, Q, S, T, V*

BOOK 3

C.1–4: Semitone is Not Half a Tone and the Implications Thereof
Sources: *B, I, K, P, Q, R, S, T*
Comments: The signs for the fractions in C.3 and C.4 gave scribes difficulty. *Q* is the clearest in rendering the fractions, but mainly because of the editorial work of the glossing scribe i² (see Introduction, n. 67).

C.5–14: Calculations of Intervals
Sources: *B, K, P, Q, R, S, T*
Comments: Concerning proportional spacing and direction of pitch in this series of diagrams, see book 3, n. 19.

C.15: Archytas's Proof
Sources: *B, I, Q, S, T*
Comments: C.15 is omitted in *K* and *P.*

C.16–25: Relative Sizes of Smaller Intervals and Ratios
Sources: *I, K, Q, S, T*
Comments: *R* is like other sources in every respect except that it lacks vertical lines in C.16–20. *P* is also like other sources except that there is evidence of difficulty in C.21.

BOOK 4

D.1–9: Euclidian Proofs
Sources: *I, P, Q, R, S, T, V*
Comments: See book 4, n. 15, concerning problem with numbers in D.6: *P, Q,* and *S* give 6:4:3; *I* and *K* give 4:3:2; *R* and *V* have 12:8:6 written over 4:2:1; and *T* gives 12:8:6. *K* gives horizontal rather than vertical lines for D.9; *P* also had horizontal lines originally, but they have been erased and replaced by vertical lines.

D.10: Greek Notation for Lydian Mode
Source for form: *P*
Sources for notation: *I, K, P, Q,* and the descriptions in text
Comments: All manuscripts give the same basic form as far as the notational symbols are concerned, but *P* indicates the tetrachordal units by extended lines to the left. Concerning the notational signs themselves, see notes below for D.20 and D.21. *I* and *Q* serve as sources for the 28 signs in 4.3–4 only, for *Q* is incomplete, and the notational diagrams have been torn out of *I*.

D.11–12: First Division of the Monochord in Diatonic Genus
Sources: *R, S, T*
Comments: These three codices are unusually clear in the placement of divisions, letters, and notation in these diagrams. D.12^2 has been created to be analogous to D.11 and D.12 (see book 4, n. 46).

D.13–18: Second Division of the Monochord in Three Genera
Sources: *P, Q, S, T*
Comments: The spacing of the notes within the genera is particularly difficult in these diagrams, but no manuscript gives proper geometric divisions for the monochord as a whole—namely, points that would yield proper pitches when applied to a string.

   Minor inconsistencies of letters and numbers occur among all the manuscripts but cannot be recorded systematically here. The names of the notes are written out in the manuscripts but are abbreviated here in D.14–18 for the sake of clarity. The abbreviations are as follows:

Proslambanomenos   Pros

Hypate hypaton	HH
Enharmonic parhypate hypaton	*E*pH
Chromatic parhypate hypaton	*C*pHH
Diatonic parhypate hypaton	*D*pHH
Enharmonic lichanos hypaton	*E*LH
Chromatic lichanos hypaton	*C*LH
Diatonic lichanos hypaton	*D*LH
Hypate meson	HM
Enharmonic parhypate meson	*E*pH
Chromatic parhypate meson	*C*pHM
Diatonic parhypate meson	*D*pHM
Enharmonic lichanos meson	*E*LM
Chromatic lichanos meson	*C*LM
Diatonic lichanos meson	*D*LM
Mese	M
Enharmonic trite synemmenon	*E*T
Chromatic trite synemmenon	*C*TS
Diatonic trite synemmenon	*D*TS
Enharmonic paranete synemmenon	*E*pNS
Chromatic paranete synemmenon	*C*pNS
Diatonic paranete synemmenon	*D*pNS
Nete synemmenon	NS
Paramese	pM
Enharmonic trite diezeugmenon	*E*T
Chromatic trite diezeugmenon	*C*TD
Diatonic trite diezeugmenon	*D*TD
Enharmonic paranete diezeugmenon	*E*pND
Chromatic paranete diezeugmenon	*C*pND
Diatonic paranete diezeugmenon	*D*pND
Nete diezeugmenon	ND
Enharmonic trite hyperboleon	*E*T
Chromatic trite hyperboleon	*C*TH
Diatonic trite hyperboleon	*D*TH
Enharmonic paranete hyperboleon	*E*pNH
Chromatic paranete hyperboleon	*C*pNH
Diatonic paranete hyperboleon	*D*pnH
Nete hyperboleon	NH

(The instances where ambiguity arises—*E*T and *E*pH, the next-to-lowest pitches in the enharmonic tetrachords—are required because of space, but proper meaning can be determined by context.)

Abbreviations used for intervals in the division do not correspond exactly to those found in the manuscripts but are similar and function in the same way. They are:

δ   diesis of enharmonic genus
s   semitone of diatonic and chromatic genera
T   tone
sss   trihemitone of the chromatic genus
TT   ditone of enharmonic genus

The diatonic paranete hyperboleon and the nete hyperboleon are indicated as KK and LL in all diagrams in this translation. In the manuscripts, however, the nete hyperboleon is designated NN in D.16–18 which, in turn, necessitates a change in the designation of the diatonic paranete hyperboleon from NN to HH. (Concerning the use of NN for the diatonic paranete hyperboleon, see book 4, n. 53.) For the use of HH for the chromatic paranete hyperboleon, see book 4, n. 55. For the use of GG for the enharmonic paranete hyperboleon, see book 4, n. 56. For the use of G for the enharmonic lichanos hypaton, see book 4, n. 63.

D.19: Species of Consonances
Sources: *P; V* for indication of movable pitches
Comments: While the series of letters ending in H, K, L, M, N, X, O is clear both in the text and in D. 19 of *P,* the series for D.19 in *K* ends with H, I, K, L, M, N, O, P, whereas the text transmits the other series (see book 4, n. 68). The alphabet for the diagram in *R, S, T,* and *V* was originally H, I, K, L, M, N, O, P but has been altered to read H, K, L, M, N, X, O. An attempt was made to render D.19 consistent in *I,* but only M, N, X, and O were altered. A later scribe (ca. 900) has added *mobilis* to the right of notes that are movable in *V,* and, since it clarifies the explanation of species between fixed or movable notes, the word *movable* has here been placed in parentheses after the same notes.

D.20–21: Notational Diagrams for Modes
Sources: *K, P, R, S, T, V*
Comments: In these diagrams 49 Greek letters are employed: sometimes normal, sometimes turned, inverted, reversed, or otherwise altered, to represent 35 discrete pitches. Eighteen of these notational symbols also appear in 4.3–4, in which 10 additional symbols are used to represent notes in the enharmonic and chromatic Lydian tonoi. The symbols used throughout book 4 in this translation are based on the symbols used in the control manuscripts *and* the descriptions of the same symbols in 4.3 and Alypius *Eisagoge* [JanS. 359–406]. Most of the symbols in D.20 and D.21 are described only by Alypius. Since the medieval scribes were generally copying symbols for which they had no verbal descriptions, and since they did not

always understand the functions of the symbols or which musical pitches they referred to, they often distorted the signs and made mistakes. Distinctions between half-alpha, half-delta, and various positions of lambda are difficult to read or write even with textual desriptions, and without them the task is impossible for any but the most professional scholar. Restoration of consistency has served as a principle in the notational diagrams of this translation. Thus, when different symbols are found in the codices for the same pitch with the same function, the symbol from the manuscripts most consistent with the description of Alypius is used for all instances of that pitch. Nevertheless, the letters and shapes are modeled on those in the ninth-century sources, the oldest extant theoretical manuscripts containing Greek notation.

D.22–23: Modal Structures
Sources: *I, K, R, S T*
Comments: D.22 is displayed prominently in these manuscripts, whereas it is written into the text in the remaining manuscripts. D.23 is displayed in all manuscripts.

D.24: Intervallic Tests on Monochord
Sources: *R, S, T*
Comments: This diagram has been erased in *K* and was originally missing in *I* but was added subsequently in the top margin. Additional letter Ks have been added in *P* to represent the numerous intervallic tests.

BOOK 5

E.1: Ptolemy's Octachord
Sources: *I* and *R*
Comments: *I* and *R* contain letters A–H across the top, with the letters K–R in a diagonal ascending from the bottom left; but in both sources the diagonal series of letters was added at a later date. Moreover, both sources place R at a point higher than P, a placement which is not consistent with the text. R is adjusted in E.1 to conform with the argument of the text. *K, S, T,* and *V* present only A–H across the top, whereas *P* gives A–H in a row across the top, K–R in a parallel row across the bottom.

E.2–3: Aristoxenus's and Archytas's Tetrachord Divisions
Sources: *K, P, R, S, T*

Index

Adze: 165
aequisonus: 170*n*
Albinus: xxvi, 20, 46
Alypius *Eisagoge*: 123*n*–126*n*, 194–95
ἅμα κρουσθέντες: 47*n*, 116*n*. *See also* Simul pulsae
ἀναλογία: 65*n*. *See also Proportionalitas*
Ammonius *In Porphyrii isagogen sive v voces*: 6*n*
anima: 10*n*
animus: 1*n*
Anonymous III (Bellerman): 123*n*, 125*n*, 126*n*
Apollo: 30*n*
Apotome (major semitone): differs from minor semitone by a comma, 113–14; differs from minor semitone by two schismata, 97; larger than four commas, smaller than five, 111–12; larger part of a tone, 84–85; perceiving space of, 100–101; perceiving two, 103; Philolaus's definition, 96; remainder after minor semitone subtracted from tone, 82*n*, 84; smallest numbers containing, 85
Apuleius of Madaura: xx
ἀραιός (*rarus*): 116*n*
Archytas: demonstration concerning division of superparticular ratios, 103, 105; division of genera, 177–78; mentioned, xxxiii, xxxvi, 66*n*, 106*n*
Arion of Methymna: 6
Aristides Quintilianus: 34*n*, 131*n*

Aristotle: on parts of the soul, 10; the Organon and Boethius's commentaries, xix; source of Boethius's logical works, xxv
—*De anima*: 10*n*
—*Nicomachean Ethics*: 10*n*
Aristoxenus: the Aristoxenian tradition, xxviii*n*, xxxvi, xxxvii*n*, 31*n*, 173*n*, 175*n*; diapason consists of six tones, xxxii, xxxvi, 87, 92, 173–74; diatessaron consists of two and a half tones, 92, 173; disagreements with Pythagoreans, 162*n*; division of genera, 174–77; harmonic rule according to, 165–66; Ptolemy's criticism of, 178–79; reliance on senses, 87, 88, 165; theory of intervals, 173; theory of sound, 166; mentioned, xxxvi, 160*n*
—*Harmonica*: 5*n*, 16*n*, 86*n*, 88*n*, 92*n*, 165*n*, 166*n*, 172*n*
Arithmetic (the discipline): xix, xx, 54, 74, 78
armonia (ἁρμονία): 5*n*. *See also* Genera, enharmonic; Harmony; Mode
armonicus: 165*n*
Art: 50
Astronomy: xix, 54
Athenaeus *Deipnosophistae*: xxix, 1*n*, 3*n*, 4*n*, 6*n*, 31*n*, 34*n*
Atys, King of Lydians: 30
Augustine *Contra Julianum*: 6*n*
Aulete: 6, 6*n*, 50
auloedus: 51*n*
Aulos: 6, 8, 9–10, 51